Stephen Dillaye

**Our Presidential Candidates and Political Compendium**

Vol. 2

Stephen Dillaye

**Our Presidential Candidates and Political Compendium**
*Vol. 2*

ISBN/EAN: 9783744731133

Printed in Europe, USA, Canada, Australia, Japan

Cover: Foto ©ninafisch / pixelio.de

More available books at **www.hansebooks.com**

# OUR
# PRESIDENTIAL CANDIDATES

AND

# Political Compendium.

ALSO CONTAINING LIVES OF THE CANDIDATES FOR VICE-PRESIDENT—THE PROCEEDINGS OF THE THREE NATIONAL CONVENTIONS—THE THREE PLATFORMS AND THE THREE LETTERS OF ACCEPTANCE.

### LIFE OF GENERAL J. A. GARFIELD,
By E. B. Kennedy, of the New York Bar.

### LIFE OF GENERAL J. B. WEAVER,
By Hon. S. D. Dillaye, of the New Jersey Bar.

### LIFE OF GENERAL W. S. HANCOCK,
By Henry Hill, Journalist, of Newark, N. J.

### POLITICAL COMPENDIUM,
By F. C. Bliss, Author of "Citizen's Manual," etc.

*ILLUSTRATED.*

NEWARK, N. J.:
F. C. BLISS & COMPANY.
1880.

# INTRODUCTION.

We are on the eve of another Presidential Election and the passions, prejudices, favoritism and enthusiasm of the masses, are beginning to be exercised and exhibited in a thousand forms. This is natural, and perhaps not to be condemned if properly controlled, kept within reasonable bounds, and exercised in a just and honorable manner. Every citizen should act honestly and conscientiously after having thoroughly examined the subject matter, in every possible light, and from different standpoints.

There are three political parties in our country, and each at its National Convention nominated a candidate for the Presidency. Every party has its great and good men, and he who does the most for the preservation and welfare of his country, should be considered the greatest and best. Men make positions; positions don't make men. Honorable, enterprising, intelligent and resolute persons, out of fragments and bits of opportunities, will oftimes march onward to honor and renown.

As political parties, we are fortunate in having now in nomination for the highest office in the gift of the people the three most popular men of their respective parties, and we may say their recognized leaders; men, all of whom have carved, with their own swords, their name imperishably on the facade of the republic; men, whose military and political careers have been distinguished by marked ability, political sagacity and executive force.

# INTRODUCTION.

Again, the publishers are fortunate in securing the services of three so able gentlemen, each of whom from his party standpoint, has presented the case of his chosen candidate in a manner and with an ability we must all admire. Each champion differs from his fellow-champions, chiefly in this, that he sees or believes what they do not.

We have been impartial to each of the Candidates and Parties, inserting the proceeding of the Conventions and Lives of the Candidates in the order of time, in which they took place.

From the facts and arguments presented, the reader must be the sole judge of the merits and qualifications of each Candidate ; and having so judged it is his duty to act according to the dictates of his own judgment and conscience. We trust the book will be found readable, interesting, and of permanent value to every American citizen ; no matter to what party he may belong.

THE PUBLISHERS.

# CONTENTS OF PART I.

|  | PAGE. |
|---|---|
| PROCEEDINGS OF THE NATIONAL REPUBLICAN CONVENTION | 7 |
| THE REPUBLICAN PLATFORM | 11 |
| NOMINATION OF GEN. JAMES A. GARFIELD | 16 |
| GEN. GARFIELD'S LETTER OF ACCEPTANCE | 17 |
| LIFE AND SERVICES OF GEN. GARFIELD | 25 |
| GEN. GARFIELD'S CONGRESSIONAL RECORD | 41 |
| LIFE OF GEN. CHESTER A. ARTHUR | 69 |
| PROCEEDINGS OF THE NATIONAL GREENBACK-LABOR CONVENTION | 74 |
| THE GREENBACK PLATFORM | 80 |
| NOMINATION OF GEN. JAMES B. WEAVER | 85 |
| GEN. WEAVER'S LETTER OF ACCEPTANCE | 88 |
| LIFE AND SERVICES OF GEN. WEAVER | 95 |
| GEN. WEAVER'S CONGRESSIONAL RECORD | 121 |
| LIFE OF COL. BENJAMIN J. CHAMBERS | 144 |
| PROCEEDINGS OF THE NATIONAL DEMOCRATIC CONVENTION | 150 |
| NOMINATION OF GEN. WINFIELD S. HANCOCK | 158 |
| THE DEMOCRATIC PLATFORM | 159 |
| GEN. HANCOCK'S LETTER OF ACCEPTANCE | 162 |
| LIFE AND SERVICES OF GEN. HANCOCK | 166 |
| GEN. HANCOCK'S MILITARY CAREER | 173 |
| GENERAL HANCOCK'S CIVIL SERVICES | 201 |
| LIFE OF WM. H. ENGLISH | 219 |

# ILLUSTRATIONS OF PART I.

|  | PAGE. |
|---|---|
| THE NATIONAL CAPITOL.................Frontispiece. | |
| THE EXPOSITION BUILDING, CHICAGO................ | 7 |
| PORTRAIT OF GEN. JAMES A. GARFIELD.............. | 25 |
| " " " CHESTER A. ARTHUR............. | 69 |
| " " " JAMES B. WEAVER................ | 95 |
| " " COL. BENJAMIN J. CHAMBERS.......... | 144 |
| THE EXPOSITION BUILDING, MUSIC HALL, CINCINNATI | 150 |
| PORTRAIT OF GEN. WINFIELD S. HANCOCK.......... | 166 |
| " " WILLIAM H. ENGLISH................ | 219 |

FOR OTHER ENGRAVINGS SEE PART II.

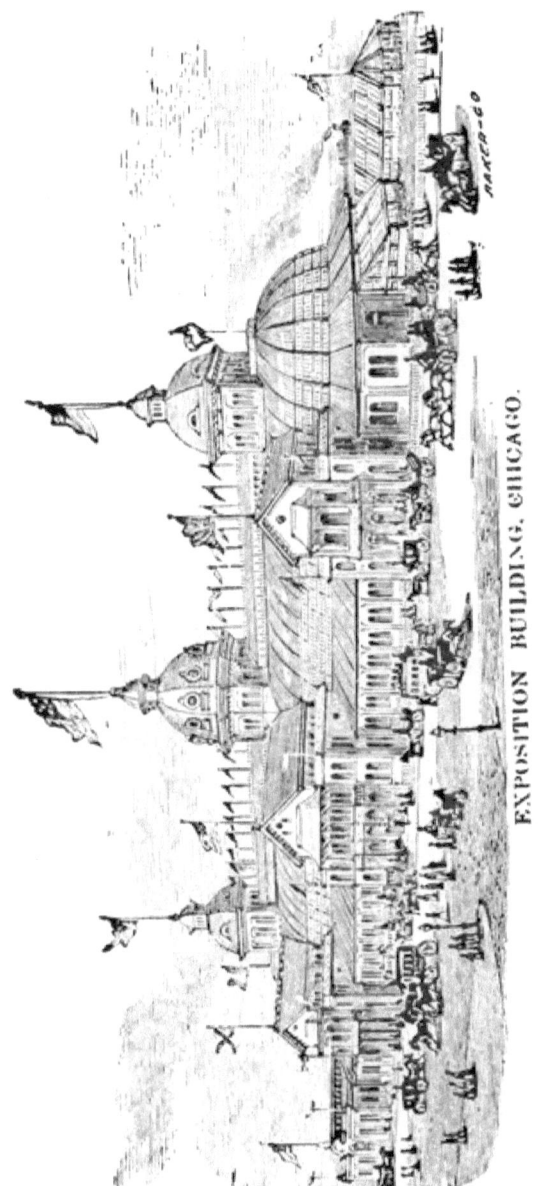

EXPOSITION BUILDING, CHICAGO.

# CHAPTER I.

### PROCEEDINGS OF NATIONAL REPUBLICAN CONVENTION.

During the present year, three political parties have held their conventions, declared their principles, and nominated their candidates for the offices of the President and Vice-President. Two of these were held in Chicago, and one in Cincinnati. We will briefly refer to the proceedings of each, in the order of time they took place.

### THE NATIONAL REPUBLICAN CONVENTION.

#### HELD AT CHICAGO, JUNE 2D–8TH, 1880.

The Seventh National Convention of the Republican party met on the 2d day of June, 1880, in Exposition Hall, at Chicago, and at five minutes past one o'clock, P. M., the Hon. J. Don Cameron, of Pennsylvania, Chairman of the National Republican Committee, called the Convention to order, and, at his request, the Rev. Dr. Kittredge, of Chicago, opened the proceedings with prayer, and Secretary Keogh read the call for the Convention.

Previous to the opening of the proceedings, the vast building and hall presented a scene of striking interest. Situated on the lake shore, within a short distance of the very heart of the city, it is within a few minutes' walk of all the great hotels. The roof, the sides, and every available point of the building were decorated with flags and banners of every size and description, and within the Hall were innumerable decorations, consisting of the flags of the nation, the coats-of-arms of the States, portraits of the Republican fathers, busts of national men—irrespective of party, and emblems of American achievements.

The portrait of the late Senator Chandler was placed over the Chairman's platform, and on the rear wall was Mr. Lincoln's portrait, surrounded by his own words, "And that government of the people, by the people, and for the people, shall not perish from the earth." There were portraits of eminent Republicans; there were busts of Franklin, Webster, Jackson, Douglas, Washington, Clay and others, set in brackets against the wall.

Large baskets of flowers ornamented the Chairman's desk, and plants were everywhere in profusion, while in the centre was stationed a military band, playing patriotic and other strains of music.

After the call had been read, Mr. Cameron briefly addressed the Convention, referring to the bitterness which had attended the preliminary canvass, and which he hoped would now disappear in the desire and determination to nominate for President the strongest candidate, and one who would command the respect of the civilized world. He counselled harmonious and united action. In conclusion, he announced that he had been instructed by the National Committee to put in nomination for temporary Chairman, the Hon. George F. Hoar, of Massachusetts.

The nomination was unanimously ratified, and Messrs. Davis of Texas, Frye of Maine, and Raum of Illinois, were appointed a committee to conduct him to the chair.

Judge Hoar addressed the Convention at some length. He said the function of the Convention, if wisely used, was that of naming the man whom the people would make President. His reference to the nomination of Mr. Lincoln, twenty years ago, was greeted with applause. Lincoln had gone to rest, but his associate on the ticket, Hamlin, was here to-day in full figure, still discharging actively his duty to the country and the party.

He reviewed briefly the history of the late war and its political incidents and consequences, and criticised the policy of the Democratic party in that connection. That party, he claimed, was to-day actuated by the old rebel spirit, and North, South, East and West was the party of fraud and injustice. In Maine, it ambitiously sought to pilfer a whole State, while on the other hand, the Republican party tells us of rebellion subdued, of slaves enfranchised, sound currency restored, and our flag floating everywhere, honored and respected. In conclusion, he said that the duties of the chair would be discharged fairly, and without respect of persons.

The Secretaries, and other temporary officers of the Convention, were then appointed. The call of the States was then proceeded with, and the regular committees appointed.

On June 3d, the Convention was called to order at 11.45 A. M., and during the morning session, the permanent organization was completed by the promotion of Mr. Hoar to be the President of the Convention, and the election of Vice-Presidents and Secretaries.

Much sparring, and some telling hits were made

between Mr. Conkling, of New York, who was the leader of the Grant or third term faction, and Mr. Frye, of Maine, who was working in the interests of Mr. Blaine, which created at times immense excitement and applause; but very little business was accomplished during the sessions of the day.

When the Convention was called to order on the third day, the great Hall was crowded, and presented a brilliant spectacle. Every seat, every place where standing room could be invented or appropriated, was filled. Prince Leopold, of England, and suite, were seated as spectators upon the platform, and watched all the proceedings with keen interest.

Senator Conkling began the business of the morning session, by moving a resolution, pledging each delegate to support the nominee of the Convention. The resolution was adopted, three West Virginia delegates alone voting against it. Mr. Conkling then moved that these delegates be declared unworthy to sit in the Convention, but after an animated discussion, in which General Garfield took a leading part, the Senator withdrew his resolution, and the coercion game failed. The evening session was a stormy one, and District representation was upheld, by a vote of 449 against 306.

On Saturday, the fourth day of the Convention, Hon. Edwards Pierrepont, of New York, Chairman of the Committee on Resolutions, reported the same, and they were adopted, having first been amended by the insertion of a civil service plank, and are as follows:

## THE PLATFORM.

The Republican party, in National Convention assembled, at the end of twenty years since the Federal Government was first committed to its charge, submits to the people of the United States this brief report of its administration. It suppressed a rebellion which had armed nearly a million of men to subvert the National authority. It reconstructed the union of the States, with freedom instead of slavery as its corner-stone. It transformed 4,000,000 of human beings from the likeness of things to the rank of citizens. It relieved Congress from the infamous work of hunting fugitive slaves, and charged it to see that slavery does not exist. It has raised the value of our paper currency from thirty-eight per cent. to the par of gold. It has restored, upon a solid basis, payment in coin for all the National obligations, and has given us a currency absolutely good, and equal in every part of our extended country. It has lifted the credit of the Nation from the point where six per cent. bonds sold at 86c., to that where four per cent. bonds are eagerly sought at a premium. Under its administration, railways have increased from 31,000 miles in 1860, to more than 82,000 miles in 1879. Our foreign trade has increased from $700,000,000 to $1,150,000,000 in the same time, and our exports, which were $20,000,000 less than our imports in 1860, were $264,000,000 more than our imports in 1879. Without resorting to loans it has, since the war closed, defrayed the ordinary expenses of Government, besides the accruing interest on the public debt, and has annually disbursed more than thirty millions for soldiers' pensions. It has paid $888,000,000 of the public debt, and by refunding the balance at lower rates, has reduced the annual interest charge from nearly $151,000,000 to less than $89,000,000. All the industries of the country have revived, labor is in demand, wages have increased, and throughout the entire country there is evidence of a coming prosperity greater than we have ever enjoyed.

Upon this record, the Republican party asks for the continued confidence and support of the people, and this Convention submits for their approval the following statements of the principles and purposes which will continue to guide and inspire its efforts:

First—We affirm that the work of the last twenty-one years has been such as to commend itself to the favor of the Nation, and that the fruits of the costly victories which we have achieved through immense difficulties should be preserved; that the peace regained should be cherished; that the dissevered Union, now happily restored, should be perpetuated, and that the liberties secured to this generation should be transmitted undiminished to future generations; that the order established and the credit acquired should never be impaired; that the pensions promised should be extinguished by the full payment of every dollar thereof; that the reviving industries should be further promoted, and that the commerce, already so great, should be steadily encouraged.

Second—The Constitution of the United States is a supreme law and not a mere contract; out of confederated States it made a sovereign Nation. Some powers are denied to the Nation, while others are denied to the States, but the boundary between the powers delegated and those reserved, is to be determined by the National, and not by the State tribunals.

Third—The work of popular education is one left to the care of the several States, but it is the duty of the National Government to aid that work to the extent of its constitutional duty. The intelligence of the Nation is but the aggregate of the intelligence in the several States, and the destiny of the Nation must be guided, not by the genius of any one State, but by the average genius of all.

Fourth—The Constitution wisely forbids Congress to make any law respecting an establishment of religion, but it is idle to hope that the Nation can be protected against the influence of sectarianism while each State is exposed to its domination. We therefore recommend that the Constitution be so amended, as to lay the same prohibition upon the Legislature of each State, and to forbid the appropriation of public funds to the support of sectarian schools.

Fifth—We affirm the belief avowed in 1876, that the duties levied for the purpose of revenue should so discriminate as to favor American labor; that no further grant of the public domain should be made to any railway, or other corporation; that slavery having perished in the States, the twin barbarity—polygamy—must die in the Territories; that everywhere the protection accorded to citizens of American birth must be secured to citizens by American adoption, and that we esteem it the duty of Congress to develop and improve our watercourses and harbors, but insist that further subsidies to private persons or corporations must cease; that the obligations of the Republic to the men who preserved its integrity in the hour of battle are undiminished by the lapse of the fifteen years since their final victory—to do them perpetual honor is, and shall forever be, the grateful privilege and sacred duty of the American people.

Sixth—Since the authority to regulate immigration and intercourse between the United States and foreign nations, rests with Congress, or with the United States and its treaty-making powers, the Republican party, regarding the unrestricted immigration of the Chinese as an evil of great magnitude, invoke the exercise of those powers to restrain and limit that immigration by the enactment of such just, humane and reasonable provisions as will produce that result.

Seventh—That the purity and patriotism which characterized the earlier career of Rutherford B. Hayes in peace and war, and which guided the thoughts of our immediate predecessors to him for a Presidential candidate, have continued to inspire him in his career as

Chief Executive, and that history will accord to his Administration the honors which are due to an efficient, just and courteous discharge of the public business, and will honor his interposition between the people and proposed partisan laws.

Eighth—We charge upon the Democratic party the habitual sacrifice of patriotism and justice to a supreme and insatiable lust of office and patronage; that to obtain possession of the National and State Governments and the control of place and position, they have obstructed all effort to promote the purity and to conserve the freedom of suffrage, and have devised fraudulent certifications and returns; have labored to unseat lawfully elected Members of Congress, to secure at all hazards the vote of a majority of the States in the House of Representatives; have endeavored to occupy by force and fraud the places of trust given to others by the people of Maine, and rescued by the courageous action of Maine's patriotic sons; have, by methods vicious in principle and tyrannical in practice, attached partisan legislation to appropriation bills, upon whose passage the very movements of the Government depends, and have crushed the rights of individuals; have advocated the principles and sought the favor of rebellion against the Nation, and have endeavored to obliterate the sacred memories of the war, and to overcome its inestimably valuable results of nationality, personal freedom and individual equality.

The equal, steady and complete enforcement of the laws, and the protection of all our citizens in the enjoyment of all privileges and immunities guaranteed by the Constitution, are the first duties of the Nation. The dangers of a Solid South can only be averted by a faithful performance of every promise which the Nation has made to the citizen. The execution of the laws and the punishment of all those who violate them, are the only safe methods by which an enduring peace can be secured and genuine prosperity established throughout the South. Whatever promises the Nation makes the Nation must perform, and the Nation cannot with safety regulate this duty to the States. The Solid South must be divided by the peaceful agencies of the ballot, and all opinions must there find free expression; and to this end the honest voter must be protected against terrorism, violence or fraud.

And we affirm it to be the duty and the purpose of the Republican party to use every legitimate means to restore all the States of this Union to the most perfect harmony that may be practicable, and we submit it to the practical, sensible people of the United States to say whether it would not be dangerous to the dearest interests of our country at this time to surrender the administration of the National Government to the party which seeks to overthrow the existing policy under which we are so prosperous, and thus bring distrust and confusion where there are now order, confidence and hope.

The Republican party, adhering to the principles affirmed by the last National Convention, of respect for the constitutional rules governing appointment to office, adopts the declaration of President Hayes that the reform in the Civil service shall be thorough, radical and complete; to that end it demands the co-operation of the legislative with the executive departments of the Government, and that Congress shall so legislate that fitness, ascertained by proper practical tests, shall admit to the public service.

The next order of business was the selection of a candidate for the Presidency, and the names of James G. Blaine, Ulysses S. Grant, John Sherman, George F. Edmunds, Elihu B. Washburn and William Windom, were duly presented, with forcible and appropriate remarks.

On Monday, the 7th of June, the balloting commenced. On the first ballot, Grant received 304, Blaine 284, Sherman 93, Edmunds 34, Washburn 30, and Windom 10. Whole number of votes, 755—necessary to a choice, 378.

There being no choice, balloting was resumed after a brief discussion, and during the day at both sessions *twenty-eight* ballots were taken, with but little change, as on the 28th ballot Grant received 307, Blaine 278, Sherman 91, Edmunds 31, Washburn 35, Windom 10, and Garfield 2.

On Tuesday, June 8th, the Convention was called to order at 10.30 A. M., and balloting was resumed at once, with but little change. On the 34th ballot, however, Garfield received 17 votes, and on the next he received 50. When the roll was called for the 36th ballot, the Blaine and Sherman States began to cast their votes for General Garfield, from the beginning of the call. It soon became plain that the contest was between Grant and Garfield.

A feeling of intense excitement soon reigned, and the crowd broke out repeatedly into tremendous cheering, interrupting the call. The band began to play "Hail to the Chief," and cannon began to fire a salute before the call was finished. General Garfield rose to a point of order, and said his name could not be used without his consent; but the call went on without heeding it.

The ballot resulted as follows:

   Whole number of votes, 755
   Necessary to a choice,  378
   Grant, . . .  306
   Blaine, . . . .  42

| | |
|---|---|
| Sherman, | 3 |
| Washburn, | 5 |
| Garfield, | 399 |

A scene of great enthusiasm followed. Congratulatory speeches were made by Conkling, Logan, Hale, Pleasants and others, and the nomination was made unanimous, and after singing "Rally Round the Flag," etc., a recess was taken.

After recess, at the evening session, Mr. Frye, of Maine, was called to the chair. Nominations were made for Vice-President, and the name of Chester A. Arthur, of New York, being presented by General Woodford, one ballot was taken, resulting as follows:

| | |
|---|---|
| Whole number of votes, | 743 |
| Necessary to a choice, | 373 |
| Washburn, | 193 |
| Jewell, | 44 |
| Maynard, | 30 |
| Bruce, | 8 |
| Arthur, | 468 |

The nomination was then made unanimous, and at 7.35 P. M. the Convention adjourned, *sine die*.

The following is General Garfield's Letter of Acceptance, addressed to Hon. George F. Hoar, Chairman, &c.:

### LETTER OF ACCEPTANCE.

MENTOR, O., July 12.

DEAR SIR: On the evening of the 8th of June last I had the honor to receive from you in the presence of the committee of which you were chairman, the official announcement that the Republican National Convention at

Chicago had that day nominated me as their candidate for President of the United States. I accept the nomination with gratitude for the confidence it implies, and with a deep sense of the responsibilities it imposes. I cordially indorse the principles set forth in the platform adopted by the Convention. On nearly all the subjects of which it treats, my opinions are on record among the published proceedings of Congress. I venture, however, to make special mention of some of the principal topics which are likely to become subjects of discussion.

Without reviewing the controversies which have been settled during the last twenty years, and with no purpose or wish to revive the passions of the late war, it should be said that while the Republicans fully recognize and will strenuously defend all the rights retained by the people, and all the rights reserved to the States, they reject the pernicious doctrine of State supremacy which so long crippled the functions of the National Government, and at one time brought the Union very near to destruction. They insist that the United States is a nation with ample power of self-preservation; that its Constitution and the Laws made in pursuance thereof, are the supreme law of the land; that the right of the Nation to determine the method by which its own Legislature shall be created, cannot be surrendered without abdicating one of the fundamental powers of Government; that the National laws relating to the election of Representatives in Congress, shall neither be violated nor evaded; that every elector shall be permitted, freely, and without intimidation, to cast his lawful ballot at such election and have it honestly counted, and that the potency of his vote shall not be destroyed by the fraudulent vote of any other person.

The best thoughts and energies of our people should be directed to those great questions of National well-being, in which all have a common interest. Such efforts will soonest restore perfect peace to those who were lately in arms against each other; for justice and goodwill will outlast passion. But it is certain that the wounds of the war cannot be completely healed, and the spirit of brotherhood cannot fully pervade the whole country until every citizen, rich or poor, white or black, is secure in the free and equal enjoyment of every civil and political right guaranteed by the Constitution and the laws. Wherever the enjoyment of these rights is not assured, discontent will prevail, immigration will cease, and the social and industrial forces will continue to be disturbed by the migration of laborers and the consequent diminution of prosperity. The National Government should exercise all its constitutional authority to put an end to these evils; for all the people and all the States are members of one body, and no member can suffer without injury to all. The most serious evils which now afflict the South, arise from the fact that there is not such freedom and toleration of political opinion and action that the minority party can exercise an effective and wholesome restraint upon the party in power. Without such restraint, party rule becomes tyrannical and corrupt. The prosperity which is made possible in the South by its great advantages of soil and climate, will never be realized until every voter can freely and safely support any party he pleases.

### POPULAR EDUCATION.

Next in importance to freedom and justice, is popular education, without which neither freedom nor justice can be permanently maintained. Its interests are intrusted to the States and to the voluntary action of the people. Whatever help the Nation can justly afford, should be generously given to aid the States in supporting common schools; but it would be unjust to our people and dangerous to our institutions to apply any portion of the revenues of the Nation, or of the States, to the support of sectarian schools. The separation of the Church and the State, in everything relating to taxation, should be absolute.

### THE NATIONAL FINANCES.

On the subject of National finances, my views have been so frequently and fully expressed, that little is needed in the way of additional statement. The public debt is now so well secured and the rate of annual interest has been so reduced by refunding, that rigid economy in expenditures and the faithful application of our surplus revenues to the payment of the principal of the debt, will gradually but certainly free the people from its burdens, and close with honor the financial chapter of the war. At the same time, the Government can provide for all its ordinary expenditures, and discharge its sacred obligations to the soldiers of the Union, and to the widows and orphans of those who fell in its defence. The resumption of specie payments, which the Republican party so courageously and successfully accomplished, has removed from the field of controversy many questions that long and seriously disturbed the credit of the Government and the business of the country. Our paper currency is now as National as the flag, and resumption has not only made it everywhere equal to coin, but has brought into use our store of gold and silver. The circulating medium is more abundant than ever before, and we need only to maintain the equality of all our dollars to insure to labor and capital a measure of value from the use of which no one can suffer loss. The great prosperity which the country is now enjoying, should not be endangered by any violent changes or doubtful financial experiments.

### THE TARIFF.

In reference to our custom laws, a policy should be pursued which will bring revenues to the Treasury, and will enable the labor and capital employed in our great industries to compete fairly in our own markets with the labor and capital of foreign producers. We legislate for the people of the United States, and not for the whole world; and it is our glory that the American laborer is more intelligent and better paid than his foreign competitor. Our country cannot be independent unless its people, with their abundant natural resources, possess the requisite skill at any time to clothe, arm and equip themselves for war, and in time of peace to produce all the necessary implements of labor. It was the manifest intention of the founders of the Government to provide for the common defence, not by standing armies alone, but by raising among the people a greater army of artisans, whose intelligence and skill should powerfully contribute to the safety and glory of the nation.

### INTERNAL IMPROVEMENTS.

Fortunately for the interests of commerce, there is no longer any formidable opposition to appropriations for the improvement of our harbors and great navigable rivers, provided that the expenditures for that purpose are strictly limited to works of National importance. The Mississippi river, with its great tributaries, is of such vital importance to so many millions of people, that the safety of its navigation requires exceptional consideration. In order to secure to the Nation the control of all its waters, President Jefferson negotiated the purchase of a vast territory, extending from the Gulf of Mexico to the Pacific Ocean. The wisdom of Congress should be invoked to devise some plan by which that great river shall cease to be a terror to those who dwell upon its banks, and by which its shipping may safely carry the industrial products of 25,000,000 of people. The interests of agriculture, which is the basis of all our material prosperity, and in which seven-twelfths of our population are engaged, as well as the interests of manufacturers and commerce, demand that the facilities for cheap transportation shall be increased by the use of all our great watercourses.

### CHINESE IMMIGRATION.

The material interests of this country, the traditions of its settlement and the sentiment of our people, have led the Government to offer the widest hospitality to emigrants who seek our shores for new and happier homes, willing to share the burdens as well as the benefits of our society, and intending that their posterity shall become an undistinguishable part of our population. The recent movement of the Chinese to our Pacific coast, partakes but little of the qualities of such an immigration, either in its purposes or its results. It is too much like an importation to be welcomed without restriction ; too much like an invasion to be looked upon without solicitude. We cannot consent to allow any form of servile labor to be introduced among us under the guise of immigration. Recognizing the gravity of this subject, the present Administration, supported by Congress, has sent to China a Commission of distinguished citizens, for the purpose of securing such a modification of the existing treaty, as will prevent the evils likely to arise from the present situation. It is confidently believed that these diplomatic negotiations will be successful without the loss of commercial intercourse between the two Powers, which promises a great increase of reciprocal trade and the enlargement of our markets. Should these efforts fail, it will be the duty of Congress to mitigate the evils already felt, and prevent their increase by such restrictions as, without violence or injustice, will place upon a sure foundation the peace of our communities and the freedom and dignity of labor.

### THE CIVIL SERVICE.

The appointment of citizens to the various executive and judicial offices of the Government is, perhaps, the most difficult of all duties which the Constitution has imposed on the Executive. The Convention wisely demands that Congress shall co-operate with the Executive Departments in placing the Civil Service on a better basis. Experience has proved that with our frequent changes of administration no system of reform can be made effective and permanent without the aid of legislation. Appointments to the military and naval service are so regulated by law and custom as to leave but little ground for complaint. It may not be wise to make similar regulations by law for the civil service. But, without invading the authority or necessary discretion of the Executive, Congress should devise a method that will determine the tenure of office, and greatly reduce the uncertainty which makes that service so uncertain and unsatisfactory. Without depriving any officer of his rights as a citizen, the Government should require him to discharge all his official duties with intelligence, efficiency and faithfulness. To select wisely from our vast population those who are best fitted for the many offices to be filled, requires an acquaintance far beyond the range of any one man. The Executive should, therefore, seek and receive the information and assistance of those whose knowledge of the communities in which the duties are to be performed, best qualifies them to aid in making the wisest choice.

The doctrines announced by the Chicago Convention are not the temporary devices of a party to attract votes and carry an election; they are deliberate convictions resulting from a careful study of the spirit of our institutions, the events of our history, and the best impulses of our people. In my judgment, these principles should control the legislation and administration of the Government. In any event, they will guide my conduct until experience points out a better way.

If elected, it will be my purpose to enforce strict obedience to the Constitution and the laws, and to promote, as best I may, the interest and honor of the whole country, relying for support upon the wisdom of Congress, the intelligence and patriotism of the people, and the favor of God. With great respect, I am very truly yours,

J. A. GARFIELD.

*To the* HON. GEORGE F. HOAR, *Chairman of Committee.*

GEN. JAMES A. GARFIELD.

## CHAPTER II.

### LIFE AND SERVICES OF GEN. JAMES A. GARFIELD,

#### BY EDWARD B. KENNEDY.

On June 8th, 1880, the Republican party in National Convention assembled, nominated JAMES A. GARFIELD, of Ohio, as its candidate for the office of President of the United States.

It is but natural that, as soon as a citizen is nominated for that high office, all thinking men should wish to learn his past history in order that they may judge of his mental and moral endowments and qualifications, and so be able to judge intelligently whether or not he is worthy of their suffrages. It is to meet such a want that this sketch has been written.

It is one of our proudest boasts that our republican institutions offer an opportunity for any person, no matter how poor or how humble his origin, to rise to the highest position within the gift of the people, provided he possesses the elements of character necessary to achieve success.

The life of General Garfield is a practical illustration of the fact that neither poverty nor obscurity, nor both combined, can succeed in conquering the man who is possessed of intellect, perseverance and integrity, and who meets a difficulty only to surmount it.

On both his father's and his mother's side, General

Garfield comes of old New England stock. The family records do not go back of his great-grandfather, Solomon Garfield, who lived at Weston, Massachusetts. Abraham Garfield, a brother of Solomon, was in the fight at Concord Bridge, and was one of those who sent affidavits to the Continental Congress to prove that the British were the aggressors in that affair. At the close of the Revolutionary War, he moved to Otsego county, New York. He bought wild land in the township of Worcester, where he settled. He had five children, one of whom, Thomas, was General Garfield's grand-father.

Thomas Garfield grew up in Worcester, married there, and had four children. He died when only thirty years old, of small-pox, which he had contracted during a journey to Albany. His son, Abram, the father of General Garfield, was but two years of age when his father died, and was bound out to James Stone, a relative on his mother's side. He left his guardian when only fifteen years old, and went to Madrid, St. Lawrence county, New York, where he resided for about three years.

At the age of eighteen he made his way to Newburg, Ohio, where he succeeded in obtaining employment.

There had resided in the township of Worcester at the same time with the Garfields, a family of Ballous. They were of Huguenot origin, and were directly descended from a Huguenot fugitive who had settled in Rhode Island. The Ballou and the Garfield children had been educated together in the same district school in Worcester. In 1814 they removed from Otsego county to Perry Township, near Zanesville, Ohio.

In 1820, Abram Garfield left Newburg, Ohio, to join

his Otsego county friends and former neighbors. Here he renewed his acquaintance with Eliza Ballou, and on the third of February, 1820, they were married, he being at this time a few months short of his majority, and she but eighteen.

Immediately on his marriage, Abram Garfield removed to Newburg, Ohio, now a part of the city of Cleveland, where he continued to reside for nearly six years. Three children were born here, Mehetable in 1821, Thomas in 1822, and Mary in 1824. In 1826 he procured a contract to construct three miles of canal, and with his family he removed to New Philadelphia, Tuscarawas county. They resided there for three years, during which time one son was born, James B., the only child they ever lost. He died in 1830.

In January, 1830, Abram went to Orange Township, Cuyahoga county. His half-brother, Amos Boynton, the child of his mother by her second marriage, lived there. They each bought a tract of wild land of about eighty acres in extent at $2.00 an acre, and proceeded to cut out their farms. For a few weeks the families lived together in a log house, built by the joint labor of the two men; but Garfield soon erected a house of his own near by. It was of the prevailing pattern of log houses. Its walls were of logs, its roof of rudely split shingles, and its floor of rough planking. The house had only one room, one end of which served as a kitchen, while at the other stood the bedstead. The younger children at night occupied a trundle-bed, which, during the day, was put under the parents' bed to be out of the way and give more room, while the older children climbed a ladder to a small loft where they found sleeping accommodations. In this house, on November 19, 1831, was born James Abram Garfield.

By constant toil, his father was clearing his land, planting fields, where but a short time since the forest had stood, and the future seemed all bright, when suddenly he was removed by death. During the Spring of 1833, a fire broke out in the woods, and Abram Garfield exerted himself to the utmost to keep the fire from his fences and fields. He became over-heated, and sitting down to rest where a cold wind blew, contracted a violent sore throat. By means of blisters, a country doctor succeeded in choking him to death. He was buried in a corner of a wheat field on his farm.

His death threw the family into great distress. They were deeply in debt, and Thomas, the oldest son, was but ten years of age. It seemed as though the homestead must be sold, and the family broken up.

Against the advice of her neighbors, Mrs. Garfield determined to keep her family together, sold fifty acres of the farm to pay the debts left by her husband, and managed by hard work and the exercise of the most rigid economy to rear her children.

Thomas did not marry until he was thirty, and now resides in Michigan. The two sisters are married, and live in Salem, Ohio.

During the Winter months, young Garfield received some tuition in the district schools, and in the Summer season he worked upon the farm, or in a carpenter's shop. Early in life he was ambitious to secure a good education, and all his efforts were bent in that direction.

Finding that the men employed on the Ohio and Erie Canal, which ran near his house, procured better wages than could be earned at the carpenter's bench, he became when seventeen years old a driver, and was subsequently advanced to the position of boatman.

Early in the year 1849, he determined to ship as a sailor on the lakes. From this he was dissuaded by his mother, after much labor. In March, his mother and his brother Thomas furnished him with $17, and in company with his cousins, William and Henry Boynton, he went to Chester, in order to attend the Academy at that place.

As they were not able to pay the price asked for board —$1.50 per week—they took a few cooking utensils, and hiring a room in an old, unpainted farm-house, they prepared their own meals. Here he first saw his future wife, Lucretia Randolph, a student at the same Academy with him. There was no association between them at this time, however, save in the classes.

There was a literary society connected with the Academy, and young Garfield began to take part in the debates, though not without many misgivings.

At the end of the term of twelve weeks, James went home, helped his brother on the farm, and worked at harvesting for day's wages. With the money he earned, he paid off the balance of a doctor's bill incurred during a fever brought on by hard work and exposure during his labors on the canal. When he returned to Chester in the fall, he was almost penniless. He made an arrangement with a carpenter to board him for $1.00 per week, and this sum he expected to earn by helping the carpenter on Saturdays. He succeeded in this arrangement, and at the close of the term returned home with $3.00 of his earnings in his pockets, and his debts all paid.

He now thought himself competent to teach school, and spent some time in searching for a position, but he met with so many rebuffs, that at last, thoroughly discouraged, he resolved never to seek another position, a resolution to which he has strictly adhered, all of his many civil, military and political positions having been conferred upon him without any solicitation on his part. While in this state of mind, he was offered the position of teacher at the district school at the "Ledge." The school had been broken up for two winters by the ruffianism of the larger scholars. He accepted the offer, took charge of the school, came out victor in a severe tussle with the district bully, and succeeded by patience, firmness and ingenuity in acquiring the affection and respect of both parents and scholars. As was the custom in those days, he boarded around the district.

In the Spring he had $48—more money than he had before possessed at any one time. He had long wished to secure a college education, but had regarded it as beyond his reach. But when he returned to Chester for his third term, he met a college graduate who furnished him with such information, that he resolved to bend all his energies to that one purpose. He thought that by hard work, both to prepare himself to enter, and to furnish himself with means to pay his expenses, he could get through in twelve years. He now began to study such things as were required to fit him for college. Before returning to Chester in the spring, he had united with the Disciples' Church, and his religious experience, together with the prospect of procuring the object of his desire, caused him to forever abandon his boyhood's idea of becoming a sailor.

When the spring term ended, he returned home, and during the summer worked at harvesting and carpentering. In the fall he again returned to Chester, and in the winter he taught school in Warrensville for $16 a month and board. One of the scholars wished to study geometry, and Garfield, who had never advanced so far in mathematics, bought a text book, studied nights and took his pupil through, without its once being suspected but that the master was fully informed.

In the spring he went with his mother to visit some relatives in Muskingum county, and during this journey rode for the first time on a railroad. While on this visit he taught a spring school on Back Run, in Harrison township.

In the summer he returned to Orange and decided to continue his education at Hiram College, a new institution just established by the Disciples at Hiram, Portage county, Ohio, and in August, 1851, he entered there. He lived in a room with four other pupils, and continued energetically to prepare himself for college. During this term he made rapid progress in Latin and Greek. In the winter he again taught school at Warrensville, earning $18 a month. When the spring came, he returned to Hiram to prosecute his studies, and during the summer vacation he worked at his trade as a carpenter.

At Hiram, he met two women, who both exercised a large influence over his future life. One, Miss Almeda A. Booth, was a teacher in the school, and possessed a mind of remarkable strength and range. She guided and accompanied him in his studies, and the friendship established here continued until her death a few years since. The other was his former fellow-student at Chester, Lucretia Randolph, now his wife. Her father had settled at Hiram to educate his four children. A strong mutual attachment sprung from their association, and they entered into an engagement to marry as soon as Garfield succeeded in establishing himself.

At the beginning of his second year at Hiram, one of the teachers was forced to suspend his labors by reason of illness, and young Garfield was made a tutor in his place, and during his subsequent stay there was both teacher and scholar, and was working all this time to fit himself for college. His future wife recited to him two years in Greek.

When Garfield commenced his course at Hiram, he had studied Latin only six weeks, and had just commenced Greek, and was therefore just ready to begin his four years preparatory course to fit himself to enter the Freshman class at college. Yet in *three* years he fitted himself to enter the Junior class, two years further along, thus crowding the work of six years into three, and at the same time earning his own living by teaching.

In the Spring of 1854, he wrote to the Presidents of Yale, Williams and Brown, stating what his studies had been, and enquiring what class he could enter, provided he passed satisfactory examinations in them. They all wrote that he could enter the Junior class. President Hopkins added this sentence to the business part of his letter: "If you come here, we shall do what we can for you," and this seemed to Garfield to extend a helping hand to him and caused him to decide to enter Williams College. He had been pressed to go to a college in Bethany, Virginia, which had been founded by Alexander Campbell, and was under the auspices of the Disciples. But wishing to secure better opportunities for learning and culture, he resisted all endeavors to dissuade him from entering Williams.

How to get the money necessary to pay his college expenses, was a problem which caused him much anxiety. During his stay at Hiram he had been able to put aside a small amount, but not sufficient to carry him through his two years course. A kind-hearted gentleman, many years his senior, loaned him the amount, and so set at rest his fears on that point. Garfield was so scrupulous about the payment of this debt, that he procured an insurance on his life for its amount, and gave the policy to his creditor, telling him that if he lived he would pay the debt off, and if he died, the policy would be security against loss. Soon after he was graduated, the debt was repaid.

He went to Williams in the Fall of 1854, and passing a satisfactory examination entered the Junior class. His college course was marked by the same unflagging zeal and unwearied application which has always characterized him in every undertaking. He pursued his studies closely and carefully, and entered on a course of reading in general literature, which served to broaden his mind and furnished him with much valuable information which was of great service to him in after years. Here he first became acquainted with the works of celebrated novelists, and his enjoyment and appreciation of them was very great. Prior to this time, he had been disposed to regard the reading of light literature, as a waste of precious time. Now, however, he was forced to turn to it as a means of rest and recreation, to a mind wearied and worn by constant and unremitting toil, with weighty matters.

During his stay at Williams, he occupied his vacation time by teaching, and during one winter it is said he taught a district school at North Pownal, Vt., which during the preceding winter had been taught by Chester A. Arthur, now his associate on the Republican ticket. At one time he taught a school at Poestenkill, Rensselaer county, New York, a small village near Troy. While there he often visited Troy, and became well acquainted with many persons residing in that city. He received a very tempting offer of a position as a teacher in one of the schools in that place, and although it offered him an opportunity to discharge his debts, and to at once obtain a situation of comparative comfort, he refused it, because it involved his relinquishing his cherished plan of completing his college course. In 1856 he was graduated from Williams with honor. Ex-President Hopkins has said of him that while his college life was not marked by any remarkable occurrence, it was so because it was a fully and perfectly rounded life, and in all respects just such a life as that of every college student should be. Among his classmates he was noted for his wonderful industry as a student, his physical activity in college games, and his heartiness and cordiality in social matters.

After the close of his college course he returned to

Ohio, and in a short time he became Professor of Latin and Greek at Hiram College. During the following year, when only twenty-six years old, Garfield was made the President of this institution. His influence in his new position was remarkable. He more than doubled the attendance, raised the standard of scholarship, strengthened the faculty, and inspired all with his own enthusiasm, energy and zeal.

It has been said that at one time General Garfield was a minister, but this is not so. The only foundation for the statement rests on the fact that he used to speak in the churches of the denomination of which he was a member. The Disciples had no regular ministers, but supported a few traveling elders, and very often were addressed by their own lay members who had the ability to preach.

During all of General Garfield's connection with Hiram College, he followed closely and with his accustomed energy and zeal, the study of his chosen profession of the law, and at the same time read largely of general literature.

It seemed now as though his place in life was won, and he was united to the object of his youthful affections, Lucretia Randolph. Miss Randolph was a well educated, refined and affectionate young lady. She shared with her husband his thirst for learning, and his ambition for culture, and has been his companion in all his studies. Much of General Garfield's success in his subsequent career, may justly be attributed to his fortunate marriage.

In 1857 and 1858, General Garfield had taken quite an **active part** in the political campaigns, and had acquired a reputation as a vigorous, eloquent and logical orator. In 1859 he was elected to the Ohio State Senate, to represent the counties of Portage and Summit. He did not think a few weeks during the winter, spent at Columbus, would seriously break in upon or interfere with his work at Hiram College, and so accepted the position. His most intimate friend in the Senate was Jacob D. Cox, afterwards Major-General, Governor of Ohio, and Secretary of the Interior under President Grant. During the session of 1860-61, Garfield vigorously aided the State to prepare to assist the general government in the conflict which was approaching. When the cloud of civil war descended upon the country, Garfield put aside everything and entered the army. A company was formed consisting entirely of students of Hiram College, and was attached to the 42d Ohio Infantry. At that time the regiments when organized elected their own field officers by ballot, and Garfield was chosen by the 42d Ohio as its Colonel.

The regiment took the field in Eastern Kentucky, then under command of General D. C. Buell, and forming part of the "Department of the Ohio." The force under Buell was expected to push on in the direction of Tennessee, and occupy all of the territory included in his department. The movements of the rebels in Eastern Kentucky caused a brief diversion from this object, and seriously threatened to inflict severe injury to him if he moved. Humphrey Marshall was in the field, and at the beginning of January, 1862, was in the command of about 2,500 insurgents, intrenched in the neighborhood of Paintsville, in Johnstown county, on the main branch of the Big Sandy River, that forms the boundary line between Kentucky and Virginia. Colonel Garfield was assigned to the command of the 18th Brigade, and was ordered by General Buell to drive Marshall out of Kentucky. His force was outnumbered two to one, and he was entirely without any military experience, while opposed to him was a force well intrenched, and commanded by an officer who had served, during the Mexican war, with distinction.

Colonel Garfield's force was composed of the 42d Ohio and 14th Kentucky Regiments of Infantry, and 300 of the 2d Virginia Cavalry. By a forced night march along the course of the river, a march of great danger and difficulty, and undertaken at an inclement season of the year, he succeeded in reaching Marshall's position, only to find that Marshall on hearing of his approach had fled in alarm up the river in the direction of Prestonburg. Garfield's cavalry was at once dispatched in pursuit, and succeeded in overtaking Marshall's cavalry at the mouth of Junio Creek, from which point, after a brief encounter, they drove them several miles.

On the following day, Colonel Garfield set out in pursuit with about 1,100 of his men, and succeeded in overtaking Marshall in the Forks of Middle creek, where he was strongly posted. Here they fought a battle which lasted from one o'clock in the afternoon until dark, and resulted in the entire defeat of Marshall, and the driving him from all his positions. Garfield having been reinforced by 700 men, was enabled to make victory at the Battle of Prestonburg complete. Marshall fled, after having destroyed all his baggage. He left, however, a small force in Pound Gap, which was well fortified, and held as a post of observation.

On March 14, 1862, Colonel Garfield, with a force of 500 Infantry and 200 Cavalry, started to dislodge them. After a hard march of ten days, he succeeded in reaching the Gap, and at once proceeded to attack the position. Sending his cavalry ahead on the road to attract the enemy's attention, he with his infantry scaled the rocks to their post unobserved. A few volleys sufficed to scatter the force left to hold the Gap, and it fled. The services here performed were of vastly more importance, strategically considered, than the number of men employed in them would seem to indicate. They put an end to a flank movement which was seriously interfering with Buell's plans, and served to clear Eastern Kentucky entirely. For his services in this brief campaign, Colonel Garfield was rewarded with the commission of Brigadier-General of Volunteers.

He was now ordered to join Buell, and was assigned to the command of the 20th Brigade. He was in command of this Brigade when Buell reached Grant at Pittsburgh Landing, and took part in the second day's battle. He also commanded it at the seige of Corinth. In August, he was forced by reason of ill health to abandon for a time active operations in the field, and at this time he was made a member of the Court-Martial to try Fitz John Porter.

In January, 1863, he was again ordered to active duty, and directed to report to General Rosecranz, who had been placed in command of the "Army of the Cumberland."

General Rosecranz offered him the position of Chief of Staff, which he accepted. At the battle of Chickamauga he personally wrote every order, save one, submitting each one to the Commanding General for approval. That one was the fatal order which lost the day. The officer who wrote it failed to express it clearly, and General Wood, to whom it was sent, misunderstood its meaning, the result being that the movement made in consequence of it, opened a gap in the line, through which the rebels poured, flanking and annihilating General Rosecranz's right wing.

Trying vainly to check the retreat of Rosecranz, General Garfield was swept with his Chief back beyond Rossville. But he could not concede that the defeat had been entire, and obtained permission of Rosecranz to proceed to General Thomas's head-quarters. Not knowing the precise position of Thomas, he took his course in the direction indicated by the sound of the guns. It was a perilous ride. His horse was shot under him, and his orderly killed by his side. Alone, he pushed on over the obstructed road, through pursuers and pursued, reached Thomas, told him of the disaster on the right, and explained how he could withdraw his right wing and fix it upon a new line to meet Longstreet. The movement was made just in time, but Thomas's line was too short. Longstreet poured his men into the gap, and would have destroyed Thomas, but for the timely arrival of General Granger, with Steedman's division.

After a terrible struggle, unequalled even upon this terrible day, Longstreet was driven back. As night closed in upon the gallant Army of the Cumberland, Generals Garfield and Granger on foot, and enveloped in smoke, directed the loading and pointing of a battery of Napoleon guns, whose flash as they thundered after the retreating column of the assailants, was the last light that shone upon the battle field of Chickamauga.

For his services at Chickamauga, General Garfield was promoted to be Major-General of Volunteers.

*"General Garfield's military career was not of a nature to subject him to trials on a large scale. He approved himself a good, independent commander in the small operations in the Sandy Valley. His campaign there opened our series of successes in the West; and though fought against superior forces, began with us the habit of victory. After that he was only a subordinate. But he always enjoyed the confidence of his immediate superiors, and of the Department. As a Chief of Staff, he was unrivalled. There, as elsewhere, he was ready to accept the gravest responsibilities in following his convictions. The bent of his mind was aggressive; his judgment of purely military matters was good; his papers on the Tullahoma campaign will stand a monument of his courage, and his far-reaching, soldierly sagacity; and his conduct at Chickamauga will never be forgotten by a nation of brave men."

---

*Whitelaw Reid's "Ohio in the War."

## CHAPTER III.

### HIS CONGRESSIONAL RECORD.

In the Summer of 1862, when every one was looking for the speedy termination of the War, a number of officers who had achieved distinction by reason of services in the field, were selected at home for Representatives in Congress.

Among the number was General Garfield. He was elected from the district which had formerly been represented by Joshua R. Giddings, by a large majority. This honor which had been conferred upon him while he was serving with his brigade in Kentucky, and had been entirely unsought by him, and which was therefore all the more valued, caused him considerable trouble. To leave his command and return to peaceful scenes, while there was still work to do in the field, even though it would only be a change of duty, seemed to him almost like desertion. He nearly resolved on several occasions that he would resign his seat in Congress, and remain in the military service. But the earnest solicitation and advice of his friends, coupled with the fact that there was no prospect of any active military operations during the winter months, finally decided him to take his new office. He retained his position in the Army, however, until it was absolutely necessary for him to resign in order to take his seat. General Garfield has often expressed regret that he did not serve through the war.

In Congress, General Garfield at once became eminent. His natural sagacity and discernment, his studiousness, his logic and eloquence, all combined to place him in the front rank of the Republican leaders. He was placed on the Military Committee, of which General Schenck was Chairman, and by his intelligence and untiring energy, was of great service in carrying through the measures which recruited the armies during the closing years of the war.

Here, as elsewhere, General Garfield prosecuted his studies with a zeal which nothing could abate. Finding himself called upon to legislate on matters concerning the finances, tariff, internal revenue, and all questions of political economy and public policy which can come before a legislative body, he entered upon an arduous course of study in order that he might not only be himself informed on all these matters, but that he might be able to inform others who had not his opportunities for study, of the true principles which should guide and control their action. All with whom he came in contact saw that he was destined to make his mark upon the politics of the country.

In 1864, he was renominated without opposition, and re-elected by an increased majority. He served on the Committee of Ways and Means.

In 1866, his renomination was opposed by a few of his constituents, on the ground that he did not favor as high a tariff on iron as they wished. He was, however, renominated by the Convention, and was re-elected by a large majority. During this term, he was Chairman of the Committee on Military Affairs, and took an active part in remodeling the Army, and looking after the demands of discharged soldiers for pay and bounty, of which many had been deprived.

In 1868, General Garfield was again re-elected, and was appointed Chairman of the Committee on Banking and Currency, and was also on the Committee on the Ninth Census.

In 1871, General Garfield was made Chairman of the Committee on Appropriations, which post he held until 1875, when the Democrats gained control of the House of Representatives. Under his leadership, the expenditures of the Government were largely reduced, and a new and better system of estimates and appropriations devised, which provided a closer accountability on the part of those who disbursed the money, and full information on the part of those who should vote to appropriate it of its intended use.

When James G. Blaine went to the Senate, General Garfield was chosen by the Republicans as their candidate for Speaker, and by custom, became the acknowledged leader of that party in the House. This position he had really long held by virtue of his well known probity of character and acknowledged ability. In January last he received an honor never before conferred upon any Ohio Republican, that of a unanimous nomination by the Republicans of the Ohio Legislature to the office of Senator of the United States. He was elected to succeed Hon. Allen G. Thurman, whose term of office expires on March 4, 1881.

As General Garfield has been before the country for twenty years, eighteen years of which time have been spent in the House of Representatives, and as during all of that time he has been one of the leaders of the Republican party, his views on all important topics have been expressed again and again in his public utterances, and we can best gain a knowledge of those views on matters of policy which are now of so much moment, by turning to those utterances and weighing fairly and candidly their meaning and their bearing.

His financial views, always sound, have been strengthened by his studies. At all times has General Garfield been an advocate of honest money; at all times has he stood up and manfully striven against the assaults of the inflationists. As early as 1866, when the din of carnage had scarcely subsided, he began to advocate the payment and retirement of the Greenbacks. On March 19, 1866, in a speech on a bill introduced for that purpose, he said:

"I am an advocate of paper money, but that paper money must represent what it professes on its face. I do not wish to hold in my hand the printed lies of the Government; I want its promise to pay signed by the high officers of the Government, sacredly kept in the exact meaning of the words of the promise. Let us not continue this conjurer's art by which sixty cents shall discharge a debt of one hundred cents. I do not want industry everywhere to be thus crippled and wounded, and its wounds plastered over with legally authorized lies. * * * * *

"I propose, sir, to let the house take the responsibility of adopting or rejecting this measure. On the one side, it is proposed to return to solid and honest values; on the other, to float in the boundless and shoreless sea of paper money, with all its dishonesty and broken pledges.

\* \* \* \* Choose the one, and you float away into an unknown sea of paper money that shall know no decrease, until you take just such a measure as is now proposed to bring us back again to solid values. Delay the measure, and it will cost the country dear; adopt it now, and with a little depression and a little stringency in the money market, the worst will be over and we shall have reached the solid earth. Sooner or later, such a measure must be adopted. Go on as you are now going, and a financial crisis, worse than that of 1837, will bring us to the bottom."

In an article on "The Currency Conflict," published in the *Atlantic Monthly* for February, 1876, General Garfield discusses the financial question at length. We give a few extracts:

"Three thousand years of experience have proved that the precious metals are the best materials of which to make the standard of value, the instrument of exchange. They are themselves a store of value; they are durable, divisible, easily transported, and more constant in value than any other known substances. In the form of dust and bars, as merchandise, their value is precisely equal to their declared value as money, less the very small cost of coinage. Coin made of these metals measures wealth, because it represents wealth in itself, just as the yard-stick measures length, and the standard pound measures weight, because each has, in itself, that which it represents.

"Again, the precious metals are products of labor, and their value, like that of all other merchandise, depends upon the cost of production. A coin represents and measures the labor required to produce it; it may be called an embodiment of labor. Of course this statement refers to the average cost of production throughout the world, and that average has varied but little for many centuries. It is a flat absurdity to assert that such a reality as labor can be measured and really represented by that which costs little or no labor. For these reasons the precious metals have been adopted by the common law of the world as the best materials in which to embody the unit of money.

\* \* \* \* \* \*

The word 'dollar' is the substantive word, the fundamental condition of every contract, of every sale, of every payment, whether at the Treasury or at the stand of the apple woman in the street. The dollar is the guage that measures every blow of the hammer, every article of merchandise, every exchange of property. Forced by the necessities of war, we substituted for this dollar the printed promise of the government to pay a dollar. That promise we have not kept. We have suspended payment, and have compelled the citizen to receive dishonored paper in place of money.

\* \* \* \* \* \*

In all such transactions, capital is usually able to take care of itself. The laborer has but one commodity for sale, his day's work. It is his sole reliance. He must sell it to-day or it is lost forever. What he buys must be bought to-day. He cannot wait till prices fall. He is at the mercy of the market. Buying or selling, the waves of its fluctuations beat against him. Daniel Webster never uttered a more striking truth than when he said : 'Of all the contrivances for cheating the laboring classes of mankind, none has been more effectual than that which deludes them with paper money. This is the most effectual of inventions to fertilize the rich man's field by the sweat of the poor man's face.'

\* \* \* \* \* \*

"The duty of the government to make its currency equal to real money, is undeniable and imperative. First, because the public faith is most solemnly pledged, and this alone is a conclusive and unanswerable reason why it should be done. The perfidy of one man, or of a million men, is as nothing compared with the perfidy of a nation. The public faith was the talisman that brought to the Treasury thirty-five hundred million dollars in loans, to save the life of the nation, which was not worth saving if its honor be not also saved. The public faith is our only hope of safety from the dangers that may assail us in the future. The public faith was pledged to redeem these notes in the very act which created them, and the pledge was repeated when each additional issue was ordered. It was again repeated in the act of 1869, known as the 'act to strengthen the public credit,' and yet again in the act of 1875, promising redemption in 1879.

"Second. The government should make its currency equal to gold, because the material prosperity of the people demands it. Honest dealing between man and man requires it. Just and equal legislation for the people, safety in trade—domestic and foreign, security in business, just distribution of the rewards of labor—none of these are possible until the present false and uncertain standard of value has given place to the real, the certain, the universal standard. Its restoration will hasten the revival of commercial confidence, which is the basis of all sound credit.

"Third. Public morality demands the re-establishment of our ancient standard. The fever of speculation which our fluctuating currency has engendered, cannot be allayed till its cause is destroyed. A majority of all the crimes relating to money that have been committed in public and private life since the war, have grown out of the innumerable opportunities for sudden and inordinate gains which this fluctuation has offered.

\* \* \* \* \* \*

"Our public faith is the symbol of our honor and the pledge of our future safety."

General Garfield has been the constant and untiring enemy of all classes and character of political jobbery and corruption. During his term of service as Chairman of the Appropriations Committee, the famous act for increasing the salaries of Congressmen, known as the "Salary grab," and which was made to operate retroactively, was introduced by General B. F. Butler, of Massachusetts, and was strenuously opposed at every step by General Garfield, he both speaking and voting against it, and only consenting to its final passage when it became necessary to save bringing on an extra session of Congress. His name is fourth on the list of those who covered their "back pay" into the Treasury.

It has been charged against him that he was bribed to make large appropriations on behalf of the Board of Public Works of Washington, by a fee of $5,000 paid by certain persons interested in the notorious "De Golyer" pavement patents. The facts in regard to the case are very simple. In 1874 a gentleman in General Garfield's district wrote to Hon. J. M. Wilson, who was chairman of the Joint Committee on the part of the House, a letter of inquiry as to the testimony affecting Garfield, and received in answer the following letter, which fully states all that was adduced before the committee, which in any way related to or affected General Garfield:

CONNERSVILLE, Ind., August 1, 1874.

*Hon. George W. Steele:*

DEAR SIR: To the request for information as to whether or not the action of General Garfield in connection with the affairs of the District of Columbia was the subject of condemnation by the committee that recently had those affairs under consideration, I answer that it was not; nor was there, in my opinion, any evidence that would have warranted any unfavorable criticism upon his conduct.

The facts disclosed by the evidence, so far as he is concerned, are briefly these:

The Board of Public Works was considering the question as to the kind of pavements that should be laid. There was a contest as to the respective merits of various wooden pavements. Mr. Parsons represented, as attorney, the De Golyer & McClelland patent, and being called away from Washington about the time the hearing was to be had before the Board of Public Works on this subject, procured General Garfield to appear before the Board in his stead and argue the merits of this patent. This he did, and this was the whole of his connection in the matter. It was not a question as to the kind of contract that should be made, but as to whether this particular kind of pavement should be laid. The criticism of the committee was not upon the pavement in favor of which General Garfield argued, but was upon the contract made with reference to it; and there was no evidence which would warrant the conclusion that he had anything to do with the latter.

Very respectfully, &c.,

J. M. WILSON.

During the Greeley campaign of 1872, charges of bribery and corruption in connection with the "Credit Mobilier" were brought against a number of Republican Congressmen. It was alleged that they had accepted stock in that corporation, which was of great value, as pay for their official action. Among those whose names were so used was General Garfield.

At the opening of the next session of Congress a committee was appointed to investigate the charges. After a long and thorough examination of all the witnesses, documents, and facts, the committee reported, distinctly acquitting General Garfield of all charges of a corrupt nature. General Garfield testified before this committee on January 14th, 1873, "I never owned, received, or agreed to receive any stock of the Credit Mobilier or of the Union Pacific Railroad, or any dividend or profits arising from either of them." He also said in substance that Oakes Ames offered him some of the stock; that he enquired as to the liability of stockholders, and Mr. Ames could not then inform him. Subsequently learning that there was a question as to Mr. Ames' right to sell the stock, he informed Ames that he had concluded not to buy; that the only money transaction he had ever had with Ames was that on his return from a European trip, being in need of money, he had borrowed $300 from Ames, which he had repaid. Against this testimony is set the testimony of Oakes Ames. Mr. Ames had testified on December 17th, 1872, "I agreed to get 10 shares of stock for him, and hold it until he could pay for it. He never did pay for it, or receive it." When asked if Garfield ever received any dividends he said, "No, sir; I think not. He says he did not. My own recollection is not very clear." When questioned in regard to the loan he said, "Yes, I am willing to so understand it. I do not recollect paying him any dividend, and have forgotten that I paid him any money." This testimony entirely corroborates that of General Garfield. Ames agrees that the stock was never paid for, or received; that there was a loan of $300, and that he can remember no payment of dividends.

After General Garfield had testified, Ames was recalled, when he testified: "In June (no year given) I received a dividend in cash on his stock of $600—which left a balance due him of $329—which I paid him."

The conflict between this and Ames' earlier testimony is obvious. Then he had no recollection of paying any dividend. Now he speaks precisely of $329. Then he recalled a loan of three hundred or four hundred dollars. Now, when asked if he ever made such a loan, he says: "Not to my knowledge, except that he calls this a loan."

The points of agreement and difference between General Garfield's testimony and Mr. Ames' may thus be stated: They agree that soon after the session of 1867-8, Mr. Ames offered to sell General Garfield ten shares of Credit Mobilier stock at par and accrued interest; that General Garfield never paid him any money on that offer; that General Garfield never received a certificate of stock; that after the month of June, 1868, General Garfield never received, demanded or was offered any dividend in any form on that stock. They also agreed that General Garfield once received from Mr. Ames a small sum of money. On the following points they disagreed: Mr. Ames claims that General Garfield agreed to take the stock. General Garfield denies it. Mr. Ames claims that General Garfield received from him $329 and no more, as a balance of dividends on the stock. General Garfield denied it, and asserted that he borrowed from him $300 and no more, and afterward returned it, and that he never received anything from him on account of stock.

Now as to the proof. Part of the memoranda offered by Mr. Ames in evidence were the entries in his diary for 1868. The account entered under General Garfield's name was one of three not crossed off, which Mr. Ames explained was because it had never been settled or adjusted. Here is the entry in full.

### GARFIELD.

| | | |
|---|---:|---:|
| 10 shares Credit M | $1,000 | 00 |
| 7 mos. 10 days | 43 | 36 |
| Total | $1,043 | 36 |
| 80 per cent. bd. div., at 97 | 776 | 00 |
| | $267 | 36 |
| Int. to June 26 | 3 | 64 |
| Total | $271 | 00 |

1,000 C. M.
1,000 U. P.

Notwithstanding he said he had no other entry in relation to Mr. Garfield on the 22d of January, Mr. Ames presented to the committee a statement of an alleged account with General Garfield, as follows:

| | J. A. G. | Dr. |
|---|---|---:|
| 1868. | To 10 shares stock Credit Mobilier of A | $1,000 |
| | Interest | 47 |
| June 19. | To cash | 329 |
| | Total | $1,376 |
| | | Cr. |
| 1868. | By dividend bonds Union Pacific Railroad $1,000 at 80 per cent., less 3 per cent | $776 |
| June 17. | By dividend collected for your account | 600 |
| | Total | $1,376 |

This account he claimed to have made up from his memorandum book, but when the memorandum book was subsequently presented it was found that the account here quoted was not copied from it, but was partly made up from memory. By comparing this account with the entry made in diary, as first quoted, it will be seen that they are not duplicates either in substance or form; and that in this account a new element is added, namely, an alleged payment of $329 in cash June 19. This is the very element in dispute. The pretended proof that this sum was paid General Garfield is found in the production of a check drawn by Mr. Ames on the Sergeant-at-Arms. The following is the language of the check as reported in the testimony:

June 22, 1868.

Pay O. A. or bearer three hundred and twenty-nine dollars and charge to my account.

OAKES AMES.

This check bears no indorsement or other marks than the words and figures given above. It was drawn on the 22d day of June, and, as shown by the books of the Sergeant-at-Arms, was paid the same day. But if this check was paid to General Garfield on the account just quoted it must have been delivered to him three days before it was drawn, for the account says that he received payment on the 19th of June.

General Garfield himself has made a review of the whole subject, and from it claims that the following conclusions are clearly established by the evidence:

That I neither purchased nor agreed to purchase the Credit Mobilier stock which Mr. Ames offered to sell me, nor did I receive any dividend arising from it. This appears not only from my own testimony, but from that first given by Mr. Ames, which is not overthrown by his subsequent statements, and is strongly confirmed by the fact that in the case of each of those who did purchase the stock there was produced as evidence of the sale either a certificate of stock, receipt of payment, a check drawn in the name of the payee or entries in Mr. Ames' diary of a stock account marked, adjusted and closed, but that no one of these evidences existed in reference to me. This position is further confirmed by the subsequent testimony of Mr. Ames, who though he claimed that I did receive $329 from him on account of stock, yet he repeatedly testified that beyond that amount I never received or demanded any dividend; that none was ever offered to me, nor was the subject ever alluded to in conversation. Mr. Ames admitted in his testimony that after December, 1867, the various stock and bond dividends amounted to an aggregate of more than 800 per centum, and that between January, 1868, and May, 1871, all these dividends were paid to several of those who had purchased stock. My conduct was wholly inconsistent with the supposition of such ownership, for during the year 1869 I was borrowing money to build a house in Washington, and securing my creditors by mortgages on my property; and all this time it is admitted that I received no dividends and claimed none. The attempt to prove a sale of the stock to me is wholly inconclusive, for it rests first on a check payable to Mr. Ames himself, concerning which he said several times in his testimony he did not know to whom it was paid, and, second, upon loose undated entries in his diary, which neither prove a sale of the stock nor any payment on it. The only fact from which it is possible for Mr. Ames to have inferred an agreement to buy the stock was the loan to me of $300. But that loan was made months before the check of June 22, 1868, and was repaid in the winter of 1869, and after that date there were no transactions of any sort between us, and before the investigation ended Mr. Ames admitted that on the chief point of difference between us he might be mistaken.

That the offer which Mr. Ames made to me, as I understood it, was one which involved no wrong or impropriety. I had no means of knowing and had no reasons for supposing that behind this offer to sell me a small amount of stock lay hidden a scheme to defraud the Pacific Railroad and imperil the interests of the United States, and on the first intimation of the real nature of the case I declined any further consideration of the subject. That whatever may have been the facts in the case, I stated them in my testimony as I have always understood them; and there has been no contradiction, prevarication nor evasion on my part.

In winding up his review of the whole matter General Garfield uses the following language:

If there be a citizen of the United States who is willing to believe that for $329 I have bartered away my good name, and to falsehood have added perjury, these words are not addressed to him. If there be one who thinks that any part of my public life has been gauged on so low a level as these charges would place it, I do not address him. I address those who are willing to believe that it is possible for a man to serve the public without personal dishonor. I have endeavored in this review to point out the means by which the managers of a corporation wearing the garb of honorable industry have robbed and defrauded a great national enterprise, and attempted by cunning and deception for selfish ends to enlist in its interests those who would have been the first to crush the attempt had their objects been known.

Hon. Jeremiah S. Black, of Pennsylvania, a prominent Democrat, bears testimony to General Garfield's entire innocence in this matter. In a letter written to Hon. James G. Blaine, he says:

PHILADELPHIA, Feb. 13, 1873.

MY DEAR SIR:—From the beginning of the investigation concerning Mr. Ames' use of the Credit Mobilier, I believed that General Garfield was free from all guilty connection with that business. This opinion was founded not merely on my confidence in his integrity, but on some special knowledge of his case. I may have told you all about it in conversation, but I desire now to repeat it by way of reminder.

In the winter of 1869-70, I told General Garfield of the fact that his name was on Ames' list: That Ames charged him with being one of his distributees; explained to him the character, origin and object of the Credit Mobilier; pointed out the connection it had with Congressional legislation, and showed him how impossible it was for a member of Congress to hold stock in it without bringing his private interest in conflict with his public duty. That all this was to him a perfectly new revelation, I am as sure as I can be of such a fact, or of any fact which is capable of being proved only by moral circumstances. He told me then the whole story of Train's offer to him and Ames' subsequent solicitation and his own action in the premises, much as he details it to the committee. I do not undertake to reproduce the conversation, but the effect of it all was to convince me thoroughly, that when he listened to Ames he was perfectly unconscious of anything evil. I watched carefully every word that fell from him on this point, and did not regard his narrative of the transaction in other respects with much interest, because, in my view, everything else was insignificant. I did not care whether he made a bargain technically binding or not: his integrity depended upon the question whether he acted with his eyes open. If he had known the true character of the proposition made to him, he would not have endured it, much less embraced it.

The utter groundlessness of the charges against General Garfield is clearly demonstrated. But for the fact that some of those politically opposed to him thought they saw a chance to remove a powerful and much feared opponent, and with a recklessness and malice which nothing can even palliate, endeavored to do so by destroying what is more precious to him than life—his honor, we never should have heard of these accusations. But acting on the principle that a "lie well stuck to is as good as the truth," these charges have been again and again repeated, notwithstanding the fact that their utter falsity and baselessness has been repeatedly demonstrated.

In the course of one of his masterly speeches, General Garfield, in speaking of President Johnson's course, alluded to General Hancock, who had then recently been placed in command of Louisiana, as follows:

"Mr. Speaker, I will not repeat the long catalogue of obstructions which he has thrown in the way by virtue of the power conferred upon him in the Reconstruction law of 1867, but I will allude to one example where he has found in a Major-General of the Army a facile instrument with which more effectually to obstruct the work of reconstruction. This case is all the more painful because an otherwise meritorious officer, who bears honorable scars earned in battle for the Union, has been made a party to political madness which has so long marked the conduct of the President. This General was sent into the District of Louisiana and Texas with a law of Congress in his hand,—a law that commands him to see that justice is administered among people of that country, and that no pretence of civil authority shall deter him from performing his duty,—and yet we find that officer giving lectures in the form of proclamations and orders on what ought to be the relation between the civil and military departments of the Government. We see him issuing a general order in which he declares that the civil should not give way before the military. We hear him declaring that he finds nothing in the laws of Louisiana and Texas to warrant his interference in the civil administration of those States. It is not for him to say which should be first, the civil or the military, in that rebel community. It is not for him to search the defunct laws of Louisiana and Texas for a guide to his conduct. It is for him to obey the laws which he has sent there to execute. It is for him to aid in building up civil governments, rather than preparing himself to be the Presidential candidate of the party which gave him no sympathy when he was gallantly fighting the battles of the country."

It will be born in mind that this speech was delivered on January 17, 1868,—over twelve years ago.

In 1870, Mr. Niblack, of Indiana, in speaking for the Democrats, insisted that the expenditures and burdens of the War were properly chargeable to the Republican party. General Garfield at once replied, and a few words of his are well worth quoting :

"I desire to ask that gentleman and his party one question. Suppose that in the year 1861 every Democrat north of the Potomac and the Ohio had followed the lead of Grant, and Douglas, and Dickinson, and Tod, and all the other great lights of the Democratic party ; had thrown away the Democratic name ; said that they would be Democrats no longer, as we said we would be Republicans no longer, but all would be Union men, and stand together around the flag until the rebellion had been put under our feet. I desire to ask the gentleman if these things had happened, how long the war would have lasted, and how much the war would have cost? I do not hesitate to say that it could not have lasted a month, and the expenditures of the war would never have exceeded $10,000,000. I say, as a matter of current history, that it was the great hope of the rebels of the South that the assistance of the Democratic party of the North would divide our forces and overcome all our efforts; that at the ballot-box the Democrats at home would help the cause which they were maintaining in the field. It was that, and that alone, which protracted the war and created our immense debt. I come, therefore, to the door of your party, gentlemen on the other side, and I lay down at your threshold every dollar of the debt, every item of the stupendous total which expresses the great cost of the war; and I say if you had followed Douglas there would have been no debt, no blood, no burden."

During the long session of Congress in 1876, Hon. L. Q. C. Lamar of Mississippi, then a Member of the House, but since elected to the Senate, endeavored to prove that the best interests of the country would be promoted by the elevation to power of the Democratic party, and sharply arraigned the Republican party for many alleged short-comings. On August 4th, 1876, a few days after Mr. Lamar had spoken, General Garfield replied. After stating Mr. Lamar's position, he considered the origin of the ideas which had controlled the parties in the past. He stated that nearly two centuries before this time two utterly irreconcilable and antagonistic ideas had been implanted in this Continent. One was landed with the Pilgrim fathers, at Plymouth, and was, that all men were created free and equal, and were entitled to the fruits of their own labor. The other was landed with a colony in Virginia, and was, that one man had a right to own another, and possess himself of the fruits of his labor. After tracing down the career of these two ideas, and showing how though at first they lived, and grew and strengthened alongside of each other, yet, as the country filled up, there was found not to be room for both, and the irrepressible conflict finally broke forth. He showed the connection of the Democratic party with the latter of these two ideas. He then went on to say:

"MR. CHAIRMAN: It is now time to inquire as to the fitness of this Democratic party to take control of our great nation, and its vast and important interests for the next four years. I put the question to the gentleman from Mississippi (Mr. Lamar), what has the Democratic party done to merit that great trust? He tries to show in what respects it would not be dangerous. I ask him to show in what it would be safe?

"I affirm, and I believe I do not misrepresent the great Democratic party, that in the last sixteen years they have not advanced one great national idea that is not to-day exploded, and as dead as Julius Cæsar. And if any Democrat here will rise and name a great national doctrine his party has advanced within that time, that is now alive and believed in, I will yield to him. [A pause.] In default of an answer, I will attempt to prove my negative.

"What were the great central doctrines of the Democratic party in the Presidential struggle of 1860? The followers of Breckenridge said slavery had a right to go wherever the Constitution goes. Do you believe that to-day? And is there a man on this Continent that holds that doctrine to-day? Not one. That doctrine is dead and buried. The other wing of the Democracy held that slavery might be established in the Territories if the people wanted it. Does anybody hold that doctrine to-day? Dead, absolutely dead.

"Come down to 1864. Your party, under the lead of Tilden and Vallandigham, declared the experiment of war to save the Union was a failure. Do you believe that doctrine to-day? That doctrine was shot to death by the guns of Farragut at Mobile, and driven in a tempest of fire from the Valley of the Shenandoah by Sheridan in less than a month after its birth at Chicago.

"Come down to 1868. You declared the Constitutional Amendments revolutionary and void. Does any man on this floor say so to-day? If so, let him rise and declare it.

"Do you believe in the doctrine of the Broadhead letter of 1868, that the so-called Constitutional Amendments should be disregarded? No! The gentleman from Mississippi accepts the results of the War. The Democratic doctrine of 1868 is dead.

"I walk across that Democratic camping-ground, as in a grave-yard. Under my feet resound the hollow echoes of the dead. There lies slavery, a black marble column at the head of its grave, on which I read : 'Died in the flames of the Civil War ; loved in its life, lamented in its death ; followed to its bier by its only mourner, the Demcratic party, but dead.' And here is a double grave : 'Sacred to the memory of squatter sovereignty ; died in the campaign of 1860.' On the reverse side : 'Sacred to the memory of Dred Scott and the Breckenridge doctrine ; both dead at the hands of Abraham Lincoln.' And here, a monument of brimstone : 'Sacred to the memory of the Rebellion ; the war against it is a failure.' —*Tilden et Vallandigham fecerunt*, A. D. 1864. Dead on the field of battle ; shot to death by the million guns of the Republic. The doctrine of secession, of State sovereignty, dead. Expired in the flames of civil war, amid the blazing rafters of the Confederacy, except that the modern Æneas fleeing out of the flames of that ruin, bears on his back another Anchises of State sovereignty, and brings it here in the person of the honorable gentleman from the Appomattox district of Virginia (Mr. Tucker). All else is dead.

"Now, gentleman, are you sad, are you sorry for these deaths? Are you not glad that secession is dead? that slavery is dead? that squatter sovereignty is dead? that the doctrine of the failure of the War is dead? Then you are glad that you were out-voted in 1860, in 1864, in 1868, and in 1872. If you have tears to shed over these losses, shed them in the grave-yard, but not in this House of living men. I know that many a Southern man rejoices that these issues are dead. The gentleman from Mississippi (Mr. Lamar), has clothed his joy with eloquence.

"Now, gentlemen, come with me for a moment into the camp of the Republican party, and review its career. Our central doctrine in 1860 was that slavery should never extend itself over another foot of American soil. Is that doctrine dead? It is folded away like a victorious banner; its truth is alive forever more on this Continent. In 1864, we declared that we would put down the Rebellion and secession. And that doctrine lives, and will live when the second Centennial has arrived. Freedom, national, universal, and perpetual, our great Constitutional Amendments, are they alive, or dead? Alive! thank the God that shields both liberty and union. And our national credit. Saved from the assaults of Pendleton: saved from the assaults of those who struck it later, rising higher and higher at home and abroad, and only now in doubt lest its chief, its only enemy, the Democracy, should triumph in November."

At the special session of the present Congress, which was brought on by reason of the failure of the former

Congress to pass the Appropriation Bills, General Garfield, in a speech attacking the Democracy because of its refusal to vote supplies for the Government unless certain "riders" repealing laws then in force, were allowed to be incorporated in the Appropriation Bills, said :

"I desire to ask the forbearance of the gentlemen on the other side for remarks I dislike to make, for they will bear witness that I have in many ways shown my desire that the wounds of the War should be healed, and that the grass that God plants over the graves of our dead may signalize the return of the Spring of friendship and peace between all parts of the country. But I am compelled by the necessity of the situation to refer for a moment to a chapter of history.

"'The last act of the Democratic domination in this House, eighteen years ago, was stirring and dramatic, but it was heroic and whole-souled. Then the Democratic party said : 'If you elect your man as President of the United States, we will shoot your Union to death.'

"And the people of this country, not willing to be coerced, but believing they had a right to vote for Abraham Lincoln if they chose, did elect him lawfully as President, and then your leaders, in control of the majority of the other wing of this Capitol, did the heoric thing of withdrawing from their seats, and your Representatives withdrew from their seats, and flung down to us the gage of mortal battle. We called it rebellion, but we admitted that it was honorable, that it was courageous, and that it was noble to give us the fell gage of battle, and fight it out in the open field.

"That conflict, and what followed, we all know too well ; and to-day, after eighteen years, the book of your domination is opened where you turned down your leaves in 1860, and you are signalizing your return to power by reading the second chapter (not this time an heroic one), that declares that if we do not let you dash a statute out of the book, you will not shoot the Union to death as in the first chapter, but starve it to death, by refusing the necessary appropriations.

"You, gentlemen, have it in your power to kill it by this movement. You have it in your power, by withholding these two bills, to smite the nerve centers of our Constitution to the stillness of death, and you have declared your purpose to do it if you cannot break down the elements of free consent, that, up to this time, have always ruled in the Government."

The effect of this attack was to eventually cause the Democrats to abandon their announced policy, step by step, and finally to pass the Appropriation Bills, without securing the repeal of any of the laws which they wished to expunge from the statute books. It opened the eyes of the people-at-large to the purposes of the Democracy, and caused their overwhelming defeat at the polls in the ensuing elections.

At a speech delivered at the re-union of the survivors of Andersonville, at Toledo, on October 3, 1879, General Garfield, after portraying in vivid terms the terrible ordeal through which they had been called to pass, and the steadfastness they displayed, said: "All these men, and all their comrades went out, inspired by two immortal ideas. First, that liberty shall be universal in America, and, Second, that this old flag is the flag of a nation, and not of a state; that the nation is supreme over all people and all corporations. Call it a state; call it a section; call it a South; call it a North; call it anything you wish, and yet, armed with the nationality that God gave us, this is a nation against all State sovereignty and secession, whatever. It is the immortality of that truth that makes these re-unions, and that makes this one. You believed it on the battle-field, you believed it in the hell of Andersonville, and you believe it to-day, thank God, and you will believe it to the last gasp."

On April 14, 1866, the anniversary of the death of Abraham Lincoln, General Garfield moved, in the House of Representatives immediately after the opening prayer, that the reading of the journal be dispensed with; and that motion having been carried, he moved that the House adjourn, and in the course of a few remarks on that motion, said: "In the great drama of the Rebellion there were two acts. The first was the war, with its battles and seiges, victories and defeats, sufferings and tears. That act was closed one year ago to-night, and just as the curtain was lifting on the second and final act, —the restoration of peace and liberty; just as the curtain was rising upon new characters and new events, the evil spirit of the rebellion, in the fury of despair, nerved and directed the hand of the assassin to strike down the chief character in both.

"It was no one man who killed Abraham Lincoln; it was the embodied spirit of treason and slavery, inspired with fearful and despairing hate, that struck him down in the moment of the nation's supremest joy."

At the Chicago Convention, on the night of June 5th, 1880, General Garfield, in a speech of wonderful eloquence and power, nominated John Sherman as a candidate for the Presidential nomination. In the course of that speech, after stating the condition of the country at the time the Republican party came into power, he said: "The Republican party changed all this. It abolished the babel of confusion, and gave to the country a currency as national as its flag, based upon the sacred faith of the people. It threw its protecting arm around our great industries, and they stood erect as with new life. It filled with the spirit of true nationality all the great functions of the Government. It confronted a rebellion of unexampled magnitude, with slavery behind it, and under God, fought the final battle of liberty, until victory was won. Then, after the storms of battle, were heard the sweet, calm words of peace, uttered by the conquering nation, and saying to the conquered foe that lay prostrate at its feet: 'This is our only revenge, that you join us in lifting to the serene firmament of the Constitution, to shine like stars forever and forever, the immortal principles of truth and justice, that all men—white or black, shall be free and stand equal before the law.'"

In the course of the same speech he described the necessary qualifications of the person who should be chosen as candidate, and, unconsciously, in attempting to describe another, described himself. He said: "We want a man whose life and opinions embody all the achievements of which I have spoken. We want a man who, standing on a mountain height, sees all the achievements of our past history, and carries in his heart the memory of all its glorious deeds, and who, looking forward, prepares to meet the labor and the dangers to come. We want one who will act in no spirit of unkindness toward those we lately met in battle. The Republican party offers to our brethren of the South the olive branch of peace, and wishes them to return to brotherhood on this supreme condition,—that it shall be admitted, forever and forever more, that in the war for the Union, we were right and they were wrong. On that supreme condition we meet them as brethren, and on no other. We ask them to share with us the blessings and honors of this great Republic."

General Garfield is the possessor of two homes: a house in Washington, and a farm at Mentor, Ohio. His entire property may amount to $20,000, and consists entirely of that just mentioned. This he has earned by his own exertions. When he entered Congress he owned a house at Hiram, worth about $1,500; and by saving a little of his salary, and an occasional legal fee, has accumulated the remainder. Seven children have been born to him, of whom, five are living, two having died in infancy. In person, he is six feet high, broad shouldered and powerfully built. His head is of an immense size, and his forehead very high. His hair and whiskers are of a light brown color, and his eyes are blue.

He dresses plainly, and cares nothing for luxurious living. He is exceedingly temperate in all things, save brain work, and is a devoted husband and father.

As a statesman, General Garfield stands in the foremost rank. His great knowledge, firm convictions, clear perception, uprightness of character, and unflagging energy and zeal, all combine to make him the foremost man of his day.

In this short and imperfect sketch, we have seen how a man may rise superior to his circumstances, and by prudence, energy, honesty and intelligence, may succeed in overcoming all obstacles which are encountered, and advancing step by step on the ladder of fame, be selected by a great political party as its candidate for the highest office the Republic can bestow.

General Garfield himself has said, that "The man who wants to serve his country, must put himself in the line of its leading thought; and that is the restoration of business, trade, commerce, industry, sound political economy, hard money, and the honest payment of all obligations; and the man who can add anything in the direction of accomplishing any of these purposes, is a public benefactor." Certainly he fulfills his own requirements to the very letter.

## CHAPTER IV.

### LIFE OF GEN. CHESTER A. ARTHUR.

The candidate of the Republican party for Vice-President, is General Chester Allan Arthur, of New York.

General Arthur was born in Fairfield, Franklin County, Vermont, on the 15th of October, 1830. His father,— Rev. Dr. William Arthur, was a Baptist clergyman, and a native of the north of Ireland. He achieved considerable eminence as a pulpit orator, and also as an author of philological works.

Young Arthur received part of his early education at a school at Greenwich, Washington County, New York. At one time he taught a district school at a place then known as Whipple's Corners, and at the present time as North Pownal, Vermont, occupying the same school-room in which, a year or two subsequently, General Garfield also taught. Arthur was, however, mainly prepared for college under the tuition of his father.

He entered Union College, at Schenectady, New York, and was graduated therefrom in 1848, when only eighteen years of age.

While in College, he was a hard student; was very popular among his classmates, and was regarded by all who knew him, as a young man of ability and promise.

Soon after leaving College, he commenced the study of law, and subsequently entered the office of Eratus D. Culver, who afterwards became Minister to one of the South American States, and later on a Judge of the City Court of Brooklyn.

Mr. Culver had at one time been a Member of Congress from Pennsylvania, and had been closely identified with the anti-slavery struggles of his day, and General Arthur received his early training in politics during their association. As a young man, he became deeply interested in and identified with, the Free-Soil agitation. He was a delegate from Brooklyn to the first Republican State Convention held in New York.

After Mr. Culver became a judge, Mr. Arthur became associated in business with a Mr. Gardner, their partnership lasting for some ten years, and until the death of Mr. Gardner, when Mr. Arthur conducted the business alone. In 1871 he became senior member of the firm of Arthur, Phelps, Knevals and Ransom. Mr. Benjamin K. Phelps, his partner, has been the District-Attorney of New York County for nearly nine years.

A Virginian, named Jonathan Lemon, landed eight slaves in New York, intending to ship them from there to Texas. Mr. Arthur thought he would see whether or not the State of New York would submit to the indignity of being used as a transfer station for the traffickers in human flesh and blood, and sued out a writ of *Habeas Corpus* in their behalf. After listening to an extended argument from the counsel on both sides of the case, Judge Paine, before whom the writ was returnable, decided that the slaves should be released, as they were not within the terms of the fugitive slave law. The State of Virginia directed its Attorney-General to appeal from this decision, and the Legislature of New York requested the Governor to employ counsel to defend the case. Mr. Arthur was employed as counsel, pursuant to this request, and associated with himself Hon. William M. Evarts, now Secretary of State, and together they argued the case in the General Term. Opposed to them, was that veteran advocate and defender of slavery —Charles O'Connor.

The decision of Judge Paine was sustained, and Lemon appealed to the Court of Appeals, where the judgment was also affirmed; and ever afterwards slave-holders gave New York a wide berth.

In 1856, Lizzie Jennings, a colored woman of good character and reputation, was rudely expelled from a Fourth Avenue horse-car, wholly on account of her color. Through General Arthur, she brought suit against the railroad company to recover damages. The case was tried before Judge Rockwell and a jury in Brooklyn, and the jury awarded the woman $500 as damages. The company appealed, but the decision was sustained in all the higher courts, and it was forced to pay the damages. This settled for all time a then much vexed question, and thenceforward, colored people were allowed to ride on all the street cars in the city.

It required no small amount of moral courage to stand up in the face of the prevailing sentiment of the community, and espouse and advocate the cause of the despised and down-trodden black man; and General Arthur is deserving of the highest praise, for his daring and chivalrous services.

General Arthur continued to actively practice his profession, until in January, 1861, when Governor Morgan appointed him Inspector and Quartermaster-General. In this position he rendered highly efficient services in the work of preparing and forwarding troops to the seat of war.

In the fall of 1871, General Arthur was appointed by President Grant, Collector of the Port of New York, to succeed Thomas Murphy. Upon the expiration of his term of four years, his services had proved so acceptable that he was reappointed, and the nomination was unanimously confirmed by the Senate, without being referred to a committee, a compliment usually paid only to ex-Senators. In July, 1878, he was succeeded by Collector Merritt.

General Arthur has always taken a great interest in

politics, and since its formation, has been one of the leaders of the Republican party in New York. During the Gubernatorial campaign in that State in 1879, he served as Chairman of the State Committee, and to his skillful and judicious management, was, in a large measure, due the success of the party.

In personal appearance, General Arthur is a portly gentleman, with a pleasant face, bright eyes, and heavy hair and whiskers, now quite gray. Socially, he is a genial companion and a great favorite. He is a public spirited but unobtrusive citizen, and a pleasant and ready speaker. He has been very successful as a lawyer, and has a large and extensive practice. He has two children —a son of about fourteen, and a daughter of eight years of age. Early in the present year, he had the misfortune to lose his wife, to whom he was devotedly attached. Her death was very sudden and unexpected. She was the daughter of Capt. Herndon, the explorer of the Amazon river, who was lost while in command of the steamship "Central America," while on the trip between Havana and New York.

## CHAPTER V.

### THE NATIONAL GREENBACK LABOR CONVENTION.

#### HELD AT CHICAGO, JUNE 9TH, 1880.

On Wednesday, the 9th day of June, 1880, the National Greenback Labor Convention met in the Industrial Exposition Building, at Chicago, and in the same hall where the Republican Convention had just previously been held, and at 12:30 p. m. the Hon. F. P. Dewees, Chairman of the National Executive Committee, called the Convention to order.

In a brief and forcible manner he spoke of the Convention that had adjourned, referring to the fact that it was a struggle of men against each other, who had no principle to contend for, and were therefore left to divide into factions and fight for spoils.

He congratulated the delegates that this Convention promised well for a union of all elements opposed to the old parties, and grandly for the labor and industrial interests of the country. He then called upon Rev. Mr. Ingalls, of Iowa, to open the proceedings with prayer.

The large hall at this time presented quite an animated and business like appearance. There were about one thousand delegates and alternates in attendance, and every State but Oregon was represented in the Convention. The delegates were from all ranks of industry, laboring men, mechanics, farmers, lawyers, clergymen, physicians, men of intelligence and brains.

After the reading of the call for the Convention, the Hon. Gilbert De La Matyr, of Indiana, was unanimously chosen temporary chairman, and in a brief but forcible speech he laid down the principles which had brought the party into life and developed it as a great political organization, which had representatives on the floor of the Convention at its opening, from nearly every State and Territory in the Union.

Charles Litchman, of Massachusetts, and Perry P. Maxsom, of Kansas, were then chosen Secretaries. After the call of the roll of States and their appointment of committees, Mrs. Gage, President of the National Woman's Suffrage Association, addressed the Convention, urging that a plank in their behalf be inserted in the platform. She was followed by Susan B. Anthony and Miss Lucinda B. Chandler, of Pennsylvania.

At the evening session the hall was crowded to overflowing, there being at least 10,000 persons present. In the absence of regular business, and while waiting for reports of the committees, calls were made for prominent men of the party to address the Convention.

Among others, Mr. Wallace, of Canada, Member of Parliament, was introduced, and made a speech that called forth enthusiastic applause. The gentleman spoke for half an hour, and held the vast audience spell-bound by the force and clearness of his remarks. At the conclusion the vast audience rose to their feet and gave three rousing cheers for the Canadian Greenbacker.

He was followed by a Mr. Wright, Secretary of the

Canadian Currency Reform League, who spoke for an hour, and logic, anecdote and illustration were made to tell for the great cause he advocated.

Cries of "Kearney," "Kearney," were then heard from all parts of the house. The great agitator of the sand lots refused for some time to leave his seat in the California delegation, but at last ascended the platform. His speech was wholly free from objectionable or inflammatory language, and was listened to with interest.

He thanked God that even the Republican Convention had the grace to reject imperialism, in the candidacy of Grant, and prophesied that General Garfield, in consequence of the weakness of the Republican platform on the subject, and his record on the Chinese immigration bill, would not receive one-third of the vote of California. He predicted that the Greenback and Workingingmen's party would carry California, Nevada and Oregon.

He went into a description of the Chinese coolie system, as it exists in California, and showed conclusively that it was the African slave trade limited to a term of years. "We will not harm a hair of any Chinaman in California," said Kearney, "but we intend to stop this slave traffic." He then described how contracts are made for the poor serfs of China, with the ruling classes there who own them, and the Six Chinese Companies who buy them by the thousand for a term of years, bind themselves to return their slaves dead or alive at the end of that time.

On Thursday, the 10th of June, the Convention was called to order at 10 o'clock a. m., when the Committee on Credentials reported. They also submitted some resolutions recommending that those who were not elected under the call of the National Greenback-Labor Committee be furnished seats in the Convention with the respective delegations to which they may belong, and that they have a voice in casting the vote of the State, but the vote of no State be thereby increased. They also recommended that the accredited delegates present from each State or Territory be authorized to cast the full vote to which such State and Territory is entitled under the call of the Convention.

The minority of the committee presented an adverse report, the object being to keep out the Farwell Hall delegates. But to understand this let us go back a little.

At the same time that these proceedings were going on in the regular Convention, another Convention, composed of representatives from the Greenback Labor Clubs of the country, and known as the Pomeroy wing of the party, had assembled in Farwell Hall, not far distant, to the number of 187. They had previously, at a Convention held in St. Louis, nominated for President, S. D. Dillaye, of New Jersey, and B. J. Chambers, of Texas, for Vice-President, and adjourned to meet in Chicago, June 9th, with a view to forming a union of the two conflicting parties.

The spirit which prevailed was excellent and friendly, and union and fraternity were the earnest wish of both.

During the discussion of the resolutions, and of the majority and minority reports above mentioned, Chairman De LaMatyr asked the privilege of saying a few words. "They were organizing," he said, "the grandest movement of ages. Everywhere the toiling masses felt oppression, and were organized under various forms. While divided, they would remain powerless. They must have harmony and unity to over-throw the well-disciplined forces of their enemies. It was useless to think they could achieve any great result if they were split into several factions. It was a solemn hour. They must lay aside personal preferences, and be prepared to offer up their prejudices on the altar of this sublime movement. Indiscretion would enfeeble them, and invite certain defeat. If they could unite the different elements, for the purpose of lifting from labor the burden that bound it to the earth, they would accomplish a grand result."

He recommended that each State delegation be left to settle the matter of voting in their own ranks. He asked them to rise to the sublimity of the movement without an embittering word. He besought them not to utter an unkind word. The eyes of millions were upon them gauging their work. He would lay his life on that altar. He knew the better sentiments of their hearts would prevail, and they would go from the Convention organized for victory. The people were aroused, and when they were, their voice was the voice of God.

This brief address was delivered feelingly and forcibly and it had a most soothing, pacifying and satisfactory effect.

The minority report was withdrawn, and the resolutions unanimously adopted.

The report of the Committee on Permanent Organization was then presented and adopted, as follows: President, Capt. Richard F. Trevellick, of Michigan; Secretary, Charles H. Litchman, of Massachusetts, with several assistant secretaries.

A committee was appointed to conduct Mr. Trevellick to the Chair as its Permanent President, and after the applause had subsided, he made a brief speech, thanking the Convention for the honor tendered him to preside over such a large, intelligent, but noisy body, and accepting the gavel as an emblem for authority, asked the pleasure of the Convention.

A motion was made that a committee be appointed by the Chair to wait on the Farwell Hall delegates and the Socialistic party, and inform them of the action of the Convention, invite their attendance, and to escort them to seats on the floor of the Convention.

The committee appointed, consisted of W. P. Parks, of Arkansas, Hon. Gilbert De LaMatyr, of Indiana, Hon. Stephen D. Dillaye, of New Jersey, Z. M. Brunn, of Pennsylvania, and G. F. Bynall, of Virginia.

The committee proceeded at once with a band of music to Farwell Hall, and upon their re-appearance in the Convention with the Farwell Hall delegates, the whole vast assemblage rose, the wildest enthusiasm prevailed, and the greatest joy was manifested over the reunion of those who were working for the same grand results, but had temporarily labored apart.

Speeches of welcome and congratulation were made, and after the speeches, the delegates broke away from all restraint. Flags and State banners were waved, cheer after cheer rent the air, and at last a grand burst of enthusiasm greeted one of the Southern delegates, who lifted the banner of his State higher than all the rest. Order was at last restored, and the Convention again commenced work.

The Committee on Platform was next called for, and its report was presented through its chairman, Congressman Gillette. The report on motion of Congressman Murch, of Maine, was unanimously adopted. It is as follows:

### THE PLATFORM.

Civil government should guarantee the divine right of every laborer to the results of his toil, thus enabling the producers of wealth to provide themselves with the means for physical comfort, and the facilities for mental, social and moral culture; and we condemn as unworthy of our civilization the barbarism which imposes upon the wealth producers a state of perpetual drudgery as the price of bare animal existence.

Notwithstanding the enormous increase of productive power, the universal introduction of labor-saving machinery, and the discovery of new agents for the increase of wealth, the task of the laborer is scarcely lightened, the hours of toil are but little shortened, and few producers are lifted from poverty into comfort and pecuniary independence.

The associated monopolies, the international syndicates and other income classes demand dear money and cheap labor, a "strong government" and hence a weak people.

Corporate control of the volume of money has been the means of dividing society into two classes; of the unjust distribution of the products of labor, and building up monopolies of associated capital, endowed with power to confiscate private property. It has kept money scarce, and scarcity of money enforces debt trade, and public and corporate loans—debt engenders usury, and usury ends in the bankruptcy of the borrower.

Other results are deranged markets, uncertainty in manufacturing enterprise and agriculture, precarious and intermittent employment for the laborer, industrial war, increasing pauperism and crime, the consequent intimidation and disfranchisement of the producer, and a rapid declination into corporate feudalism.

Therefore we declare :

1. That the right to make and issue money is a sovereign power to be maintained by the people for the common benefit. The delegation of this right to corporations is a surrender of the central attribute of sovereignty void of constitutional sanction, conferring upon a subordinate, irresponsible power, absolute dominion over industry and commerce. All money, whether metallic or paper, should be issued and its volume controlled by the government, and not by or through banking corporations, and when so issued should be full legal tender for all debts, public and private.

2. That the bonds of the United States should not be refunded, but paid as rapidly as is practicable, and according to contract. To enable the government to meet these obligations, legal tender currency should be substituted for the notes of the national banks, the national banking system abolished, and the unlimited coinage of silver as well as gold established by law.

3. That labor should be so protected by national and State authority, as to equalize its burdens, and insure a just distribution of its results; the eight-hour law of Congress should be enforced; the sanitary condition of industrial establishments placed under rigid control; the competition of contract convict labor abolished; a bureau of labor statistics established; factories, mines and workshops inspected; the employment of children under 14 years of age forbidden, and wages paid in cash.

4. Slavery being simply cheap labor, and cheap labor being simply slavery, the importation of Chinese serfs necessarily tends to brutalize and degrade American

labor; therefore, immediate steps should be taken to abrogate the Burlingame treaty.

5. Railroad land grants, forfeited by reason of non-fulfillment of contract, should be immediately reclaimed by the government ; and henceforth the public domain reserved exclusively as homes for actual settlers.

6. It is the duty of Congress to regulate inter-State commerce, all lines of communication and transportation should be brought under such legislative control as shall secure moderate, fair and uniform rates for passenger and freight traffic.

7. We denounce, as destructive to prosperity, and dangerous to liberty, the action of the old parties in fostering and sustaining gigantic land, railroad and money corporations and monopolies, invested with and exercising powers belonging to the government, and yet not responsible to it for the manner of their exercise.

8. That the Constitution, in giving Congress the power to borrow money, to declare war, to raise and support armies, to provide and maintain a navy, never intended that the men who loaned their money for an interest consideration should be preferred to the soldier and sailor, who perilled their lives and shed their blood on land and sea in defense of their country ; and we condemn the cruel class legislation of the Republican party which, while professing great gratitude to the soldier, has most unjustly discriminated against him and in favor of the bondholder.

9. All property should bear its just proportion of taxation, and we demand a graduated income tax.

10. We denounce as most dangerous, the efforts everywhere manifest to restrict the right of suffrage.

11. We are opposed to an increase of the standing army in time of peace, and the insidious scheme to establish an enormous military power under the guise of militia laws.

12. We demand absolute democratic rules for the gov-

ernment of Congress, placing all representatives of the people upon an equal footing, and taking away from committees a veto power greater than that of the President.

13. We demand a government of the people, by the people, and for the people, instead of a government of the bondholder, by the bondholder, and for the bondholder; and we denounce every attempt to stir up sectional strife as an effort to conceal monstrous crimes against the people.

14. In the furtherance of these ends, we ask the co-operation of all fair-minded people. We have no quarrel with individuals, wage no war upon classes, but only against vicious institutions. We are not content to endure further discipline from our present actual rulers, who, having dominion over money, over transportation, over land and labor, and largely over the press and the machinery of government, wield unwarrantable power over our institutions and over life and property.

The great majority of those comprising the Convention were men unused to the tricks and subterfuges of the politician; men who had grown sick of the machine politics of the day, and were resolved to break their old allegiance. They came together to found a new party, to raise a new standard, to formulate a new Declaration of Independence from old party trammels.

The material of the Convention was of such as heroes are made. There were young men, also men with gray heads and young hearts, whose voices have been and will still continue to be heard in the defence of vital truths.

Alexander Campbell, of Illinois, whose life-long battle against injustice and oppression has given courage to so many younger in the fight, was there to inspire them with his presence and aid them with his smile of approval and words of cheer and counsel. There was E. P. Allis, of Wisconsin, one of nature's noblemen, with a solid delegation of as brave and true men as ever honored a reform movement, with but one ambition—the maintenance of principles.

New Jersey sent Stephen D. Dillaye and John G. Drew, whose able articles on the essential principles of the reform movement the "Irish World" has made household words. She also sent J. A. Beecher, whose bold, sharp and ringing articles in "The Press," denouncing the money power and gigantic corporations, have opened the eyes of many to discern the truth, and to whom we are indebted more than to any other for a full and correct report of the proceedings of this Convention.

There was also John A. Thompson, of West Virginia, Alfred Taylor of Kansas, E. H. Benton, of Nebraska, S. F. Norton, of Illinois, J. M. Devine, of Massachusetts, Stephen Maybell, of California, Stanley H. Bell, of Tennessee, Major Harman, of Mississippi, and a host of others, including our representatives in Congress and other progressive men too numerous to mention.

It was 12 o'clock, at midnight, Thursday, when a motion was made and carried that the Convention proceed to nominate a candidate for President of the United States. Motions had been made to adjourn, but were voted down, as a majority of the delegates seemed determined to get through their work before adjournment.

On the roll call of States, C. P. Judd, of Colorado, nominated Gen. J. B. Weaver, of Iowa ; S. F. Norton, of Illinois, nominated Alexander Campbell, of Illinois;

James Buchanan, of Indiana, nominated Benj. F. Butler, of Massachusetts; Mr. Fogg, of Maine, nominated Solon Chase; P. H. Talbott, of Missouri, nominated Stephen D. Dillaye, of New Jersey; Edward P. Allis, of Wisconsin, was nominated by the delegation of that State; Hendrick P. Wright, of Pennsylvania, was also put in nomination, which was ably seconded by Mr. Dillaye; the Hon. Mr. Murch, of Maine, was also nominated, but promptly declined.

Able speeches were made in behalf of all the nominees on the presentation of the names and in seconding the same, but by reason of the lateness of the hour they were necessarily brief and to the point.

At 3.25 A. M. it was moved and carried that the Convention proceed to ballot for the Presidental candidate. An informal ballot was first taken, the result of which was announced at 4.10 o'clock A. M., just as daylight was breaking. It stood: Weaver $224\frac{1}{2}$; Wright $126\frac{1}{2}$; Dillaye 119; Butler 95; Chase 89; Allis 41; and Campbell 21.

The first formal ballot then commenced, but before its announcement it was evident that Weaver had a clear majority, and all the delegates hastened to change their votes to that candidate. Motions sprang up from all parts of the house to make his nomination unanimous, and, just as the sun shone through the eastern windows, the result of the ballot was announced as 718 for James B. Weaver. His nomination was made unanimous.

Through the east windows of the hall the first rays of the morning sun were shining under the arched canopy. The day had come.

Alfred Taylor, of Kansas, rising and pointing toward the streaming sunlight, said: "My heart throbs with gratitude when I see the darkness of night give way to the light of the sun, symbolical of the mission of our party." The Convention rose to their feet, and with cheers upon cheers hailed the bright omen.

A committee of five were appointed by the chair to proceed to the Palmer House to notify General Weaver of his nomination, and to conduct him to the hall. This was soon effected, and when the committee appeared on the platform conducting the General to the Chairman's desk, the scene can be imagined better than described.

The delegates rose as one man to greet their chosen head, and manifested, in the most unmistakable terms, that they then and there, swore fealty and allegiance to the dauntless young leader. The man who nobly fought the Congressional syndicate of the money power and kept them at bay, quivered with suppressed emotion as he was almost carried to the front of the platform.

Dead silence followed as suddenly as the storm of enthusiasm had arisen. In the hushed stillness General Weaver said:

"Mr. Chairman and gentlemen of the convention: I highly appreciate the great honor you have conferred upon me, and I appear before you in greater trepidation than ever before experienced in my life, for the reason that, without any desire on my part, you have seen fit to place me at the head of your ticket. In this informal manner I say, that relying on a Divine Providence and the patriotism of the American people, I accept the trust you have confided in me.

In my judgment we have reached a juncture in the

history of our country, which, in all time to come will be regarded as an historic epoch: an epoch when the people must decide whether we shall degenerate like the European aristocracies, and the many be ruled, so that the few may hold the emoluments of office and accumulate the wealth of the country.

I accept your trust thus informally, but in the near future will give you my acceptance and my views at length; and I now thank you most heartily for the honor you have shown me."

Congressman Gillette offered the following resolution which was adopted. "Resolved, that it is the sentiment of this convention that our gallant candidates for President and Vice-President shall advocate our principles on the stump everywhere."

Nominations of candidates for Vice-President were then made. Gen. Horace P. Sergeant of Massachusetts presented the name of Gen. A. M. West of Mississippi. Col. B. J. Chambers of Texas, the nominee of the St. Louis Greenback convention was also put in nomination.

On the first ballot Chambers received 403 and West, 311. Gen. West at once arose and moved that the nomination of Col. Chambers be made unanimous. He spoke highly of Col. Chambers, and in conclusion declared that nothing now remained for the delegates to do but to go to their homes and do their duty as patriots and Greenbackers, and victory would perch on their banners in November. The nomination of Col. Chambers was then made unanimous.

At 6.10 A. M. the Convention adjourned, *sine die*, and the delegates retired from the Hall with cheers for the whole ticket.

LETTER OF ACCEPTANCE.

BLOOMFIELD, Iowa, June 23, 1880.

*Hons. S. F. Norton, E. P. Allis, Solon Chase, S. D. Dillaye, E. H. Gillette.*

GENTLEMEN—It is my pleasure to acknowledge the receipt of your letter of June 23d, 1880, formally notifying me of my nomination for the office of President of the United States, by the united Greenback Labor party, whose representatives convened at Chicago, June 9, 1880.

I am profoundly grateful for the honor conferred. Fully realizing the high responsibility to which I have been called, and conscious that the position was unsought by me, I accept the nomination as a solemn duty. The Convention is to be congratulated upon the great work accomplished, in the unification of the various Greenback and Labor elements, into one compact organization. This was of first importance, and thoroughly prepares our forces to strike a decisive blow for industrial emancipation during the impending struggle.

Our party has this great significance : it is a great labor movement, composed of earnest people, who earn their bread by honest toil, whether of hand, head or heart ; and as the world depends for the comfort of life upon the various departments of human toil, so will every part of society feel the vivifying influence of the grand achievements of our organization that lie just in the future ; for when labor is prosperous, every other element of society tells the impulse of vigorous life.

The three great political parties have selected their candidates and made formal declarations of their principles. It is now the high duty of every citizen of the United States to judge between them ; and after careful inquiry into the aims and purposes of each, to determine the organization, with which duty calls him to act.

The admirable platform adopted by the Convention, meets my cordial approval. It is comprehensive, reasonable and progressive—containing those principles of economic reform essential to the preservation of the liberty and prosperity of the whole people.

It being the duty of man to earn his bread in the sweat of his face, it becomes the first duty of civil government to foster industry. All laws, therefore, which place a premium upon idleness, whether of men or money, unjustly discriminate in favor of capital, or withhold from honest men the full and just reward for their labor, are simply monstrous. Capital should be the servant of labor rather than its master.

This great truth can never be realized until there is an adequate circulating medium. Inasmuch as this circulating medium is for the benefit of all, its issue and volume should be sacredly kept under the control of the people, without the intervention of banking corporations. All money, whether gold, silver or paper, should be issued by the supreme authority of the nation, and be made a full legal tender in payment of all debts—public and private.

The system which now prevails, gives into the hands of banking corporations absolute control over the volume of the currency, and through this they have the power to fix the price of the labor and property of fifty millions of people. By provision of law, the method is clearly defined whereby they may, without limit, inflate or contract the currency at will. Cognate to this, and a part of the same scheme, stands the system of funding the public debt. Like national banking, this was borrowed from the English monarchy. By this system an enormous non-taxable, interest-bearing debt is to be perpetuated. The bonds support the banks, and the banks foster the public debt. If you pay off the bonds, the banks must cease to exist. Hence, if the national banks are to continue, we must have a perpetual bonded debt. Both patriotism and sound statesmanship loudly call for the abolition of banks of issue, and the substitution of legal tender Treasury notes for their circulation. Pay the bonds according to contract, and as rapidly as possible.

Seven hundred millions of the public debt become redeemable, at the option of the Government, during this and the ensuing year. Two funding bills are now pending before Congress—one introduced by the Democratic, and the other by the Republican leader of the House, whereby it is proposed to deprive the people, for twenty and thirty years, of the lawful right to pay said bonds. This is a crime against the laborer and the taxpayer, and should cause wide-spread alarm among all classes.

The annual surplus revenues, and the idle coin now in the Treasury, and that which must continue to accumulate, if the silver law approved Feb. 28, 1878, shall be honestly enforced, are ample to pay every dollar of the seven hundred millions, both principal and interest, within the next six years. There is not the slightest excuse for funding these bonds, except to perpetuate the debt as the basis of an iniquitous banking monopoly. It must be apparent to all that the great moneyed institutions and other corporations now have control of nearly every department of our Government, and are fast swallowing up the profits of labor, and reducing the people to a condition of vassalage and dependence. These monopolies, of whatever class, headed by the associated banks, are interlocked in purpose, and always act in closest sympathy.

There are three industrial classes in America: First, the producers; second, those who manufacture our raw materials and prepare them for use; third, the distributers of these products. Each should be protected in the legitimate fruits and profits of their labor, but should not be permitted to extort from and enslave the others.

The great problem of our civilization is how to bring the producer and consumer together. This can only be done by providing an adequate circulating medium, and by rigid regulation of inter-State commerce and transportation. This was wisely foreseen by the framers of the Constitution, and accordingly, by the eighth section of Article 1, Congress is clothed with power "to regulate commerce with foreign nations and among the States." This power imposes a corresponding duty upon Congress to see that it is enforced.

The two great agents of commerce are money and transportation. It is undeniable that both of these agents are under absolute control of monopolies. By controling the volume of money, the banks fix the price of all labor and property; and the railroads, by combination, render competition impossible, and control absolutely the price of transportation.

This places the people between the upper and nether millstones, and grinds them to poverty and ruin. It results in the wholesale robbery of both producer and consumer. Who is able to controvert this stupendous fact? Farmers, planters and laboring men of the United States, I beseech you to open your eyes at once to this alarming condition of things.

I am especially thankful that the platform of the party which placed me in nomination is open, bold and unmistakable on these great questions.

The Republican and Democratic platforms are either silent with regard to these vital issues, or they have pronounced in favor of the monopolies and against the people. With fifty million of people looking them in the face and pleading for relief, they utter not one word of promise or hope. Their leaders and platform makers are in the toils of the syndicate, gigantic bank corporations and railroad monopolies, and have neither the disposition nor the courage to strike one generous blow for industrial emancipation.

An area of our public domain, larger than the territory occupied by the great German empire, has been wantonly donated to wealthy corporations ; while a bill introduced by Hon. Hendrick B. Wright, of Pennsylvania, to enable our poor people to reach and occupy the few acres remaining, has been scouted, ridiculed and defeated in Congress. In consequence of this stupendous system of land grabbing, millions of the young men of America, and millions more of industrious people from abroad, seeking homes in the new world, are left homeless and destitute. The public domain must be sacredly reserved to actual settlers, and where corporations have not complied strictly with the terms of their grants, the lands should be at once reclaimed.

The immigration of persons from foreign countries, seeking homes and desiring to become citizens of the United States, should be encouraged, but the importation of Chinese servile laborers should be prohibited by stringent laws.

While the bondholder has been paid gold in return for his depreciated currency, the soldiers and sailors who saved our Union, our homes, our money and our altars, and whose blood consecrated every battlefield from Belmont and Donelson, to Gettysburg and Appomatox, are denied the pittance justly due them under their contract with the Government, as though soldiers and sailors could live on gratitude alone,

By the answer of Secretary Sherman of June 10, 1880, to the Senate resolution of inquiry, it appears that the Government paid the soldiers in greenbacks during the war of the rebellion $1,249,519.135.16.

The total interest paid in gold on the public debt from July 1, 1861, to June 30, 1879, is $1,809,301,485.19, and still we owe the principal of the debt. The soldier has been taxed to pay this interest, while the bondholder, as usual, has gone free.

During the present Congress, it has been impossible to induce the committees to report a single bill to remedy existing evils. The important committees of the House are so constituted, and the despotic rules of that body so interpreted as to render relief impossible. Under these rules the Speaker is as much the dictator of the country as though he were an emperor, and ruling in the most despotic government on the globe.

One of the grand missions of our party is to banish forever from American politics that deplorable spirit of sectional hatred, which, for base purposes, has been fostered by the leaders of the old parties. This has greatly deceived and embittered the public mind, both North and South.

Our civilization demands a new party, dedicated to the pursuits of peace, and which will not allow the war issues ever to be reopened, and will render the military strictly subordinate to the civil power. The war is over, and the sweet voice of peace, long neglected, calls us to worship at her altars; let us crown her temples with willing votaries. Let us have a free ballot, a fair count, and equal rights for all classes—for the laboring man in Northern manufactories, mines and workshops, and for the struggling poor, both white and black, in the cotton fields of the South.

I most earnestly and solemnly invoke united action of all industrial classes, irrespective of party, that we may make a manly struggle for the independence of labor, and to re-establish in the administration of public affairs, the old time Democracy of Jefferson and Jackson, and the pure Republicanism of Abraham Lincoln and Thaddeus Stevens.

In consequence of the great avenues to public opinion, the press, the bar, and the pulpit, being mainly under the control of the enemies of our movement, your convention thought proper to request its candidates to visit the various sections of the Union and talk to the people. It is my intention to comply with this request to the extent of my ability.

And now, eschewing all violence and tumult as unworthy of the cause we represent, and relying upon Divine Providence and the justice of our cause, let us go forth in the great struggle for human rights.

With high regard, I am your obedient servant,

J. B. WEAVER.

GEN. JAMES B. WEAVER.

# CHAPTER VI.

## LIFE AND SERVICES OF GEN. JAMES B. WEAVER.

### BY HON. STEPHEN D. DILLAYE.

James Baird Weaver, the nominee of the National Greenback Labor Party for President of the United States, English by origin, and American by birth, was born at Dayton, Ohio, June 12, 1833. His ancestors emigrated from England and settled in New York early in the century. The grandfather of the subject of this sketch, Henry Weaver, moved to Ohio while it was yet almost an unbroken wilderness. His probity, intelligence and activity as a citizen, secured him the appointment, then a distinguished honor, as one of the Judges of the State Courts, an office he filled with credit to himself and to his constituents.

Active in all the duties of a pioneer, he was placed in command of a fort on the Ohio river, located where the city of Cincinnati now stands, which post he occupied during the savage war of the Indians with conspicuous bravery.

Abram Weaver, the son of Henry, and father of James B., was a native of Ohio. His mother, Susan Imlay, was a native of New Jersey, and owed her origin to one of the oldest of its Revolutionary families. In 1835, Abram Weaver moved to Cass County, Michigan. His occupation was that of a farmer, a tiller of the soil. He remained in

Michigan until 1842, when he started West in pursuit of a new home. He crossed the Mississippi, and on the 1st of May, 1843, settled in Davis County, Iowa, and resumed his occupation as a farmer. Active, intelligent and well educated for practical life, he was made Clerk of the Courts of Davis County, a position he filled for ten years. He continued his farm life until 1848, when he removed with his family to the village of Bloomfield, where James attended district school for two years, and carried the mail, on horseback, from that place to Fairfield, his father being the Government contractor for that route. Ambitious to secure the means of future support while yet a boy, and determined to make his way in the world, knowing that he had to depend upon himself, in 1850, he commenced the study of law in the office of Hon. Samuel G. McAchran, of Bloomfield. He had no means of support but what he earned by his own efforts, for he had determined from the first that he would support himself without trenching upon the means, or in anywise burthening his father. To this end, he secured employment as a clerk in the store of C. W. Phelps, but continued his legal studies, devoting mornings and evenings, late into the night, to his books.

In 1853, he was induced to drive an ox team across the plains to California. It was an undertaking at which an older and stouter heart might well hesitate, but he was poor, needed the reward the toil would secure, and performed the long, slow, and dangerous pilgrimage as if he was a veteran in the service. The journey was full of hardships, but it was invigorating to the body, as it was inspiring to the energies and ambition of the dauntless boy who had undertaken it. Having safely reached his destination and delivered up his charge, he returned by the water routes to Bloomfield. From thence he went to Bonaparte, a village near by, to enter the store of Edwin Manning, where he spent the winter of 1854, performing his duty to his employer with such fidelity as to receive his unqualified commendation and the offer of increased wages, and a partnership if he would remain, but young Weaver felt that he owed a higher duty to himself, and to the profession to whose labors and honors he aspired.

In the fall of 1854, he secured a loan, *at* $33\frac{1}{3}$ *per cent. annual interest*, of sufficient means to enable him to pursue a Course at the Cincinnati Law School, and he entered upon it with a devotion to his studies, and an energy in the daily acquisition of legal knowledge which left no room to question his future success. He remained at the law school until he had finished the course of studies, prescribed for elemental preparation, and received the honorary degree of LL.B. This gave him admission to practice, and he proceeded at once to open an office at Bloomfield.

For six years he labored with unremitting zeal in the grand profession to which he had devoted his life. They were years of struggle,—full of labor, with a daily increasing business and support.

On the 13th of July, 1858, he was married at Keasaqua, Iowa, to Clara Vinson, a native of St. Marys, Ohio. He commenced keeping house at once, and made his home the palace of his soul. Educated in the West, to the full limit of its nowise inferior advantages, blessed with health, full of the attractive beauty of youth, industrious and ambitious, Mrs. Weaver became the cheerful, affectionate and devoted helpmate of her husband. Practising the most rigid economy, making her home the sympathetic resting-place for companionship, she entered with enthusiasm into all the labors and trials of her husband's active life. When the voice of duty called him to the battle-field of the Rebellion, she yielded to the demand of her country with womanly heroism, and yet with that anxiety and grief no pen can describe. During his absence on the field, she took charge of his affairs, and watched his progress—his courageous devotion to his duties and his promotion, as a young wife and mother of a first-born child yet clinging to her breast only could. This daughter is now twenty-one years of age, and married to E. A. Robinson, Esq., a young lawyer at Ottumna, Iowa. They have also been blessed with two sons— James B., Jr., and Abram C., and four younger daughters.

The home life of General Weaver is all an accomplished and devoted wife—whose whole existence is dedicated to his comfort, the care of his family, and to his ambition, surrounded by children educated to the affectionate devotion of every-day companionship—can make it. General Weaver and his wife are active members of the Methodist church. He has been for many years the efficient Superintendent of the Sunday-school connected with his church. Thoroughly temperate, zealous in good works, the family and family life of General Weaver is that of a citizen seeking, by his benevolence and Christian charities, to deserve the respect, and merit the confidence of his neighbors and friends.

In personal appearance, General Weaver is commanding, graceful and easy. Tall, well-built, compact and energetic with the glow of health, he is just in the ripening strength of manhood. His features are regular in the symmetry of form, and display the natural vigor of perfect health. His face is full of expression. Always lighted up with the sunshine of good nature, it yet carries with its smile the will which shows the inflexible character of the man. Easy of access, affable, courteous and quick to comprehend, he is socially a favorite in society. In debate, he is electric in manner, and often powerfully eloquent in expression. Careful in his positions, determined to be just, and quailing before no opposition, he speaks with the daring boldness of a man who knows his rights and is determined to maintain them. Possessing many of the characteristics of Douglass, in the fervid fluency of Western force and logical compactness, and in the determined zeal of his advocacy; he, like that lamented statesman, leaves no room for friend or foe to doubt his positions, or question the integrity of his purpose.

General Weaver's normal life, as a citizen and as a man, may be said to have commenced on his return from the battle-field of the Rebellion, and yet, a clear insight into his character and his career, will be but promoted by tracing somewhat more minutely his earlier characteristics and position.

Almost immediately on leaving the law school at Cincinnati, young Weaver, then but about twenty-three years of age, opened a law office at Bloomfield. His whole capital consisted of his physical vigor and bodily health with the mental, moral, intellectual and legal acquirements he had been able to secure in the seven years of labor and study, which formed the novitiate of his self-sustained career. But bold in heart, and determined in purpose, he crossed the threshold from student to active life, feeling that there was no such word as failure in the lexicon of his future.

In the midst of friends who had learned to appreciate his industrious ambition and his moral worth, in the very heart of the rapidly increasing State in which he had grown into manhood, and to whose future he had dedicated his fortune, he felt that confidence in himself, that conscious integrity and determined energy always inspire. Iowa was developing its rich fields of productive industry with a prosperity and progress without a parallel in the history of States, unless it might be found in the rapid growth of some of her sister empires in the west. Free from all the hindrances and prejudices of older civilizations, she was full of opportunities for the industrious and honest. Young Weaver had wedded his life to its life, determined to make himself a part of its growth, its prosperity and its character.

Intensely American, he worked for bread and for fame, as if every day's life was the dependent necessity of every day's labor. He could not help succeeding, for he was diligent in the performance of every duty and was quick to show that he bore within him the oratory and genius of intellectual power. Combining this, with the talent wrought from years of studious labor and the varied experiences of his life, he appeared to be able to judge and compare as if he comprehended the event he pursued, by intuitive perceptions of all its logical results.

Genius is the child of originality, a strange and powerful current springing fresh and clear from invisible fountains of good sense in the man who possesses it, and which at the right hour is poured forth in copious streams, rolling limpid and pure into the daily current of life.

Young Weaver, in the very commencement of his professional career, displayed that seemingly intuitive knowledge, which, finding its expression in an oratory full of the genius of command, assured his success at the bar. He had worked his way to a successful practice, won to his affections a wife to comfort, aid and encourage him in his daily labors and aspirations; mastered the trials of the first years of practice, and was vigorously at work in performing the daily increasing demands for his professional services, when the startling echo of that relentless cry for civil war reverberated through the land, as the loud-mouthed cannon of South Carolina belched forth their defiant challenge at Fort Sumpter.

Young Weaver heard the summons. It was the South against the North to sustain human slavery. It was the North defending its flag to sustain human liberty. He was for liberty. He did not wait for requisitions for men, or for position to command, but with his great heart swelling with devotion to the old flag under which, friendless and poor, he had been able to march to manhood, respectability and professional success, he enlisted in the ranks, enlisted to give his life and blood, his hopes and his manhood to his country and its cause. He was elected first lieutenant to company G, of the Iowa infantry, and soon promoted as Major. This was October 3, 1862. The regiment was a reality; it was at the work of life and death for liberty.

They were engaged in deadly strife at the battle of Corinth, October 12, 1862. The Colonel and the Lieutenant-Colonel were killed; it was a hand to hand fight, in which, the desperate courage and savage will of the South were pitted against men who were on the field of battle with but one purpose, liberty or death—and they won. The gallant part taken in that bloody and eventful battle by General Weaver, promoted him to the Colonelcy. Shortly after he was promoted to position of Brigadier-General for gallantry on the field.

General Weaver was not educated for military life, but he led the gallant Second until the expiration of the term of service, on the 27th of May, 1864, when he was mustered out. He never missed a march, a skirmish, or a battle, and came near to being hit at Fort Donelson, when a ball passed through the top of his cap and plowed a furrow through his hair. At the battle of Reseca, Georgia, he led the brigade that crossed the Oostanala, found the enemy's position there, laid the pontoon bridges under fire, and after crossing the brigade, jumped into the rifle pits and drove the enemy before him. He makes no claim to the laurels of the victor, or to any great achievement on the field of battle. He was called to combat; he answered the call, did his duty manfully, boldly, nay even brilliantly. All time will entwine his name, as inseparably connected with the hard fought triumph of the battle of Corinth; what is more, from the hour he enlisted until the war closed, he was always at the post of duty, a living soldier of patriotism, honest to himself, honest to his country, his home and his God.

The war closed, General Weaver with the whole five hundred thousand veterans, then better than ever prepared to defend their country, passed almost without attracting public attention, into the avocations of peace and the labors of active life. After devoting their very being to the noble and genuine patriotism of elevating the nation to the level of its untold privileges as a political power, they resumed the industries of peace to heal the wounds the war had inflicted, and set in motion the energies of a renewed life to develop the commerce, agriculture and manufacturing of the country, until the whole God blessed heritage of freemen was energetic in the activities of enterprise.

General Weaver at once returned to Bloomfield and entered with his new manhood and the experience the wide diversities of situation and acquaintance the war had given to him, into the practice of the law. He was recognized everywhere as a man of the people. He was popular because he was bold and just, and always ready to do unto others as he would that others should do unto him. Right was his rule and justice his aim.

Appointed District Attorney, one of the most arduous and responsible of public offices, he performed the duties with careful fidelity to the demands of justice, and the no less imperative claims of humanity. Firm without obstinacy, prompt without haste, and confident without arrogance, he filled the duty of public prosecutor with universal satisfaction to the courts and with the most deserved applause by the people. He retired from the District Attorneyship to accept the office of United States Assessor of Revenue for the district of Iowa. He performed the responsible duties of this office with fidelity to the Government and to the people and continued to administer its affairs until the office was discontinued.

General Weaver, from the moment of the appearance of the Greenback as the national fiat that it had taken a new step in the financial policy of the country, was its open, unqualified and determined advocate. He felt that while the Government was struggling to rid itself from the barbaric infamy of human slavery, that it had broken another chain which held it enthralled to as tyranical usurpers of human property, as the slave dealer and owner was of human flesh.

Gold and silver had for centuries been the instrument of universal brigandage and usury. Limited in quantity, controlled by the powerful and the rich, they were the one power to which all political power had been forced to yield. He was convinced of these facts, and that men and governments were slaves to coin and its owners; that all Asia and India, excepting the privileged owners of coin, were kept in servitude to its oligarchic power. That England was a living mass of pauperism and imbecility under the domination of coin, wherever it enslaved; that England had under its iron-heeled tyranny descended from *1,000,000 of comparatively independent property owners in a population of 15,000,000, in three-quarters of a century, to less than 70,000 comparatively independent property owners in a population of 36,000,000.*

He knew that when coin reigned in finances, public debts and taxation reigned over the people. He knew that the few could and always did control it. He knew that he who has the power to control, has the power to tyrannize over those he has the power to control ; and all time and all history had taught him that the money power was the most heathen, relentless and unscrupulous power that ever dominated over a prostrate people. Pity cannot reach it. Starvation cannot move it. Ireland tells its story!

When he first received the Greenback, it passed like gold, for *it represented the Nation—was the nation—its property, its law, its honor, its power.* Shylock had forced its issue. It had said to Secretary Chase, "Gold and silver there is none." It had skulked away to Europe, or hid itself in the double-locked safe of the calculating usurer, to make profit out of blood and quadrupled usury out of the demands of war. It said to Secretary Chase, "take our bills, our paper money, and we will supply your wants. It is true we don't pay or redeem our bills in specie, but we are the bankers and money kings of the land."

Secretary Chase, and the great and good but timid men who surrounded him, said: "You ask us to take your individual promise to pay ; your individual credit to use as money to meet the demands of the United States." And he said: "I will take the credit of the Government, the people, the nation, bottomed on taxes, and I will issue Treasury certificates as money, precisely as Franklin had done in Pennsylvania; precisely as Thomas Jefferson had over and over again recommended."

After discussing the whole subject of finance and weighing all schemes, Jefferson had declared "that bank paper must be suppressed, and the circulating medium must be restored *to the Nation to whom it belongs.* It is the only fund on which they can rely for loans; it is the only recourse which can never fail them, and it is an abundant one for every necessary purpose. Treasury bills bottomed on taxes, to any extent that may be found necessary, thrown into circulation will take the place of gold and silver, and so the nation may continue to issue its bills as far as its wants require and the limits of circulation will admit." Jefferson, Madison, Jackson, Calhoun, Webster and Clay sustained this doctrine; General Weaver adopted it.

The Greenback was issued as a full legal tender, but it could only be issued by virtue of a law of Congress, establishing the amount and time and circumstances of the issuing. The amount issued by virtue of the first appropriation was exhausted. It was always at a par with gold, simply because it was made a full legal tender. No money was more eagerly or confidently received by the people. No desire was ever so eagerly or so madly attached by the bankers and money power.

A new and a large appropriation was demanded. The Treasury was empty. The army was in the field. To rely on gold or banks was to give up the battle. Government credit was the sole recourse. We had to issue *bonds* bearing interest to get money, *and sell them in the market for what they would fetch*, or issue Treasury certificates as money to the full limit of our wants, as Jefferson recommended.

In this emergency, Mr. Chase and the Committee on Ways and Means prepared a bill with timid care, not yet indoctrinated into the grandeur, safety and incomparable superiority of such money over that of all other systems ever devised, to issue $150,000,000 as a full legal tender for all debts, public and private, redeemable in bonds of the United States in sums of $50, or any multiple of that sum, instead of issuing them as Jefferson recommended bottomed on taxes.

This bill, after the most elaborate efforts to defeat it, on unconstitutional and bug-bear grounds, coined out of the fruitful brains of the money power, passed the House. It went to the Senate. Then the great bankers prepared to kill it—cripple it, or load it down with such marks of inferiority as should make it the easy instrument of their nefarious designs.

Bankers, money hessians, usurers, and the whole tribe of Israelitish knaves who grow oppulent on misfortune and become rich out of the misery they create, combined to defeat the bill, or so amend it as to place the Treasury and finances of the nation completely in their power. These worse than Hessians saw that if the bill passed as it was it would render the people financially independent. They saw that it would cut off all chances for them to rob the people. They were astute enough to see that to carry out the policy this bill established would transfer the control of the money of the nation from bankers and usurers, to the people. It was emancipation of the masses. It was the hand writing on the wall for the money kings.

It was therefore the battle of the giants for control.

The great bankers of New York, with Coe at their head, sustained by Gallatin and Martin as leaders, Bates and Walley and their coadjutors of the Boston banks, with Rogers, Mercer and Patterson and their assistants of the Philadelphia banks, associated themselves as representing the capital, the wealth and monied power of the nation, as bankers and brokers, to influence the Committee of the Senate to report against the bill. This they well knew they could not accomplish. To kill the bill then was figuratively to kill the nation, for the life of the bill was the credit, which is the next thing to the life of the nation.

The bankers then culminated in the bond policy, and they determined the bill should be so amended as to make reliance upon the Greenback an impossibility, and *dependence on the bond policy an absolute necessity.*

How was this to be done? The first step was to frighten the Committee of the Senate into the belief that capitalists would utterly repudiate and discredit the Greenback if it was issued in such quantities as the Government demanded. That the only line of policy capitalists could or would sustain, was to issue bonds, *interest and principal payable in coin.* That if the Government adopted this course capital would aid it, and stand by it. If it issued a full legal tender Greenback they would oppose and discredit it. *That bonds could only be negotiated, the interest of which was payable in coin. That coin to pay this interest so that the purchasers of bonds would feel secure, could only be relied upon by making the duties on foreign merchandise payable in coin alone.*

To accomplish this, it was necessary for the Committee

*to consent to an amendment which should repudiate our own credit, discredit our own legal tender money and place it on the market to be carped at by jews, discarded by bankers and slandered by the whole gambling throng of curbstone brokers.*

But the money power was omnipotent. The Senate yielded to its mandates,—consented to so amend the bill *as to print repudiation on the back of every bill, in these words:* "*Not receivable for Duties on Imports, or for Interest on the public debt.*" They further so amended the bill as to make the gold value of the Greenback the market value of United States bonds.

This infamy,—the most damnable that ever disgraced Congress, and the most costly to the tax-burthened producer ever enacted to impose upon a confiding but swindled people,—became a law; but not till these money lords had made complete the subjugation of the people, by exempting the bonds to be issued from all taxation.

The great mass of the people did not comprehend the aim and purpose with which their own and their country's money was thus insultingly disgraced. It was as diabolical as if Congress had voted to print, in burning words of shame across every flag of stars that floats to the breeze on land or sea: "The nation has yielded to its Shylocks. The people are subjugated to the Hessians of the money market."

The result was soon seen. The repudiated Greenback was proclaimed as worthless as the French Assignat or the Continental money of the Continental Congress. Wall street, New York; Third street, Philadelphia and

Boston, vilified it, slandered it, and exhausted the whole vocabulary of financial lies to undervalue it on the market. Gold went up, Greenbacks went down, and yet no bonds were sold. Gold was magnified as an unqualified necessity,—Greenbacks as a disgraceful cheat, till gold went up to 200, Greenbacks down to 50, and still the work of depreciation went on in the exact ratio as our demand for money was intensified. Gold reached 285 ; Greenbacks down to 38.

At this point of our financial history, Capital hit upon the grand expedient of offering to come to the aid of the country, provided bonds could be made the basis for bank circulation, and further providing the Government would give a monopoly of banking to National Banks, and furnish ninety per cent. of the face value of the bonds in United States currency, guaranteed by the Government, without charge, to be lent as money at discount rates by the banks. A deeper plan of public robbery was never imposed upon an intelligent people ; but the banks got just what they demanded.

The sale of bonds then commenced. $400,000,000 were sold at 42 cents on the dollar. Thus, at one stroke, $232,000,000 were paid as a share to get $168,000,000 of gold. The sales went on, till $410,000,000 more bonds were sold to be made the basis for banking for the aggregate sum of $197,250,000, giving to the bankers $212,750,000, as a share—more than doubling their capital before they started. Besides this, the Government gave the banks $350,000,000 in currency, to lend on compound interest.

This was but the initiatory step. Capital had usurped

the banking monopoly of the nation. It had $350,000-000 in currency, for which it had not paid a dollar; and it had $410,000,000 of bonds drawing gold interest, for which it had paid but $197,250,000.

This was not enough. The bonds issued had been drawn payable in legal currency. The capitalists now clamored, with the whole metropolitan press subsidized to sustain them, for a Congressional declaration that the whole indebtedness should, and of right must be, payable in coin. The people had no voice,—Congress was controlled by capital. Capital said, "pass the *Credit Strengthening Act*." Congress passed it. Two hundred millions were thus imposed upon the taxpayer, by a robbery without a single palliating excuse to mitigate its outrageous effrontery, for the benefit of foreign Jews and American usurers, who had purchased their bonds at less than fifty cents on a dollar, and who had already received back the full amount they had paid in interest.

Capital, by this bill had secured a Congressional declaration, that all the bonds should be paid in coin, yet greedy with the usurious greed of the vampire, it took another step, and through the aid of five hundred thousand dollars paid by the agent of the Rothchilds, these lines were introduced into a bill foreign to the subject, demonetizing silver, leaving the people and the United States no means of liquidating their debts but by payment in gold.

The necessary result of these bills, all dictated and passed under the controling influence of foreign capital and the overpowering combination of the banks, associated into a confederated oligarchy to rule the finances of the nation, was contraction ; for the whole country saw that as gold was soon to be the the only medium of legal payment, that immediate measures must be taken to provide for the financial crisis so near at hand.

And yet one more step was necessary to place the people, the property and the credit of the country completely under the power of the banks, and gamblers at the stock board,—that was, to force on a law demanding a resumption of specie payment ; and that at a time when the whole specie in the United States was not equal to the business demands of a single city. Gold not to exceed $200,000,000, all told ; with government obligation reaching the sum of $2,500,000,000; with private and business indebtedness double this amount.

The fact that the National Banks, the Bank Association, Bondholders, and foreign speculators controlled our finances was not alone the result of the bond inflation into which Congress had been drawn, but the same reasons which had led to the infamous privileges granted to the National Banks and to the unheard of usury by which we had sold "our bonds for what they would fetch," and *by which we had in a single transaction paid $232,000,000, as an absolute share to get $168,000,000 in gold*, led us to those enormous land grants and charters, and money advances, which robbed the people and the nation of 300,000,000 acres of our public domain, to give it to gambling knaves,—subsidised Congressmen and speculators in our national disgrace.

With these enormous land grants, were money or bond grants (bonds exempt from taxation) to the extent of

$60,000,000; with a practical monopoly of the highways of the nation from the Atlantic to the Pacific. Out of these grants, utterly without Constitutional support, procured by the basest frauds which ever tarnished the legislation of Congress, grew up corporate combinations and corporate powers which, in extent of their franchises, in magnitude of capital and insolence of control, surpass any monopolies that have ever before trampled upon the rights of government or people in the history of the world. They ruled States, Legislatures, Congress and the people. Arrogant with power, insolent with wealth, and in possession of the highways and the transportation from ocean to ocean, and from regions of eternal snows in the north to regions of perpetual flowers in the south, they combined with the banks, bond-holders and usurers, to centralize the government to their control.

The crisis they sought commenced its culminating power in 1873. We had contracted our circulating medium from $1,944,710,294.51, Jan. 1, 1865, to $702,-794,487.51, in 1875. The result was almost unusual bankruptcy. Failures went from 662 in 1866, to 10,000 in 1876, and 12,000 in 1877. Factories were closed; three million of men were out of employment; millions were without home, bread or hope; and nothing but the illimitable grandeur of our unequalled resources kept us from revolution and despair. But the great West poured its products in bounteous profusion, to meet the necessities of the people at home and supply the demands from abroad, while our mines in the mountains through the whole auriferous region, literally stocked with minerals from Dakota, Nebraska, Colorado, New Mexico, Arizona,

Utah, Nevada and California, were giving us annually a hundred million of treasures. These resources, supported by the indomitable will of our people who, like the old guard of Napoleon know how to die but can never learn how to surrender, kept us from yielding to that infernal system of political economy which makes an infinitesimal part of our production more omnipotent to control the destinies of our people, than the united grandeur of the whole, by this yielding to gold the favored few—the monopolent banks. The corporations, the tax-exempt bond holders, grow into enormous riches, while the struggling tax-paying producer and worker is reduced to an enslaved dependence on capital.

General Weaver had been an ardent Republican,—circumstances had made him one,—but he was no idle slave to political dogmas. He saw that the Republican party had trafficked away the great purposes for which it was organized; that it had leagued with capital to secure political power; that it had sold its loyalty to corporate knaves, to make sure of winning the support of corporate combinations; that it had degenerated from a great party, devoted to human liberty, to become a monied power, devoted to centralization, aristocracy and monopolies; that it was ruled by cliques, managed by "bosses," and run by the bank association, and he cut the cable, and put himself in open, defiant and manly opposition to its leaders, its purposes and its legislation.

During the progress of the legislation so palpably antagonistic to all of the industrial and productive interests of the country, men all over the land began to discuss and inquire into the object and purpose of it; and there were not wanting brave and manly souls to denounce it. Among others, the Hon. Peter Cooper,—a man above ambition, beyond want, on the very pinnacle of commercial fame, honored for a long and active life, devoted to the best interests of his fellow man, yet too much in love with his country and the welfare of his countrymen to remain silent when experience and a disinterested judgment, based upon the activities of the largest and most successful enterprise of the land, bade him denounce the financial system which was overwhelming the nation with debt, bankruptcy, forced idleness and despair.

Through his exertions and those of Henry Cary Baird, Henry C. Carey, Moses Field and other liberal and disinterested patriots, the Greenback party sprang into existence. Its first object was purely financial. Gradually it enlarged its philosophies, its objects and its views, until it became the avowed champion of those human rights which politically unite men in regulating the governments and laws under which they live. It became the Great Reform party of the time.

As land is the essential element for production, and as Government holds an immense territory in trust for the people, to be distributed in limited quantities so as to promote the welfare of all, it declares it to be the duty of Congress to hold the entire public domain for actual occupancy and homesteads; to grant no subsidies from it for individuals or corporations. That as each head of a family is legally entitled to a homestead, and as a great proportion of the laboring poor and industrious young men and women are unable to get on to homesteads and make them places of abode and cultivation without aid, that it is the duty of Congress to loan, on such terms as shall be just and secure, a sufficient sum to enable every head of a family to avail themselves of the advantages of the Homestead Act, and thus so divide our lands and encourage cultivation and thrift as to elevate labor into independence, industry into the royalty of a home and its ownership, and the people into those equalities and opportunities which leave no room for indigence, beggary and crime.

That as land without labor is fruitless, and as all the nation or the people have or possess owes its origin to labor and could not have existed without it, that it is the highest duty of government to so protect labor from unjust laws, degrading competition, and servile employment, as to make the laborer feel the honest dignity of his employment, and know that by it he can secure to himself and his family, a justly remunerative compensation.

That as land and labor produce all the varieties of natural products, markets for their distribution, exchange and sale become necessary, and therefore a medium of exchange and a measure of value becomes essential. This medium of exchange is known as money. Money is the creature or creation of law. It is just what the sovereign power declares it shall be. Congress is the sovereign representative of the people in the United States to make and declare all laws. It and it alone has the power to declare what shall constitute lawful money, how it shall be issued and what shall be its powers.

Under the old system, based upon the aristocratic and oligarchic principles of favoritism and despotic power, the authority to issue money was delegated to persons and to corporations. Paper money, and that almost exclusively has been used and issued, based on individual credit and individual liability, always bolstered into respectability by the pretense that it was at all times redeemable in coin. For two hundred years the civilized world has been duped, swindled and cheated by using this pretended money, issued not by governments, but by individuals to whom the government delegated the power. This system was exposed by Jefferson, Franklin, Madison Jackson, Benton, Calhoun, and a long list of men, eminent for their knowledge, experience and disinterested judgment. The whole system was a sham. More than fifty per cent. of all the paper money issued by banks and individuals under delegated authority has been lost —robbed from the bill-holder.

The Greenback party therefore assumed, and took the true Jeffersonian doctrine, that the Government of the United States should issue all the money used in the United States; that no banks of issue should be permitted to exist; that in whatever form the money may be issued, it shall be a legal tender for all and every purpose; that as much money should be issued as may be required to sustain labor by just rewards, fairly equalize values and confine interest to such a per cent. that the lender shall have no greater reward or annual per cent. than the average profit of the producer.

With the land, labor and money thus provided for the duties and burthens of the people which the adoption of the bonded system has imposed upon them, come next in point of importance. $2,000,000,000 of bonds and certificates of indebtedness, robbed from the Government

by the frauds of the money power, at half their value—
exempt from all taxation. More than $400,000,000 of
this amount is held by the national banks, and eight hundred
millions more become due and may be paid in the
years 1880 and 1881. The National Greenback Labor
party takes the broad ground, that it is the duty of the
Government to pay every bond as fast as it matures, or
can be paid by the terms on which it was issued; that
the Government shall issue no more bonds; that it shall
issue full legal-tender Greenbacks as money, bottomed on
taxes and on the sovereignty, power, honor, property,
public and private, in the United States.

A further fundamental theory on which this reform was
based, was that it was an unconstitutional and unparalleled
outrage to free *a rich man from the payment of taxes*,
and impose his taxes on his neighbor, a poor man. That
the Republican party has placed more than $3,000,000,-
000 of personal property, held by the richest men in the
United States, beyond the power of government to tax
it; it has made a law of privilege for a privileged class,
and has thus given $75,000,000 annually to the 300,000
bondocrats to be paid by the hard toil of the producer.

The National Greenback Labor Party have entered
their solemn protest against these outrages.

General Weaver left the Republican party, then in the
full tide of victory, when there was no position he could
not command, and no office he could not secure. He
left it in the State of Iowa, when to be a Republican and
have the confidence of the party, was to be on the highway
to any honor the State could bestow. He adopted
the principles of the National Greenback Labor party

because he believed that the future prosperity of our country and of our people depended upon it. He estimated the full extent of the indignity of having the Rothschilds manipulate our laws and control our finances. He believed that the people were as capable of managing their finances as they were to found States.

He therefore entered into the gubernatorial canvass of 1877, in the full spirit and full faith of the great reforms the Greenback movement had inaugurated; working with faultless zeal for the Greenback candidate, Hon. D. P Stubbs, until the close of the canvass. During the summer and fall which preceded the Congressional election, he was active in organizing the new party into condition for efficient work. When the Convention convened to nominate a candidate for Congress for his district, he was selected with that fire of enthusiastic zeal which leaves no room to question the popularity or the power of the candidate.

His opponent, G. S. Sampson, was a full-fledged Republican, a man of education, popularity, eloquence and wealth. The canvass was a spirited and manly duel before the people, but General Weaver fully comprehended the issues he had to discuss—he was master of them. The great mass of the voting population attended the public meetings at which he discussed the finances Mr. Sampson was then in Congress. The Republicans felt sure of his re-election, but finding that General Weaver was attracting great crowds, and winning confidence and favor wherever he spoke, they selected the strongest debater in the State, the then Attorney-General Cutts, to meet him in joint debate and discuss the issues of the campaign. These debates were full of the energy of justice and truth on the part of General Weaver, they were as masterly and able as his opponent could make the cause of monopolists. The campaign, in many of its features, was similar to that noted political duel which excited the whole American people, when Stephen A. Douglass and Abraham Lincoln discussed together the question of squatter sovereignty, through Illinois, as the great issue to determine which of the champions should win the honor of an election to the United States Senate. Douglass won the votes, Lincoln the fame of the contest; while in the battle between Weaver and Sampson, Weaver not only won the votes by a large majority, but established his fame as a public debater beyond all cavil or dispute. He received 16,366 votes against 14,308 cast for his opponent—making a clean majority of 2,056 votes in his favor.

# CHAPTER VII.

## LIFE OF GEN. JAMES B. WEAVER.—Continued.

From that day General Weaver became the admitted champion of the great reforms inaugurated by the Greenback National party in the Northwest. It is true that his colleague, Edward H. Gillette, has also won his way to Congress from the Des Moines district, by a battle little less notable, by advocating the exact reforms which had made the canvass of General Weaver destructive. Both young, in the very prime of life, both cultivated, scholarly, able and honest, they have been friends for years; as members of the bar they were often associated, and from the date of their elections they were united by the dearest ties of political sympathy and congressional effort.

Possessing ability equal to the high positions they occupied, they had no sooner reached Washington than they at once entered into the contests their position as radical reformers was certain to excite. In all, the utmost strength the Greenback National Labor party could command for Congressional battle, was fourteen. Most of these were without experience in Congressional contests. There was DeLaMatyr, the eloquent and masterly apostle of reform from Indiana; the young, ardent and clear-headed Ford of Missouri; the able and logical statesman, George W. Jones, of Texas; the representative of the stone cutters of Maine, the incorruptible and sound-headed Murch, with his colleague Judge Ladd; the young, brilliant and accomplished sons of Alabama; Judge Daniel Lindsay Russell, of North Carolina; the well-informed and able lawyer, Yocum, of Pennsylvania. These with Gillette and General Weaver were all new members.

But the National Greenback Labor party was not without its experienced legislators and acknowleged statesmen. Hon. Hendricks B. Wright was an early and an avowed advocate of its reforms. Living through half a century of our history; prominently identified with the political and progressive developments of the country from the administration of Jackson, he stood in the very van of the statesmen of the age. By his side, stood his colleague, William D. Kelly, one of the patriarchs of the House; a statesman by experience, a scholar by study, and a genius by nature; these men, with the gifted Stevenson, of Illinois, made up the representatives of the people, to advocate the reforms and establish the land, financial and industrial platform which constitutes their basis for political action.

It was thought that there was popular force enough in Republican management, to nulify any efforts which might be made to interfere with the financial policy they had inaugurated. The Democratic leaders were on the ragged edge of doubt, as to just what line of policy to pursue. Each of the old parties, while they were courting popular endorsement, yet sought to win the support of the great moneyed corporations which had so largely absorbed the capital, and were so industriously seeking to control the business interests of the country. They therefore united to meet at the outset every attempt of the reform leaders. The programme was settled, they were to be put down. They did not comprehend the power of men struggling to enforce truths and secure rights; nor yet, that each rebuff of an earnest, honest thinker was but a new spur to urge on the smouldering enthusiasm which flames forth at the first attempt to silence its evangelisms of justice.

General Weaver took his seat with his colleague and the newly elected Greenback associates, as the first distinctive representatives of the reform movement. He was not hasty to announce his position, but calmly waiting to take advantage of time and opportunity, he was ready for any emergency, and to meet the conflict which the agitation of the labor, land and financial questions was certain to excite. Just in the full vigor of manhood, commanding in appearance, electric in manner, educated by long professional encounters, to the emergencies of debate, fully imbued with the great truths he had been elected to advocate, and rich with that incomparable enthusiasm the glorious West inspires in the men who comprehend its wonderful progress—its rapid growth into States and empires of freedom, where the brutal hoof of no power but that of the usurer and the corporate knaves who had enthralled by mortgage the homes af the people, had ever trampled the liberties of man in the dust—he felt confidence in himself, and was ready to meet in the collisions of debate whatever antagonisms might place themselves in the way to obstruct the ideals of right and truth, he and his party were sworn not only to defend, but to propagate into universal acceptance.

The course of General Weaver in Congress is too recent, and too well known to be recapitulated in anything like minuteness of detail, and yet a brief reference to his votes, his speeches and his antagonisms, will serve to show how that electric current of popular opinion which culminated at Chicago, June 10th, 1880, in his nomination for the Presidency, obtained its power and produced the result.

One of the first accusations he brought against "the blaspheming past" was the action by which Congress had nullified its own law, fixing the limit of a day's work for men in the employ of the Government. It was in every sense the working-men's law. In commenting upon the defeat of the resolution, reported from the committee on education and labor, requiring Government officials to enforce the eight hour law, approved June 25, 1868, and still unrepealed, but utterly ignored and disregarded by both Republican and Democratic Congresses, General Weaver said :

"The working-men's bill to enforce the eight hour law was defeated in this house. Let me tell you that your action will recoil upon you. The eyes of the people are upon you, and you cannot escape. Remember that when the American Congress says, that we will not enforce a law which was passed in the interest and at the behest of the working men of the country, but we will allow the heads of departments to violate that law, (to meet the demand of speculating contractors,) and then turn around and say that the laboring man must obey the laws of the country, you are setting a dangerous example ; you are sowing dragons teeth ; you are sowing wind and you will reap the whirlwind. I hope the house will reconsider this motion."

Almost immediately after the eight hour bill was practically nullified by the refusal of Congress to order its enforcement, the question of restoring *the income tax on all incomes exceeding ten thousand dollars,* came before the house. It was one of those measures which should at once have commanded the attention of Congress. Direct taxation to the full extent of the requirements of the Government beyond the receipts for duties on foreign merchandise, on incomes above fifteen hundred dollars, is the doctrine of the National Greenback party. They who receive the benefits, should pay in the ratio of their receipts. This is the only mode of reaching those overgrown incomes which make their recipients dictatorial and powerful, and producing that equality among men essential to peace, the fair decrease of power and political liberty. General Weaver voted in favor of the bill; but, as it required a two-thirds vote, it failed, but it failed only for the time.

The next bill which attracted the attention of the country and awakened the liveliest interest of the reformers, was what was known as the "Silver Bill," a bill to establish free coinage of the $412\frac{1}{2}$ grain silver dollar and to place it on the same footing with gold.

On this bill General Weaver made one of those masterly speeches which not only gave him a position among the ablest orators of the house, but sent his name on telegraphic wings to every thinking and reading hamlet in the land. Members of Congress who had folded themselves in the golden robes of complacency, over the idea that they were under the wings of the Bank Association, and who had a feeling appreciation of the surplus fund devoted to the oiling of that political machinery, which it was publicly declared was now so organized that the banks could at any time control the action of Congress, began to feel that it might not, after all, be quite so easy to control Congress and the people, as the money kings had imagined.

General Weaver was master of the situation. True, he was in small minority; true, every appliance of ridicule, every shaft of wit, every power of capital with its United States treasurer ready to do its bidding, were opposed to him; but he had practical truths, facts, experiences and the common sense of mankind to sustain him, with a head, a brain and a heart nurtured in the bold and fearless spirit of the West to sustain him. There was no surplus in the National Bank fund, equal to the task of purchasing sneers, wit or sophistry enough to overawe the young Hercules of the West.

Again, on the 9th of May, General Weaver went through the ordeal to which every man who aspires to make himself the true representative, and dares to have an opinion of his own, is subjected, before he conquers his way to successful power in the House of Representatives. The question for debate was an act to amend certain sections of the Revised Statutes of the United States relating to coinage, and coin, and bullion certificates.

Fully prepared to discuss the measure, he entered upon the subject with a zeal and ability commensurate with its great importance. Among other things, he said:

"If we are to demonetize silver, and have no power to create a legal tender money, it will be readily perceived that the proposition is to hitch the car of American progress and American civilization to the decreasing product—gold, and this will lead us into inevitable decline and pauperism."

He denounced the infamous fraud by which silver was demonetised in 1873, as not only clearly unconstitutional, but as having been passed in the interest of foreign speculators in our bonds, and by the Hessians of the money market. He revived the history of the $1,500,000,000 bonds originally made payable in currency, as clearly established by the declaration of the Senators and members of Congress who took a prominent part in the passage of the law, and declared that the Credit Strengthening Act of 1869 was passed in open fraud, to get rid of that interpretation.

At this, the Republican leaders of the House defiantly interrupted him to inquire if he was not a Republican at that time, and if he had not vigorously supported General Grant and his administration? He was ready for the question. He admitted that he had been a Republican and that he had supported General Grant but he said :

"I was in the same situation then that the gentleman and many of his friends seem to be in now. I knew nothing about the question ; I had never investigated it. I was in the same condition with Paul of Tarsus, when on his way to Damascus. I have gathered some light since then, and I stand here frankly and plainly to say, having investigated this question, that a great public crime was committed against the labor of this country, by the so-called Credit Strengthening Act ; that it amounted, if not in intention, at all events in effect, to the robbery of our people, General Grant to the contrary notwithstanding."

Constantly interrupted and always ready for the attack, he repelled every effort to interfere with his argument, and met, with scorching sarcasm, each effort to confound his past with his present position. He declared that it was easy to read the animus of that Act in the opposition this bill is meeting with in this House to-day, and throughout the country, at the hands of the monomatalists; that the bill was smuggled through with a perfect knowledge that public sentiment would not tolerate it, and with the concealed and wicked purpose to deprive the people, the second time, of the right to pay the bonds, according to the terms the bond-holder had himself imposed.

He denounced the Credit Strengthening Act and the Act demonetising silver, as a conspiracy to defraud the Government and cheat the people, and declared that the cloven foot of the conspiracy was too plainly visible for gentlemen in that House, or on the stump, to cover it up. He charged directly home to the friends of those measures, that they were passed with the premeditated attempt to put the bonded debt in a condition in which it never could be paid, with the ulterior design to make the present banking system of the country, based upon the bonded debt, the great moneyed monopoly for all time to come. He said:

"This National Banking System, it is claimed, furnishes an elastic system of currency; that if the wants of trade require more money, the banks can get it by depositing more bonds, and if it becomes redundant, they can surrender it. They will regulate it solely for our good, of course. Thus, it is claimed that under the National Banking System, the amount of currency can be adjusted according to the demands of trade.

'But, sir, I maintain that the elasticity which we get at the option of the banks constitutes one of the greatest objections to the system. Such elasticity reminds me of the first piece of India rubber I ever saw. A great big fellow came to school, when I was a little boy about ten years old, holding in his hand a piece of India rubber which he was stretching. He said to me, 'Jim, did you ever see anything like this? I replied, 'I never did; what is it?' 'Why,' said he, 'they call it India rubber. Take one end of it between your teeth.' I did so. 'Now,' said he, 'pull!' I pulled and he pulled. While it was stretching out, while it was expanding, it did not hurt me a bit; but when he let loose the other end, that was contraction, and you may depend it was not pleasant. Now, the proposition is to put the rubber to the lips of the American people, and let the national banks draw it out whenever they please, or let it snap whenever they please.

"I say that it is one of the monster evils of the age and in defiance of all correct systems of finance, that we allow by law a set of men who are not elected by the people, who are not responsible to them for the management of their banking institutions, to regulate at will the volume of the currency. Such a system of finance is no better than a system of robbery; and it has had that effect practically, as a million ruined homes can testify."

The speech was not alone masterly in arrangement, logical in its unanswerable position, eloquent in its illustration, but carried with it the force of truth, which the paid advocates of capital could neither answer or refute.

On every occasion when the question of finance was before the house, General Weaver was prompt to do battle against the infamies by which the people had been subjugated to the demands of the banking oligarchy; and to the paying the taxes of the bonded nobility Republican legislation had imposed upon the people.

Side by side, and day by day, he co-operated with his Greenback associates in the House in every effort to right the wrongs which the moneyed power had imposed upon the country. His colleague, Mr. Gillette, had forcibly proclaimed the duty which devolved on reformers when in discussing the free coinage act. He said:

"Let us say to every law that has robbed labor and blasted enterprise, you must go from the statute-books. The national banks must go! the national bonds must go! the land monopolist must go! the law that bars out silver from our mints must go! the mountain of idle money in the Treasury must go into the channels of business! the millions that have been absorbed by coin bonds must go out once more to make glad the heart of the toiler, and redeem the bonds that bind him hand and foot."

In this spirit, and to this end, every energy General Weaver could bring to bear was devoted. Always in his place, always prompt in the performance of the duties devolving upon him, he commanded a position and won a triumph in the House of Representatives rarely if ever surpassed by any member in the first session of his legislative duties. Silver was remonetized; its coinage, if not to the full limit of his wishes, yet to a reasonable extent, was secured; and the idea of prolonging the payment of the public debt, by funding into long time bonds, free from taxation, for the benefit of a bonded aristocracy, and as the foundation for limitless monopoly of the national bank swindle, was resisted for the time, at least, if not for all time.

General Weaver also successfully introduced and carried the following important amendment to the coinage bill:

"The Secretary of the Treasury is hereby directed and required to cause to be paid out without discrimination, standard silver coin belonging to the Government, that may at any time be in the Treasury, the same as gold coin, in liquidation of all kinds of coin obligations against the Government."

This amendment was of the utmost importance to the whole country, and was so recognized ; but the Secretary of the Treasury has defiantly nullified its purpose, and violated its letter and spirit to win the favor of the banks, bond-holders and usurers of the land.

There is still another measure which came before the house for action, in which General Weaver placed himself in full accord with the reformers. That was a bill supplemental to the Homestead Act, by which, aid to heads of families desirous of availing themselves of the law, was to be loaned to enable them to remove, to get settled, and get in their first crops ; a measure which is destined to do more to promote general welfare, more to elevate honest poverty into self-sustaining life, labor into independence, and manhood into the equalities of a just civilization, than any measure, aside from the Homestead Act, ever passed by Congress.

To this measure General Weaver gave his hearty support. He was also active in pressing the establishment of a Bureau for Labor Statistics. With all the zeal he could command he devoted himself to the general legislation, and by his persistent advocacy of the reforms to which I have referred, won a reputation in the first session, as a member of the House of Representatives, which made him conspicuous among the active and brilliant debaters of the Forty-sixth Congress.

With the second session General Weaver found himself the target for constant attack from all the forces of the hard money, bank and bond monopolists. Almost at the outset he introduced the following:

"A Bill for the Relief of the Soldiers and Sailors who served in the Army and Navy of the United States in the late war for the suppression of the Rebellion, and to restore to them equal rights with the holders of Government bonds."

The object of this bill was to equalize the soldiers and sailors pay, by making up to them the difference between the currency in which they were paid and coin. His argument was wholly unanswerable in sustaining this measure, if the Credit Strengthening Act could be sustained on principle, or be supported by any mode of reasoning, or any rule of equity.

Capitalists had purposely degraded the Greenback, by printing repudiation on the back of every bill, till they had reduced its gold value to forty cents on a dollar; they had made the value of the Greenback the measure of the value of the bond as between the Government and the purchaser, and then had swindled the Government out of sixty cents on the dollar, or more than eight hundred millions of dollars, provided they could by any fraud, cheat it into making the bonds payable in coin. It was the surplus money of the National Banks, of the Rothschilds, and of the Jews and cut throats of the money market which bullied or intimidated Congress into the passage of this outrageous swindle.

General Weaver was indignant that Congress should yield its ready acquiescence to this robbery of the people, and insisted with unanswerable logic, that if the capitalist should be paid in coin, who had deliberately accepted the bonds paying in lawful currency, that the soldier and sailor who had given their lives to the cause and to the country at thirteen dollars per month, payable in coin, and who were obliged to take Greenbacks when they were worth but fifty cents on the dollar in coin, and thus lose one-half of their small pay, should be made good and have their pay made equivalent to gold as the bondholders had succeeded in doing with their bonds.

The bill was a fire brand in the very heart of the Republican camp. They recognized the justice of the demand but they dared not admit it, for that would be to place the soldier who had battled to save his country and sustain its credit, on a par with capitalists who had shaved it out of a thousand million of dollars, depreciated its credit, created privileged patents of nobility for an untaxed aristocracy, and played hot and cold in the days of civil war and strife. The soldier and the sailor were mere laborers, and to the average Congressman they were but hewers of wood and drawers of water to the banking and bond aristocracy.

Republicans and Democrats, while they recognized the equity of the claim but did not dare to admit it, were yet afraid to openly approve the bill, for each day from the introduction of the bill by General Weaver, there was a flood of petitions poured in from all sections of the country. Every art of cunning, every device of political knavery and every subterfuge of congressional equivocation was resorted to, to be-little, ridicule and keep the measure from consideration by the house.

More than six hundred thousand petitions demanded the passage of the act. General Weaver knew that it could bide its time; if he could not get a committee to report upon it, he could keep the subject before the people whose hearts it had warmed into enthusiastic devotion for him. They saw in General Weaver the rare object of their wonder and admiration. A member of Congress who recognized the rights of labor, and who had the manly courage to defend them in the face of all the brutal defiances of the rich and aristocratic.

They knew that every platform of the Republican party had become chronic with pretentious devotion to the soldier, but they knew as well that it was but words to catch the ear, and that they had nothing to expect. In General Weaver's bill, five hundred thousand firesides were to be made glad over a late but merited justice, and his name became enshrined in the hearts and homes of the defenders of the land from ocean to ocean.

But the great battle of the old parties in Congress did not reach its climax against the reformers, nor yet against the defiant young Hercules of the West, until he appealed to Congress to make a distinctive declaration of its principles on the financial issues of the day. For this purpose he drew up the resolutions which, it was well understood, he was to introduce for the purpose of securing a test vote of the House.

This, both Republicans and Democrats were determined to evade. It was a year for Presidential nominations. Each party was afraid to commit itself to any distinctive policy until its conventions should have met and determined upon its platform. The Greenback had become too popular for any party to entirely disavow it, and yet the Republicans were pledged for its overthrow but dared not put themselves distinctly on record for their entire withdrawal, while the Democrats, debating between their fears of offending the bank and bond aristocracy, and the known popularity of the legal tender as the exact kind of currency recommended by Jefferson, Jackson, Franklin and Calhoun, were equally averse to defining their position.

Under this state of facts, each party determined to stave off if possible, any effort on the part of General Weaver and his associate Greenback Congressmen to bring it to a distinctive vote.

To carry out this design, the Speaker of the House, then ambitious to secure the nomination for the Presidency, and at all hazards to keep his party in the strict line of a non-committal policy, not only threw every obstacle in the way of General Weaver's introducing his resolutions, but absolutely, through the intrigues of Democrats and Republicans, turned his back upon him, and stifled that freedom of speech which is the dearest and most sacred prerogative belonging to a representative of the people.

Unterrified by rebuff, every time at his post of duty, determined to maintain his right at all hazards, General Weaver, week after week, presented his resolutions, and was as often forced into silence by the arbitrary ruling of the Speaker, until the public press was forced into denouncing his insolence as opposed to the fundamental rights of every Congressional representative, and subversive of that liberty of speech which is an essential requisite of liberty itself. But like John Quincy Adams, when battling against the insolence of Southern dictation in denying the right of petition, General Weaver could neither be put down or silenced, and so maintained his manhood as a Statesman and as a patriot, as to force the Speaker and the House to listen to his resolutions and to what he had to say in introducing them. These resolutions have become historical from the very effort made to suppress them. They were in these words:

RESOLVED, That it is the sense of this House that all currency, whether metalic or paper, necessary for the use and convenience of the people, should be issued and its volume controlled by the government, and not by or through the bank corporations of the country; and, when so issued, should be a full legal tender in payment of all debts,—public and private.

2. RESOLVED, That in the judgment of this House, that portion of the interest-bearing debt of the United States which shall become redeemable in the year 1881, or prior thereto, being in amount $782,000,000, should not be refunded beyond the power of the government to call in said obligations and pay them at any time, but should be paid as rapidly as possible, and according to contract. To enable the government to meet these obligations, the mints of the United States should be operated to their full capacity in the coinage of standard silver dollars, and such other coinage as the business interests of the country may require.

The debate which was called out by the resolutions and the remarks of General Weaver in presenting them, was characteristic of the petulance and moneyed influence which so thoroughly dominates Congress. But calm, knowing exactly what he had to say, and saying it with the cool intrepidity of a veteran Statesman, he could neither be disturbed by the carping insolence of our mastered cunning, or by the no less impertinent interruptions of self-important egotists, in the pay or under the thumb of the bank association.

The resolutions were submitted to the House, and notwithstanding all the vituperation and abuse which they had excited in the ranks of the capitalistic oligarchy, they received eighty-five votes in their favor, as embodying the true financial policy of the times, against one hundred and seventeen votes in opposition, while ninety members shirked from voting,—either too timid to make known their views, or too much under the influence of the moneyed aristocracy to dare express their sentiments.

The result of this battle was universally admitted to be a masterly triumph for the intrepedity of General Weaver, and for the sound and rapidly increasing popularity of the financial policy of the National Reformers.

In the speeches of General Weaver there is a directness and force which leaves no room for equivocation, whether at the Bar, on the floor of Congress, or in those popular political gatherings where the freedom and latitude of generalization is usually indulged in. He is honest, earnest and practical in all he says and in all he does.

General Weaver took an early part in organizing the party into National unity. It was thought best to take a distinct and bold stand on the opening of the Forty-sixth

Congress, and the Reform members in organizing the House, selected their own candidate for Speaker in the Hon. Hendricks B. Wright, the veteran Statesman, whose devotion to the rights of labor, and whose ceaseless efforts to secure aid from Congress to help homeless heads of families on to homesteads under that most beneficient of all acts of Congress—the Homestead Law, made him peculiarly fit as the Congressional leader of the new party. He received the vote of every member elected as a Reformer but one, who turned traitor to honor, to his pledge and to his constituency.

This was the first organization of the party in Congress, March 18, 1879. It was felt necessary for the Greenback members of Congress to organize for political purposes, and they proceeded at an early day to form themselves into a National Congressional Committee, over which the Hon. T. H. Murch, the stone cutter, member of Congress, was made Chairman. This Committee, co-operating with a committee appointed at the Toledo conference of prominent Greenback gentlemen, as a National Committee, in a call for a conference of representative Greenback men at the City of Washington, on the 6th of January, 1880, to agree upon a time and place for holding a National Convention, to adopt a platform and select candidates for President and Vice-President of the United States.

At this conference, General Weaver was not only active in organizing and in aiding to fix upon a proper basis of representation, but upon such an address as would tend to unite the strength of the party in its support. The basis of representation was two delegates from each of the congressional districts of the United States, with four delegates at large from each State. The time for holding the convention, June 9th, 1880, and the place, Chicago.

Every one who attended the Washington conference felt that the convention would be a success, but no one for a moment dreamed that it would prove to be one of the largest, ablest and most enthusiastic national conventions ever convened in the United States.

It was well known that a branch of the party under the leadership of M. M. Pomeroy Ralph E. Hoyt and Hugo Preyer, representing what was known as the Club organization, up to that time the most efficient working element in the party, had called and held a national convention at St. Louis, March 4th, 1880. That at such convention Stephen D. Dillaye, of New Jersey, had been placed in nomination for President, and Mr. B. J. Chambers, of Texas, as Vice-President; that it had agreed upon a platform of principles and adjourned to Chicago, June 9th, to co-operate if possible, with the convention called by the congressional committee. Great anxiety was felt as to the result of this division, but Mr. Dillaye had pre-emptorily declined to be a candidate in opposition to the Chicago convention, and on being notified of his nomination, wrote a letter advising co-operation and unity of action, and accepted his nomination only to decline it with the recommendation to all to unite and harmonize for victory at Chicago, June 9th, 1880.

General Weaver was on the committee of conference named by the St. Louis convention, and through the almost universal desire for union, found but slight difficulty in agreeing upon the basis which consolidated the two organizations and the two conventions into one.

The convention at Chicago was more than a success; it was a triumphant national expression, of as able and as intelligent a body of men as ever convened in national convention; that the reforms demanded by the National Greenback Labor party were essential to our liberties, to our progress and to the perpetuity of freedom, equality and the rights of labor in the United States.

It was composed of seven hundred and eighty-five delegates, who were there to pledge their property, their honor, and their lives to the cause of reform. It was dignified in character, enthusiastic for the just and the good, and determined to so organize for political action as to secure the confidence and support of the American people.

So large a body was of necessity forced into delegating its labors to committees. The Committee on Resolutions was composed of one from each State and Territory. Its labors were immense and onerous, and were not completed until late in the evening of the second day, when the Convention was wearied and exhausted by the excessive heat of the time. The report of the Committee was read, but heard by few. Its acceptance and adoption was moved and passed without debate, under the pressure of the previous question. That the platform is able without being complete, comprehensively clear, yet wanting in definiteness; silent in some points where it should be outspoken; and timid from excessive caution of being thought radical, cannot be denied. The Convention was far in advance of the platform, but it was adopted, and in the main shadows forth the policy of the party.

Immediately on the adoption of the platform, the work of selecting a candidate was commenced. There were many names prominent before the Convention; names endeared to Greenbackers in all parts of the country: and in the fifty-four speeches eulogizing the various candidates, there was a generous enthusiasm to be just, and a universal desire to rise above all merely personal considerations, which was flattering to the patriotism of the speakers, as it was to the large-hearted magnanimity of the Convention.

However devoted and generous were the friends of Wright, Dillaye, Chase, Butler, Allis and Campbell, yet there was an invisible telegraphic fever which pervaded the whole body as if it were but one soul, and electrified every heart as if the current of expression was but waiting to break out in one full chorus, the one name that above and beyond all others, commanded the enthusiasm, the judgment and the confidence of the Convention, and that was James B. Weaver, of Iowa. There was no power to resist it; the popular heart of the nation had inscribed it on the banners of the people, and the Convention was but the echo from the heart-throbs of the reformers of the nation.

General Weaver was at once notified of his nomination and appeared before the convention to accept the great trust and thank the convention with words so full of manly emotion, as to become the sublimest expression of eloquent thanks, as the first glow of the morning sunlight filled the earth with beauty, and the hearts of the convention with thanksgiving to God for the work they had accomplished.

The committee selected to notify him formally of his nomination, addressed him a note on the 23d of June, 1880, to that effect. To this he replied, July 3d, by a letter of acceptance so frank, so full of manly truths, so ripe in the principles he adopts as his chart for political action, as to remedy nearly every omission of the platform, and give positive assurance of his devotion to the reforms demanded, and of his adherence to the rights of labor, humanity and justice.

As this masterly letter of acceptance will accompany this sketch, any attempt to analyze it would weaken its force. It speaks for itself. It is the manly deposition of the principles of a man who has nothing to conceal, and the political gospel of those reforms essential to the welfare of the people. It is worthy to be classed with the best declaration of Jefferson, and is as emphatic in the solidity of its logic and the firmness of its views, as the nullification message of Andrew Jackson.

To promote the principles, General Weaver, in compliance with the recommendation of the Convention which nominated him, has started on his way through the country to discuss the means of reform to which the National Greenback Labor party, with the aid of Divine Providence, have undertaken to introduce and enforce in the administration of our public affairs.

Thus far, his receptions have been a series of ovations, in which the great heart of the people have welcomed, with unmistaken enthusiasm, their nominee as the true representative of their rights and of their liberties.

At his own home, all parties welcomed him with a fervor and earnestness none but a great and good man could receive. His neighbors,—of all parties and all creeds, who had lived by him from his boyhood, were all aglow with Western frankness to do him honor. At New York, his frankness, his manly independence, his heroic courage, and the dignity with which he had sustained himself in his Congressional duels, won him the reluctant and yet general commendation of the press. General Weaver has opened the campaign in Alabama. The telegraph gives us his daily triumph in addressing the people. His march to the sea is described as a grand ovation. Crowds are forsaking old parties and flocking to his standard. His noble bearing, his manly form, his sun-lit face, the soul speaking through it as his great heart swells with the fire and truth of eloquence, as he pleads the cause of the people, electrifies and wins all who hear him.

March on, oh son of the West and representative of the people! With Truth for thy standard,—with the rights of labor and the liberties of your race as the evangelisms of your duty, the masses will hear you, and the nation will listen and bear you onward and upward as an apostle of the just, if they do not bear you in triumph to the grandest honor any nation or people can bestow.

## CHAPTER VIII.

### LIFE OF COL. BENJ. J. CHAMBERS.

The candidate of the National Greenback-Labor Party for Vice-President, is Col. BENJAMIN J. CHAMBERS, of Texas.

He is in the sixty-second year of his age, erect and supple of limb as an Indian, plain and unassuming in deportment. He has a fine head, gray-blue eyes, thin lips, small mouth, and well-shaped chin, and is prepossessing in his general appearance. His voice is soft, and his utterances fluent and vigorous.

Col. Chambers was born in Montgomery County, Kentucky, December 5, 1817. His father was a farmer, and emigrated from Virginia among the early settlers in that State. His mother's maiden name was Mothershead. She was born in Scott County, Kentucky. Her father was one of the Revolutionary soldiers through the whole war, and was with Washington at the storming of Trenton.

While at work on his father's farm, he embraced every opportunity of improving his mind. He also attended the common schools, and in them received a fair education. At the age of twenty he became a volunteer in the Texan-Mexican revolution, was commissioned Captain, and attached for temporary in the recuiting service, to his uncle's Gen. T. J. Chambers', staff, and landed in Texas about the 1st of April, 1837.

In 1839 he made his way to the frontier, and located in old Robertson County as a practical surveyor, which business he followed until 1847, when he was elected to the office of district surveyor of Robertson land district, comprising the territory which now includes several counties.

In his business of surveying in these early times, he had to penetrate far into the then Indian haunts, and at times he experienced many privations and hair breadth escapes.

After his term of office expired, he settled on a farm in Navarro County, where he was living when the late civil war broke out. After the close of the war, he removed to Johnson County and opened a farm, partly comprising the present site of Cleburne, donating in conjunction with Col. W. G. Henderson, one-half of a hundred acres of land for site purposes, to which the county seat was removed in 1867. He then commenced the business of merchandising in connection with his farming, which continued about three years. In 1871, he opened a private exchange and banking office, in connection with one J. W. Brown. This he closed in 1875, and retired to his farm where he now lives.

His home-place is a model farm of several hundred acres, adjoining the town of Cleburne on the west. The residence is a pretty, modern, two-story brick building, containing ten rooms, and spacious halls, elegantly furnished throughout, without ostentation, and surrounded with home comforts.

The out-buildings are numerous, including three substantial ninety feet cattle sheds, and two horse stables of the same dimensions, all inclosed and under lock and key.

The view from the mansard roof of the residence is most picturesque. Overlooking the town ten miles to the northward, the eye is caught by Caddo Peak—to the eastward lies the cross-timbers extending into the valley; to the westward the ridge of the grand valley-prairie forms the horizon, semi-circling from north-east to south-west; and twelve miles to southward lie the flats extending to Brazos river.

During the progress of the war, observing the injustice of the exemption laws, and other class legislation of the Confederate States, he lost heart in the cause, and although he was one of the exempted class, denounced the policy, and wrote directly to President Davis about it, predicting, if not arrested, the overthrow of the cause.

On the election of Grant in 1868, in an article published in the *Cleburne Chronicle* of that date, discussing the interest-bearing national debt system, he wrote as follows:

"Our fathers, as I conceive, made great political progress (towards a higher christian civilization) by breaking down legitimacy, church supremacy, and all prescriptive rights. It remains to be seen whether their children will make further progress, by breaking down this monarchial scheme of interest-bearing debts. * * * *
I hazard nothing in saying that true and free republican institutions cannot be maintained if the people allow their law makers to create an interest-bearing national debt."

In 1878 he acquired a State reputation by his "open letter" to Senator Coke, and a national reputation by his article on "Sacred Coin Contracts," and other writings. In 1878, in the face of ridicule, he boldly ran for legislative honors on the Greenback ticket, and though not elected, he received about three times the number of votes then contained in the county organization.

Col. Chambers has always held decided opinions on all political subjects that have been from time to time publicly discussed. He voted and acted with the Democratic party after the annexation of Texas until its departure, as he considers, from the true Democratic faith on the finance question at St. Louis in 1876, since which time he has been in full sympathy with the Greenbackers of the Union, and is now an enthusiastic and uncompromising member of the Greenback organization.

He was unanimously nominated as a candidate for Vice-President by the convention of the Greenback-Labor party, (known as the Pomeroy wing of that party,) which convened in St. Louis in March last, and was again renominated in Chicago as above stated.

Soon after his nomination at St. Louis, he was waited upon one evening at his residence by a large concourse of his fellow citizens, without respect to party, headed by a band of music and the Cleburne military company, to pay their respects and tender their congratulations upon the honor conferred upon him by such nomination.

After being serenaded the Colonel was called out, and after tendering thanks for such flattering evidences of their friendship and regard, he made quite a strong Greenback speech, and closed by inviting them to partake of refreshments which had been prepared. The doors were then thrown open and after the company had given three rousing cheers for Col. Chambers, as many as could flocked into the dwelling and the spacious dining hall, where they were introduced to the sweet and lovable wife of the Colonel and partook of the repast, while for more than an hour, the band, seated on the portico, continued to entertain the company with the most enchanting music.

Notwithstanding his vehement oppositions to the Republican and Democratic Leaders, by strict integrity, high sense of honor and moral rectitude, he has maintained the general respect of all classes of his fellow citizens. He is a positive man in his political and religious views. Utterly regardless of the thing called popularity, but yet by his strictly honorable and upright course has justly earned and secured the respect and confidence of all those opposed to him in his political views. He is a public spirited man, having always responded substantially to calls made upon his purse and means, in aid of churches, schools and all enterprises of a public character.

# CHAPTER IX.

## THE DEMOCRATIC NATIONAL CONVENTION.

### HELD AT CINCINNATI, JUNE 22D-24TH, 1880.

The 22d day of June, 1880, was a day long to be remembered by the people of Cincinnati. The city was literally packed with strangers; the hotels were crowded with excited, tramping men; and through the streets, bands were playing, banners flying, and clubs parading.

Around Music Hall, where the Convention was to be held, a crowd began to gather at 11 o'clock in the morning, and from that hour on it steadily increased; and although at no time before noon a jam, it was because the public square opposite afforded ample room for the overflow.

Cincinnati, with characteristic hospitality, had put on its very best and brightest face. Even the thousand and one chimneys politely held their breath, and the cloud of smoke that often darkens the air and sometimes fairly smuts the white clouds and eclipses the sun, was rolled away. The sky was of a veritable blue, and the sun smiled a smile of real Western welcome. There was little in the way of decoration besides what had been seen before, but all these had a fresh and new look, in keeping with the day. The great crowd which filled the sidewalk and the streets, were decked out with badges—

EXPOSITION BUILDING, CINCINNATI.

black and gold for Randall, dark blue for Seymour, white for Hendricks, blue again for Hancock, white again for Bayard, and still more blue and scattered badges for Tilden.

The Exposition Building, in which Music Hall is placed, is a handsome brick structure, in the modernized Gothic style. The Hall itself is almost square, and really an elegant one, being over 100 feet wide, by a little less than 200 feet long. The sides, ceiling, galleries and all, present one color to the eye; they are entirely of black ash, unpainted, its acoustic properties being thus heightened. The first gallery extends over the floor on three sides of the Hall, but is well raised, and not deep enough to darken any part of the floor. The second gallery extends only across the lower end of the Hall. Stretched across the facing of the upper gallery, was inscribed, on the day of the Convention, in gold letters on a scarlet ground, the word "Welcome." The band stand was in the first gallery, directly over the main entrance. Two large flags, with a portrait of Washington where they joined, and drapery in bunting, comprised the decorations near the stand. From each window on either side of the Hall, from the entrance to over the stage, were hung three flags.

The stage was trimmed with evergreens. Around the back of the stage were shields, fastened to the wall. Just in front of the desk, and raised a few inches above the level of the floor, so as to face the delegates and be in full view of them, stood the National coat-of-arms. A portrait of Jackson was in the centre of it, and around the outer edge the word "Democracy." The State banners were uniform in style and of neat design, the body being navy blue silk, the fringe of yellow silk, and the inscriptions in gold. Across the main aisle, at the lower end of that part of the Hall assigned to delegates, was a blue silken banner, with "Ohio Greets the Nation" on it, in white letters. The Chairman's desk stood in a little thicket of evergreens and flowers. The Hall has a sitting capacity of about seven thousand. The back of the stage was an amphitheatre of seats, reserved on this occasion strictly for ladies, and was filled with bright eyes, smiling faces and happy hearts.

At 12.45 P. M., the Hall being filled and the delegates in their seats, Senator Barnum, Chairman of the National Committee, called the Convention to order, and prayer was offered by the Rev. Charles W. Wendte, of the Unitarian Church. Mr. Barnum then, by direction of the National Committee, presented the name of Judge George Hoadley, of Ohio, for temporary Chairman. This was agreed to, and Wm. S. Scott and H. D. Mc Enery were appointed to conduct Judge Hoadley to the Chair, which they did amid great applause.

Judge Hoadley, upon taking the Chair, delivered quite a lengthy address, thanking the Convention for the great confidence reposed in him, pledging himself to act with the strictest impartiality in the exercise of the power thus conferred, during the brief period committed to him; and declared early in his speech that the Democracy there assembled were not Democrats of Congressional Districts, but representatives of indestructible, united States.

He then made reference to the duties of the convention

in connection with the formation of the platform, and warned the delegates that it was their province not to make a creed or invent a code of principles, but to promulgate those which have long been recognized as fundamental in the Democratic party. He referred to the convention of 1876, at St. Louis, and claimed that Samuel J. Tilden and Thomas A. Hendricks were elected President and Vice-President of the United States, as fairly as George Washington or James Monroe. He charged fraud upon the Republican party; of its infidelity to Republican principles; of its willingness to sacrifice the right of popular election, rather than to relax its hold upon power. He said if the Democratic party were fairly beaten in the coming election they would submit, but if successful, no cunning device of dishonest arbitration would deprive them of their rights. He referred to the Third Term movement; said it had been merely postponed, not averted, and the only way to avert it was by making powerless the only party in which it was possible. He advised vigilance,—eternal vigilance, as the price and protector of liberty.

After Judge Hoadley's speech, the customary preliminary business of the Convention proceeded. F. O. Prince, of Massachusetts, was made temporary Secretary, with several assistants. Other officers were also appointed.

Mr. Beebe, of New York, offered a resolution, adopting the rules of the last National Convention for the government of this, until it should be otherwise ordered, which was adopted. Mr. Martin, of Delaware, moved a call of the roll for Committees on Permanent Organization, on Credentials, and on Resolutions. This was adopted, and the roll call went on.

At the call for New York, John Kelly, of New York City, who was seated behind the delegates, arose and claimed to be recognized. There was great confusion for a time, but Mr. Kelly held his ground with nerve, and at each lull in the excitement and noise renewed his claim for recognition; but the Chairman called upon the Sergeant-at-Arms to restore order, and in an excited voice said: "The Chair will recognize no one but delegates on this floor. The roll call will proceed." The call then went on to the end without interruption, and the committees were named. After several resolutions of minor importance had been adopted, the Convention, after a session of an hour and twenty minutes, adjourned for the day.

On the 23d day of June, at 10.40 A. M., the Convention was again called to order. The great Hall was filled to overflowing. They came by thousands, swarmed upon the platform, filled every nook and corner, and even the ladies' amphitheatre was even more picturesque than the day previous. There was a large addition to their number, and a great multiplication of fluttering ribbons and graceful fans.

There were also a whole regiment of reporters and correspondents. Two hundred of them were in a broad zone crossing the Hall in front of the stage, fifty or more clustered on the stage, and in each of the galleries looking down on the stage, one or two hundred more. Under each of the galleries, the rival telegraph companies had their offices, and back of them, scores of operators clicking the news away the instant a vote was cast or a speech made.

After the Convention was called to order, and prayer offered, the report of the Committee on Organization was presented and read, announcing ex-Senator John W. Stevenson, of Kentucky, permanent Chairman, which was greeted with applause.

The majority report of the Committee on Credentials was then presented. It advised that both delegations from Massachusetts be seated, and that the sitting delegates from the Twenty-sixth District of Pennsylvania and from the State of New York, be allowed to retain their places. A minority report was read by Mr. Carroll, of Kansas, advising that Tammany Hall be allowed to have twenty seats.

Over the two reports, occurred an exciting struggle, one hour being allowed for the discussion. John Kelly, of New York, was called for by the Chairman to present the case of the Tammany contestants. Mr. Kelly was not in the Hall, and Mr George W. Miller, of Albany, took the platform in his behalf, amid applause. He made an earnest speech. Amasa J. Parker also spoke for the contestants. Ex-Governor Hubbard, of Texas, Colonel Fellows, of New York, Mr. Peckham, Mr. Westbrook and Mr. Young, supported the majority report.

A motion to substitute the minority for the majority report was lost, by a vote of 205½ to 457. The delegates from New York were excused from voting on the motion, at their own request. The majority report was then adopted, but a resolution was offered and unanimously approved, inviting the rejected contestants to seats on the floor during the Convention.

There was some delay in effecting the permanent

organization. Ex-Senator Stevenson did not seem to be in the Hall, when the Committee was sent to escort him to the Chair: a long pause ensued, during which time the band regaled the assemblage with music. When Mr. Stevenson did arrive and appeared upon the platform, he was greeted with the familiar strains of "Hail to the Chief," after which he returned thanks to the Convention for the honor conferred upon him personally, and upon his State by his election as permanent President of the Convention. Early in his speech he referred to the Democratic Convention held at Cincinnati twenty-four years ago, when, he said, the Democratic party named the last Democratic candidates who were elected and who took their seats, and spoke of it as a favorable omen that the Democracy of the Nation had once more met in Cincinnati. He declared that Tilden and Hendricks had been elected, but, by fraud, were excluded from their offices. That this great wrong should be resented, and they would be recreant to their duty if they did not do it.

As the Committee on Resolutions were not prepared to report, on motion of Mr. Breckenridge, of Kentucky, it was ordered that the roll of States be called, that candidates for the Presidency might be put in nomination. California was the first State to respond, and presented the name of Judge Field, who was warmly eulogized by Mr. McElrath. This nomination was seconded by Colorado. Delaware presented the name of Senator Bayard through one of its delegates—George Gray—who was a polished speaker, and who paid a glowing tribute to Senator Bayard's personal and political character.

Illinois, through ex-Congressman Samuel S. Marshall, put in nomination Col. Morrison. Indiana selected Senator Daniel W. Voorhees to present the name of ex-Senator Hendricks, which he did in a forcible and effective manner. When Ohio was called, Mr. McSweeny, who is one of the most popular stump-speakers of the West, took the platform, and made a lengthy speech in favor of Senator Thurman, whose name he presented. Hon. Daniel Dougherty, of Philadelphia, the polished and eloquent orator, took the platform when Pennsylvania was called, and presented the name of General Hancock, and eulogized him in the warmest terms. Ex-Governor Hubbard, of Texas, when that State was called, seconded the nomination of Gen. Hancock.

At a quarter before 5 o'clock, the last of the States had been called, but it was noticeable that some of the most prominent candidates had not been nominated at all. Among these were Payne, Randall, Jewett, Parker and Randolph.

Judge Hoadley then moved that the Convention adjourn until the next morning; but upon calling the roll, the Convention refused to adjourn, the vote standing $317\frac{1}{2}$ in favor and $395\frac{1}{2}$ against an adjournment.

Thereupon, one ballot was taken, resulting as follows:

| | |
|---|---|
| Whole number of votes, | $728\frac{1}{2}$ |
| Necessary to a choice, | 486 |
| Hancock, | 171 |
| Bayard, | $152\frac{1}{2}$ |
| Field, | 65 |
| Morrison, | 62 |

| | |
|---|---|
| Hendricks, | 49½ |
| Thurman, | 68½ |
| Payne, | 81 |
| Tilden, | 38 |
| Ewing, | 10 |
| Seymour, | 8 |
| Scattering, | 22 |

An adjournment was then ordered.

On Thursday, the 24th of June, the Convention was called to order, at 10.30, A. M., and after the preliminary proceedings, Mr. Peckham, of New York, took the platform, and stated that Mr. Tilden renounced all claims to the nomination, and that the New York delegates would support Mr. Randall.

The Convention then proceeded to the balloting, with the following result:

| | |
|---|---|
| Whole number of votes, | 736 |
| Necessary to a choice, | 491 |
| Hancock, | 319 |
| Randall, | 129½ |
| Bayard, | 113 |
| Field, | 65½ |
| Thurman, | 50 |
| Hendricks, | 31 |
| English, | 19 |
| Tilden, | 6 |
| Scattering, | 3 |

Before the vote was announced officially, Wisconsin asked permission to change, and cast her 20 votes for Hancock. The Convention was instantly in a state of great excitement and confusion. New Jersey at once changed her votes to Hancock. Pennsylvania changed, and cast her vote for him also. The excitement was now intense. The Hancock banner was waving and advancing to the front. The band commenced playing "Dixie" and "Hail to the Chief," and the delegates were shouting and cheering. Smith Weed finally announced that New York changed her 70 votes to Hancock. Other States followed; and when Ohio changed to Hancock, he had secured two-thirds of the Convention, and the nomination.

The result was at last announced, when Mr. Mack, of Indiana, moved to make the nomination unanimous. Speaker Randall and Senator Wallace appeared together on the platform and seconded the motion, and it was made unanimous amid great cheering.

W. H. English, of Indiana, was then nominated for Vice-President by acclamation, and after the Platform had been unanimously adopted, the Convention adjourned, *sine die*.

The Platform adopted is as follows:

### PLATFORM.

The Democrats of the United States, in convention assembled, declare:

First—We pledge ourselves anew to the constitutional doctrines and traditions of the Democratic party as illustrated by the teaching and example of a long line of Democratic statesmen and patriots and embodied in the platform of the last National convention of the party.

Second—Opposition to centralizationism, and to that dangerous spirit of encroachment which tends to consolidate the powers of all the departments in one and thus to create, whatever be the form of government, a real despotism. No sumptuary laws ; separation of Church and State for the good of each ; common schools fostered and protected.

Third—Home rule, honest money, consisting of gold and silver and paper convertible to coin on demand. The strict maintenance of the public faith, State and national, and a tariff for revenue only.

Fourth—The subordination of the military to the civil power, and a general and thorough reform of the civil service.

Fifth—The right of a free ballot is the right preservative of all rights, and must and shall be maintained in every part of the United States.

Sixth—The existing administration is the representative of conspiracy only, and its claim of right to surround the ballot boxes with troops and deputy marshals to intimidate and obstruct the electors, and the unprecedented use of the veto to maintain its corrupt and despotic power, insults the people and imperils their institutions.

Seventh—The great fraud of 1876-77, by which, upon a false count of the electoral votes of two States, the candidate defeated at the polls, was declared President, and for the first time in American history the will of the people was set aside under a threat of military violence, struck a deadly blow at our system of representative government. The Democratic party, to preserve the country from the horrors of a civil war, submitted for a time in firm and patriotic faith that the people would punish this crime in 1880. This issue precedes and dwarfs every other. It imposes a more sacred duty upon the people of the Union than was ever addressed to the conscience of a nation of free men.

Eighth—We execrate the course of this administration in making places in the civil service a reward for political crime, and demand a reform by statute which shall make it forever impossible for the defeated candidate to bribe his way to the seat of a usurper by billeting villains upon the people.

Ninth—The resolution of Samuel J. Tilden not again to be a candidate for the exalted place to which he was elected by a majority of countrymen, and from which he was excluded by the leaders of the Republican party, is received by the Democrats of the United States with sensibility, and they declare their confidence in his wisdom, patriotism and integrity, unshaken by the assaults of a common enemy, and they further assure him that he is followed into the retirement he has chosen for himself by the sympathy and respect of his fellow citizens, who regard him as one who, by elevating the standard of public morality, and adorning and purifying the public service, merits the lasting gratitude of his country and his party.

Tenth—Free ships and a living chance for American commerce on the seas and on the land. No discrimination in favor of transportation lines, corporations or monopolies.

Eleventh—Amendment of the Burlingame treaty. No more Chinese immigration, except for travel, education and foreign commerce, and therein carefully guarded.

Twelfth—Public money and public credit for public purposes solely, and the public land for actual settlers.

Thirteenth—The Democratic party is the friend of labor and the laboring man, and pledges itself to protect him alike against the cormorants and the commune.

Fourteenth—We congratulate the country on the honesty and thrift of a Democratic Congress which has reduced the public expenditure $40,000,000 a year; upon the continuation of prosperity at home and the national honor abroad, and above all, upon the promise of such a change in the administration of the government as shall insure us genuine and lasting reform in every department of the public service.

The Committee appointed by the Convention to inform Gen. Hancock of his nomination, visited Governor's Island—being the head-quarters of the General—and were formally presented to him. After the object of their visit had been announced, the written address of the Committee, notifying him of his nomination, was read and presented to him, with a copy of the Platform, by ex-Senator Stevenson, of Kentucky, to which the General briefly replied, accepting the nomination with thanks for the honor, and stating that he would send them a written acceptance. The Committee then, in the same manner, notified W. H. English, who was also present, of his nomination, who briefly replied, accepting the same.

The following letter was subsequently received by the Committee from Gen. Hancock:

LETTER OF ACCEPTANCE.

GOVERNOR'S ISLAND, NEW YORK CITY,
July 29, 1880.

GENTLEMEN: I have the honor to acknowledge the receipt of your letter of July 13, 1880, apprising me formally of my nomination to the office of President of the United States, by the "National Democratic Convention" lately assembled in Cincinnati. I accept the nomination with grateful appreciation of the confidence reposed in me.

The principles enunciated by the Convention are those I have cherished in the past, and shall endeavor to maintain in the future.

The Thirteenth, Fourteenth and Fifteenth Amendments to the Constitution of the United States, embodying the results of the war for the Union, are inviolable.

If called to the Presidency, I should deem it my duty

to resist with all of my power any attempt to impair or evade the full force and effect of the Constitution, which, in every article, section and amendment, is the supreme law of the land. The Constitution forms the basis of the Government of the United States. The powers granted by it to the legislative, executive and judicial departments define and limit the authority of the general Government; powers not delegated to the United States by the Constitution, nor prohibited by it to the States, belong to the States respectively, or to the people. The General and State Governments, each acting in its own sphere without trenching upon the lawful jurisdiction of the other, constitute the Union. This Union, comprising a general Government with general powers, and State Governments with State powers for purposes local to the States, is a polity, the foundations of which were laid in the profoundest wisdom.

This is the Union our fathers made, and which has been so respected abroad and so beneficent at home. Tried by blood and fire, it stands to-day a model form of free popular government—a political system which, rightly administered, has been, and will continue to be, the admiration of the world. May we not say, nearly in the words of Washington: The unity of government which constitutes us one people is justly dear to us; it is the main pillar in the edifice of our real independence, the support of our peace, safety, and prosperity, and of that liberty we so highly prize and intend at every hazard to preserve.

But no form of government however carefully devised, no principles however sound, will protect the rights of the people, unless administration is faithful and efficient. It is a vital principle in our system that neither fraud nor force must be allowed to subvert the rights of the people. When fraud, violence or incompetence controls, the noblest constitutions and wisest laws are useless. The bayonet is not a fit instrument for collecting the votes of freemen. It is only by a full vote, free ballot, and fair count that the people can rule in fact, as required by the theory of our government. Take this foundation away and the whole structure falls.

Public office is a trust, not a bounty bestowed upon the holder; no incompetent or dishonest persons should ever be intrusted with it, or if appointed, they should be promptly ejected. The basis of a substantial, practical civil service reform must first be established by the people in filling the elective offices; if they fix a high standard of qualifications for office, and sternly reject the corrupt and incompetent, the result will be decisive in governing the action of the servants whom they intrust with appointing power.

The war for the Union was successfully closed more than fifteen years ago. All classes of our people must share alike in the blessings of the Union, and are equally concerned in its perpetuity, and in the proper administration of public affairs. We are in a state of profound peace. Henceforth let it be our purpose to cultivate sentiments of friendship, and not of animosity, among our fellow citizens. Our material interests, varied and progressive, demand our constant and united efforts. A sedulous and scrupulous care of the public credit, together with a wise and economical management of our governmental expenditures, should be maintained in order that labor may be lightly burdened, and that all persons may be protected in their rights to the fruits of their own industry. The time has come to enjoy the substantial benefits of reconciliation. As one people we have common interests. Let us encourage the harmony and generous rivalry among our own industries which will revive our languishing merchant marine, extend our commerce with foreign nations, assist our merchants, manufacturers and producers to develop our vast national resources, and increase the prosperity and happiness of our people.

If elected I shall, with the Divine favor, labor with

what ability I possess to discharge my duties with fidelity, according to my convictions, and shall take care to protect and defend the Union, and to see that the laws be faithfully and equally executed in all parts of the country alike. I will assume the responsibility, fully sensible of the fact that to administer rightly the functions of government is to discharge the most sacred duty that can devolve upon an American citizen.

I am, very respectfully, yours,

WINFIELD S. HANCOCK.

*To the* HON. JOHN W. STEVENSON, *President of the Convention ; the* HON. JOHN P. STOCKTON, *Chairman, and others of the Committee of the National Democratic Convention.*

## CHAPTER X.

### LIFE AND SERVICES OF GEN. W. S. HANCOCK.

#### BY HENRY HILL, ESQ.

Winfield Scott Hancock was born in the city of Philadelphia, (not, as stated by many of his biographers, in Norristown,) on the 14th day of February, ("St. Valentine's Day,") 1824, and is therefore, now fifty-six years of age or in his fifty-seventh year.

His father, Benjamin F. Hancock, a lawyer of ability and probity, removed to Norristown in the year 1828, and there practised his profession till his death in 1867, commanding, for nearly four decades, the fullest confidence and profoundest respect of all who knew him.

His mother, Elizabeth Hancock, a lady of education and refinement, connected with the oldest families of Pennsylvania, died in the fullness of years at Norristown, in 1878.

He can pride himself that his blood on both sides is revolutionary and entirely heroic. During the French and Indian war before the revolution, the house of one of his mother's ancestors was attacked by Indians when all were away but the women of the household. With unyielding courage they barricaded themselves in the attic and with hatchets chopped the hands and arms of the savages as they attempted to climb up through the scuttle, until they fled, only to renew the attack in a more

GEN. WINFIELD S. HANCOCK.

horrible and barbarous form by firing the house. But the heroic defence was adequate; assistance arrived, the savages were driven off, the flames were extinguished and the family saved. His grandfather on his father's side was a soldier. He was captured by the British, claimed as a British subject, and suffered a long incarceration in Dartmoor prison, England, as the penalty of his loyalty to America. His great grandfather and his grandfather on his mother's side served under Washington. The latter enlisted at the age of fifteen, and returned five times to the field, as new levies were made in that protracted and glorious struggle. He assisted in escorting from Taneytown, Md., to Valley Forge, Burgoyne's prisoners, captured at Saratoga. His father, Benjamin F. Hancock, at the age of fifteen, joined the troops on the banks of the Delaware, when Philadelphia was threatened by the British in 1812.

Gen. Hancock has a twin brother, Hillary Hancock, a prominent lawyer in Minneapolis, Minnesota; also a younger brother, John Hancock, engaged in railroad business, and residing in Washington city. This brother served in the army of the Potomac, and the three were the only children of Benjamin F. and Elizabeth Hancock.

Before pursuing the personal history of Winfield S. Hancock, let us finish the family record. In 1850, while yet holding the rank of First Lieutenant, and but twenty-six years of age, he met, was enamored of, addressed, and was accepted in marriage by his present wife, then the accomplished Miss Almira Russell, daughter of Mr. Samuel Russell, a prominent merchant of St. Louis. The union was blessed with two children, a son and a daughter. The son has arrived at manhood, is married, had two children, until one, a bright and beautiful boy, bearing his grandfather's name, died recently at Governor's Island, while on a visit to the General. The daughter, a beautiful and accomplished girl, went to a premature grave some three years ago, leaving a void in the hearts of her parents that nothing can ever fill.

It was at Norristown, Montgomery County, Pennsylvania, beautifully situated on the Schuylkill River, not far from the historic city of Philadelphia, and in sight of Valley Forge, that spot made forever sacred in the memories of all Americans, by the sufferings of their forefathers during that awful winter, when the light of liberty on this continent, and throughout the world, seemed so nearly extinguished, perhaps forever, that young Hancock passed his boyhood, inhaling with the pure atmosphere, drinking in with the delightful scenery, imbibing with its historic traditions, that heroic patriotism which was to render such signal service in days to come. He was a pupil of the Norristown academy. He was thoughtful, studious, proficient in all his studies and a superior natural elocutionist. At the age of fifteen the citizens conferred upon him the honor of reading the Declaration of Independence at the annual celebration, and with trumpet tones he emphasized the splendid sentences of that immortal document.

Thus, all unconsciously, the tall, blue eyed, fair haired boy, his veins swelling with martial blood, was growing into his stature and his character. Bearing the great name of Hancock, the first signer of the Declaration of American Independence, and also that of the most majestic figure of the time—the idol of the people, the hero of Lundy's Lane—Winfield Scott, the responsibility expressed in the French maxim *noblesse oblige* descended upon his sinewy shoulders without dismaying his stout heart.

Of such antecedents come the highest grade of heroes. Creditable as it may be to rise from obscure and even vulgar origin, there is no such incentive to noble endeavor as well founded pride of birth—no such stimulant to true and lofty ambition, as an illustrious name bequeathed by honored ancestors, to be tarnished or kept bright by its possessor.

### HE COMMENCES HIS MILITARY CAREER.

The boy is said to be the father of the man, and as if to verify this apothegm, young Hancock at the age of 12 began his military career by organizing and commanding a boy's soldier company, whose drills, reviews, parades, reconnoissances and sham battles, are remembered by the older citizens of Norristown to this day. By his conduct on these occasions, as well as his manly deportment, graceful figure and picturesque beauty, he attracted the attention of Hon. Joseph Fornance, the Democratic member of Congress from that district. Mr. Fornance was a friend of Winfield's father, who was also a Democrat, and through his influence it was not difficult to obtain for the ambitious boy an entrance as cadet at the West Point Military Academy. This was in 1840, and when he was 16 years of age. It is therefore forty years ago that he took the oath which consecrated his life to the nation that assumed the charge of his education.

During all these years he has never wearied in the performance of his duty in peace or in war. He has never faltered when it took him up to the cannon's mouth, and has never sought other and more profitable pursuits when

> "Stern alarums changed to merry meetings,"
> "And dreadful marches to delightful measures."

His life has been sacredly devoted to his country, and by practical participation he has become proficient in every branch of military science. He is no holiday soldier, this magnificent chieftain, who has stood in the iron hail of battle from San Antonio and Cherubusco to Gettysburgh and Spottsylvania. He is no political general, this matchless hero, who has stepped upon every round of the ladder of promotion from the rank of Second Lieutenant to that of Senior Major-General of the regular army; and never asked and never received a promotion except for "gallant and meritorious conduct" on the battle field.

At West Point, with Hancock, were many young men who like him have since earned renown; among them Ulysses S. Grant, George B. McClellan, John F. Reynolds, Burnside, Reno, Franklin, Rosencrazs, Buell, Pope, Augur, Stoneman, Doubleday, Ingalls, Granger and Couch, as well as many Southern men who in the rebellion followed the Confederate standard with mistaken zeal but with sublimest courage; among them Longstreet, "Stonewall" Jackson, and A. P. and D. H. Hill.

Graduating in 1844, young Hancock was appointed Brevet Second-Lieutenant in the 6th United States Infantry. In 1846, being then twenty-two years of age, he was commissioned full Second-Lieutenant in the same regiment. He was at once sent into the Red River region of the South-west, to protect the settlers from attacks of the Indians, but was speedily transferred to Mexico, where, under General Scott,—the great soldier whose name he bore,—he participated in the glorious victories of San Antonio, Cherubusco, Molino del Rey, Contreras, Chapultepec, and in the assault and capture of the City of Mexico. Here also fought Jefferson Davis, John A. Quitman and others of the subsequent Confederate leaders, side by side with Hancock for the stars and stripes. Promotion was not as rapid then as during the Rebellion; and indeed the regular army has never been the field of rapid advancement. Instances were not rare in 1861-2, and during the early years of war for the Union, when parties entirely unskilled in the art of war commenced as colonels, and became major-generals in a few months, after a quasi participation in one or two skirmishes, which were called battles in their dispatches, resigning then to enter upon political careers.

Hancock, at the end of the Mexican War, with all its tremendous engagements, found himself only a First Lieutenant. But he had been splendidly recognized and mentioned by name in the dispatches, and he wore his shoulder-strap with a justifiable pride that made it worth more to him than the shiny but unworthily gained stars of many a general, for he had won the little trophy by "gallant and meritorious conduct in the battles of Contreras and Cherubusco," and under the immediate eye of his patronymic saint. And it was not the glory of a general's uniform which attracted the lovely girl who was to be his future wife. The daughter of the great merchant gave her heart as well as her hand, to the young Lieutenant whose fortune was yet to be gained. Doubtless she was as proud as he, of that little shoulder-strap, and of the manner in which it had been acquired.

In the fall of 1855 he was made Captain and assistant Quartermaster, and accompanied General Harney in the Florida expedition against the Indians. Subsequently he was transferred to Kansas and Nebraska, during the political troubles which attended the early settlement of those states then territories. Then with Harney to Utah. He rode overland to California long before the days of the Pacific railroad, and was stationed in California for several years, patiently bearing all this time the rank of Captain. But large trees grow slowly. All this varied experience in different parts of his native land was qualifying him for great work to be done by him in the fullness of time. He knew it not, but he knew he had consecrated his life to his country; and in all the demoralizing quiet of absolute peace, no temptation came to lure him from his adopted profession. With a philosophic mind, it is not improbable that he apprehended, if he did not foresee, that the time must come when a collision would occur between the North and the South. Self-possession has been said to be the prompt action of one who has anticipated an emergency, and decided beforehand upon the course to be pursued. Such as a competent sea captain in case of wreck, or a superior military commander in case of surprise. However this may be, when the catastrophe came and Sumpter was fired upon, and the South seceded, Hancock never for an instant wavered in his devotion to the Union.

# CHAPTER XI.

## LIFE OF GEN. W. S. HANCOCK.—Continued.

### THE GREAT REBELLION.

> "The ancestral buckler calls
> Self clanging from the walls."

When the first premonitions of civil war began to alarm the Nation in 1860, Hancock was stationed at Los Angelos, in southern California. Here, with the rank of Captain, he was attending to the important duties of the Quartermaster's department. There is no lovelier region on the earth. The climate is like that of Italy. The products are semi-tropical. The corn and the wheat of the North blend on the same plantation with the figs, and the oranges, and the sugar-cane of the South; the apple and the lemon grow side by side. Snow-clad mountains skirt the enchanted valley on the east, and the silver surf of the Pacific ocean adorns it on the west, like the rich fringe of a costly mantle.

The population was mostly from the South. The almost unanimous sentiment was for secession. Never was there a soil or climate better adapted for the reception of what the sons of chivalry considered the Patriarchal Institution of Slavery. Excitement ran high. With those hot-headed men, to differ was to incur the deadliest enmity. Social influences were all in one scale, and that the Southern.

Nothing would be easier than for the young officer to drift with the tide. Every consideration of personal ease and convenience dictated, at least, acquiescence, while illustrious examples were before his very eyes of army officers with higher rank than he could ever expect to hold, who had openly cast their fortunes with the rebel cause. Nearly twenty years he had patiently waited for his shoulder-straps. Now stars were within his instant grasp, for the South wanted experienced officers. There was no railroad or telegraph in those days between the Atlantic and Pacific States, and the news was conveyed so slowly that the election of Lincoln, in November, was not known at Los Angelos till Christmas. Let all who know how hard it is to stand alone in a tempest of public opinion, realize the position of Hancock in those trying days. To increase the embarrassment of a man who could be embarrassed, the administration of Lincoln was Republican, and Hancock had always been a Democrat, as well as his father before him, and the doctrine of State Rights had been a cardinal one with the leaders of that party. The great temptations which swept thousands into the vortex of disunion, confronted him. Even the great Republican leader—Horace Greeley —had said that a State could not be coerced, and counselled submission to the demands of the South. What easier for him than to take counsel of these older men, and at least remain inactive. What so easy as to yield to the enervating influences of the balmy atmosphere of Los Angelos and Santa Barbara.

But no, he decided with instant alacrity to stand by the Union which, so many years before, when a boy at

West Point, he had sworn to defend. There was no hesitation in his loyalty. True as the needle to the pole —steadfast as the sun in the heavens—was Hancock to the traditions of his birth, to the lessons of his youth. He made no concealment of his views. While many a northern man at home and surrounded by northern influences was hesitating and taking counsel of his fears or interests, Hancock appeared upon the rostrum, and braving public opinion, in addresses of thrilling eloquence and burning patriotism, turned back the tide, exercising, more than any other one man, that influence which prevented the breaking out of civil war on the Pacific slope. On the 4th of July, 1861, as if the spirit of old John Hancock of Massachusetts Bay hovered over the scene and inspired his utterances, he spoke at a union meeting in Los Angelos, as follows:

"We have met to commemorate that day of all among Americans, the most hallowed and cherished of the national memories—the 4th of July, 1776 ; that day when the reign of tyrants in the colonies of America ceased, and the reign of reason, of fraternity, and of equal political rights began.

Who on this continent does not know of the great event which transpired on that day, the anniversary of which we are met here to celebrate, and who among us would wish to see the day approach when that occasion should cease to be commemorated?

Can any one hear of the great events of that contest without wishing that his ancestors had been personally engaged in them?

Who can forget the names of Lexington, of Monmouth, of Brandywine and Yorktown, and who, that is so, can regret that he is a descendant of those who fought there for the liberties we now enjoy? And what flag is that we now look to as the banner that carried us through the great contest, and was honored by the gallant deeds of its defenders? The star spangled banner of America, then embracing thirteen pale stars, representing that number of oppressed colonies. Now, thirty-four bright planets, representing that number of great States. To be sure, clouds intervene between us and eleven of that number, but we will trust that those clouds may soon be dispelled and that those great stars in the southern constellation may shine forth again with even greater splendor than before.

Let us believe, at least let us trust, that our brothers there do not wish to separate themselves permanently from the common memories which have so long bound us together, but that when reason returns and resumes her sway they will prefer the brighter page of history, which our mutual deeds have inscribed upon the tablets of time, to that of the uncertain future of a new confederation, which, alas, to them may prove illusory and unsatisfactory.

Let them return to us. We will welcome them as brothers who have been estranged, but have come back. We have an interest in the battle-fields of the Revolution in those States not second to their own. Our forefathers fought there side by side with theirs. Can they, if they would, throw aside their rights to the memories of the great fields on our soil on which their ancestors won renown? No, they cannot! God forbid that they should desire it. So, to those who, regardless of these sacred memories, insist on sundering this union of States, let us who only wish our birth-right preserved to us, and whose desire it is to still be citizens of the great country that gave us birth, and to live under that flag which has gained for us the glory we boast of, say this day to those among us who feel aggrieved, your rights we will respect; your wrongs we will assist you to redress; *but the government resulting from the union of these States is a priceless heritage that we intend to preserve and defend to the last extremity."*

Unable to obtain definite intelligence but burning for active participation in the events which he knew must be pending, he made a double application for appointment to active service in the field; one to Governor Curtin of his native State, Pennsylvania, the other to General Scott, the head of the regular army. By the latter, who well knew his sterling loyalty and impetuous gallantry, he was summoned at once to Washington, where his unblemished record and martial bearing so impressed President Lincoln that he was at once commissioned Brigadier-General of Volunteers, his first command being of four magnificent regiments, one from Pennsylvania one from New York, one from Vermont and one from Maine. Gen. Scott had then retired and this appointment was made on the formal recommendation of General McClellan who had become the Commander-in-Chief.

### IN THE FIELD.

Having perfected the discipline of his new brigade, and infused into its ranks the *esprit* which his magnetism always inspired, till officers and men had almost acquired the steadiness and reliability of veterans, it is not singular that they were soon heard from in a light which will blaze forever on the pages of their country's history.

The campaign of the Peninsula commenced in April, 1862, at Yorktown. Here, for many days, the battle raged furiously against the strong intrenchments of the rebels, Hancock's Brigade covering itself with honor. On the 3d of May the enemy fell back from its lines. This movement was made under cover of the night, and was not discovered till the morning of May 4th. Pursuit was instantly made by the entire Union army. The first stand made by the retreating foe was at Williamsburgh, where the rebels had perfected another line of fortifications, reaching from the York river nearly across to the James. A powerful fort near Williamsburgh, mounted with heavy guns, constituted its central defense. The rest was a series of strong redoubts along and behind a tributary of the York river and its contiguous ravines. The position seemed almost impregnable.

THE BATTLE OF WILLIAMSBURGH—"HANCOCK WAS SUPERB."

Here the writer adopts an account so graphic, and which has come into his hands with such endorsement of its correctness, as to render its use without curtailment imperative.

Here the enemy made his stand, and by these works the Union Army, in such order as was possible, from the nature of the pursuit, found itself on the evening of the 4th of May, effectually stopped. There was rain, mud, infinite discomfort, apparent confusion, unquestionably no head to the movements of the troops, and as darkness settled down over the bivouacking army there was anything but a bright prospect for success. With the dawn of the 5th, however, matters began to assume shape and the divisions got into their positions. Hooker made his famous, bloody and ineffectual struggle in the fallen timbers before Fort Magruder. It was a gallant effort persistently made, and while reflecting honor on the division, resulted in nothing but heavy loss. Early in the forenoon General Hancock obtained permission to reconnoiter the enemy's left. With two light batteries and two additional regiments, he moved for a mile or more to the right of our line, carefully feeling the enemy's strength. Presently he came upon an opening in the woods and before him was a deep ravine, a dam across it, and on the opposite bluff a rebel fortification, the continuation of the rebel left. A glance showed the commander that the fort was not strongly manned, and by a rapid movement might be forced. This was quickly done. The troops poured across the dam, climbed the bluff and drove the enemy out of the redoubt. A road was hastily improvised up the bluff, the artillery was dragged across the dam, and Hancock formed his brigade in line of battle within the enemy's line of fortifications, and moved at once on a line parallel to the one by which he had advanced, straight back toward the rebel centre at Fort Magruder. It was a masterly movement. By one quick stroke he had completely turned the enemy's left, and unless stopped and driven back, he would render the whole rebel line untenable. The enemy fell back slowly before his advance, until a position some twelve hundred yards from Fort Magruder was reached. From this point, a gentle slope descended some distance toward the rebel centre. It was a fine position for artillery work, and Hancock sent his two batteries a short distance to the front with adequate support, and a heavy artillery duel ensued. The position, however, was a perilous one. His little command was a long distance from any supports; an almost impassable ravine was between it and the rest of the division and the army, and before it was an overwhelming force; in fact, the whole rebel army. Reinforcements were sent for, but none came. The day wore on, and the position became critical; without reinforcements it seemed madness to attempt to hold the advantage gained. With adequate support the rebel army was at our mercy. Between these conflicting views the General held on until nearly 5 o'clock in the afternoon. Then General Hancock determined to withdraw, and issued the order to retire the batteries back to the slope where the brigade line stood.

But the lynx-eyed rebel commander having repulsed Hooker in front, and realizing perfectly the danger which threatened him with his left flank turned, made his dispositions with a view of utterly overwhelming Hancock. The order to retire the artillery had not been executed, when, with a tremendous cheer, the enemy debouched from the woods on Hancock's right front, and in two splendid lines of battle two brigades of Early's troops moved on Hancock's line. There was no such thing as retreat then. Retreat meant rout, utter overthrow, capture. Whatever might be the effect of standing his ground, retreat was the worst of all possible expedients. Hancock stood his ground. Not altogether; the enemy, regardless of shell and hardly stopping for canister, swept around and almost enveloped the artillery which barely escaped from a loop in the rebel advance and went into the battery again on the slope. The brigade in perfect order, firing steadily, slowly retired before the rebel advance. The latter came on impetuously, firing and shouting "Bull Run! Bull Run! That flag is ours!" As they came slowly up the slope, flushed with certain victory, Hancock seized the opportune moment. He had been sitting close behind the centre of the line watching with imperturbable coolness the phases of the struggle. It was a supreme hour. Would his brigade respond in the presence of such overwhelming advancing numbers? The fight was, it must be remembered, in the open field. It was now at murderously short range. The thoughts of this brave commander in that crisis nobody knew. What he did all the world knows. The Little Corporal is said to have watched a similar struggle, and at the crisis to have thrown himself headlong across the bridge of Lodi. What Hancock did was a piece of the same personal daring. Dashing forward on his horse with head bared, swinging his hat and shouting "Forward! Forward! For God's sake forward!" he showed himself among his men in the line of battle. Forty yards away was the great, irregularly shaped, firing, shouting rebel force. It seemed madness to attempt to stop them. But the brigade saw and recognized Hancock's blazing form before them. Here and now he gave that historic order, "Gentlemen, Charge," and with a shout that drowned the crackling musketry, with lowered bayonets and with a line as perfect as though the men were on parade, the brigade advanced. A minute more and the conflicting forces would be hand to hand; but this did not occur.

The rebel line faltered, then stopped, then turned, as though actuated by one unpleasant, common impulse, and back they went, slowly, obstinately, fighting still, but still back the way they came, leaving the ground covered with their dead and wounded, to say nothing of some hundreds who were found retreating under fire, not so agreeable as advancing under the same conditions, and who held up white handkerchiefs and surrendered. Shortly after the struggle was over the wished for re-inforcements came in plenty, but now it was night. The great opportunity of following up the blow was lost. During the night the enemy retreated, the success of Hancock having made the Williamsburg lines untenable, although constructed to sustain a siege.

This was Hancock's first glory, and it was a shining glory, too. From an unknown subordinate in a few hours his name was heard from Maine to California.

Particular description or even mention cannot be made in this sketch, of all the brilliant deeds performed by this great soldier during the Civil War. He was almost perpetually engaged. Golding's Farm, Garnet's Hill, Savage Station, Malvern Hill, South Mountain, Antietam—where he succeeded Gen. Richardson, who fell, in command of his division—Fredricksburg, Chancellorville, Marye's Heights, and a score of others, will be names inseparably connected with his history. For his conspicuous services in the Peninsular campaign, he was recommended by the General-in-Chief for promotion to the rank of Major-General of Volunteers, and for the brevets of Major, Lieutenant-Colonel, and Colonel, in the regular army. In November, 1862, he received his commissions. As he advanced to higher rank, unlike many successful commanders, he did not avail himself of the privilege of remaining at some safe point in the rear, communicating by his aids with his subordinates. He continued his practice of being with his men and sharing their dangers. He was always at the critical point at the critical moment; and his soldiers knew that they were commanded by a man who knew no fear himself, which inspired them with the sublime courage which made the old Second Corps invincible.

### GETTYSBURG.

> "He that outlives this day and comes safe home
> Will stand a tip-toe when this day is named.
> He that shall live this day and see old age
> Will yearly on the vigil feast his friends."
> *Henry V.*

> "A combination and a form indeed
> Where every God did seem to set his seal
> To give the world assurance of a man."
> *Hamlet.*

By common consent, Gettysburg was the turning point of the war. The desperate valor of the Southern men had withstood every shock, but Lee had come to perceive that for the success of the Confederate cause, the war on their part must be more than defensive. Suddenly in June, 1863, he marched with all his available force into the Northern territory, at once threatening Washington and Philadelphia. Riots, instigated by secret emissaries, broke out simultaneously in the Northern cities. The tremendous consequences of a rebel victory at that time can only be imagined. If Washington should fall, nothing could save Baltimore and Philadelphia. New York itself might follow. Europe would at once have recognized the Confederacy, and nothing but long years of bloody warfare could have saved the Union, if indeed it was not at once and forever destroyed, with all the hopes of humanity which rested upon its existence. It was a dark hour for the nation.

The army of the Potomac, under the command of General Meade, was thrown rapidly in the same direction, to intercept the rebel progress. On the march, Hancock was selected to cover the rear, as the veteran Second Corps under their gallant leader could best be relied upon to grapple with the wily Lee, if that great strategist should make a sudden deflection toward the Capitol. Thus the contending forces swept up from Virginia, through Maryland into Pennsylvania. Neither knew the exact position or the strength of the other, but thus they rushed toward some unknown point, where they were to meet and try conclusions in one of the most momentous struggles of history. That point proved to be Gettysburg, six miles north of Mason and Dixon's line. General Mulholland, an officer in the Second Corps, thus describes the march, in a pamphlet prepared by him, commemorative of the occasion :

The march to Gettysburg was one of the longest and

most severe we had yet experienced. In thinking of war we are apt to look only at the battles ; to hear the dread sound of strife ; see the deadly, gaping wounds, and are ready to crown the survivors or give honor to those who fell ; but the hardships of the march, the heats of summer, the colds of winter, the entire absence of every comfort and luxury in active service is over-looked or forgotten by those who do not participate. Napoleon, when retreating from Moscow, lost many of his men by the excessive cold ; directly opposite was our experience on the way to Gettysburg. On one day, I think the second out from Falmouth, our corps lost more than a dozen men from sunstroke—they fell dead by the wayside. On another day we crossed the battle-field of Bull Run, where the year before Pope had met with disastrous defeat. No effort had been made to bury the dead properly ; a little earth, which the rain had long ago washed away, had been thrown over them where they fell, and their bodies, or rather their skeletons, now lay exposed to view. In some parts of the fields they were in groups, in other places singly and in all possible positions. One cavalryman lay outstreched with skeleton hand still grasping his rusted sword. Another, half covered with earth, the flesh still clinging to his lifeless bones and hand extended as if to greet us. We rested for a short time on the field and one of the regiments, our brigade (the Twenty-eighth Massachusetts) halted on the very spot on which they had fought the year previously, and recognized the various articles lying around as belonging to their own dead.

The route of the Second corps to Gettysburg was over two hundred miles in length. Some days we marched fifteen, on others eighteen miles, and on one day (June 29) this corps completed the longest march made by any infantry during the war—leaving Frederick City, Md., in the morning and halting at 11 o'clock P. M., two miles beyond Uniontown, a distance of thirty-four miles. When I look back over the almost score of years to this march of the Second corps, and think of the perfect discipline in the ranks, the cheerfulness with which the enlisted men, with their load of fifty-seven pounds weight—musket and ammunition, knapsack and cartridge box, shelter tent and blanket, canteen and rations—trudged along under the broiling sun of the hottest month in our year ; how bravely they struggled to keep up with their regiments lest they should miss the fight, and how, while on the march, no act was committed which could bring dishonor upon them as men, as citizens or as soldiers, my heart fills with admiration, and I offer a flowing measure of praise to my comrades who are yet alive and to those who are no more. There is not an inhabitant on all that line of march who can tell of a single act of vandalism by any of the men, such as we are wont to hear of other armies. In the rich and cultivated country through which we passed, life and property were respected as much as though we were in the halcyon days of peace. Old and young came to the roadside to see the army pass, and knew they were safe from insult or molestation. The fields of ripening grain waved untrampled when the corps had gone by, the men even going out of their way to avoid the gardens lest they should step upon the flowers. The perfection of discipline in the army at this period was extraordinary. The armies that fought the war of 1861 differed very widely from the armies of other nations. We had no hoardes of Cossack, no regiments of Bashi-Bazouks to burn and destroy, to insult the aged or crush the defenseless. When Hancock, at Williamsburg, said to his brigade, "Gentlemen, charge!" he did not call his troops out of their name. Our army was literally an army of gentlemen.

And so we passed on to Thoroughfare gap, to Edward's Ferry, to Frederick, Md., to Uniontown and Taneytown, where, on the morning of July 1, the Second corps was massed, and where General Meade's headquarters had been established. While the corps were filing into the fields to the right and left of the road, and settling down for a rest and to wait for orders, General Hancock rode over to General Meade and entered into conversation with him. As they were talking a mounted officer dashed up, bringing the intelligence that fighting had begun at Gettysburg—thirteen miles distant. The news was meagre—only that there was fighting. That was all; yet it caused a general surprise, unaware as we were of the near proximity of the enemy, and was enough to send a thrill throughout the veteran ranks. The road that leads to Gettysburg is scanned with anxious eyes, and soon, away in the distance, rises a cloud of dust, which comes nearer and nearer, and another messenger from the front is with us. He tells us that Reynolds is killed or mortally wounded; that the First and Eleventh corps are fighting and the battle is against us. It is now 1 o'clock, too late for the Second corps to reach the field that day to take part in stemming the tide of rebel victory; but not so with their commander. Meade orders Hancock to proceed to the front and take command of all the troops there assembled. This was ten minutes past one o'clock, and within twenty minutes Hancock, with his staff, was on the road to Gettysburg. He goes like Desaix at Marengo, to snatch victory from the jaws of defeat. (A strange coincidence. Nearly a century before, the grandfather of General Hancock, then a soldier of Washington, started from this same little village of Taneytown to escort some of the prisoners of Burgoyne to Valley Forge.) The Second corps promptly followed General Hancock and required no urging to keep the men up. The regiments moved forward solidly and rapidly, and not a straggler was to be seen. I never saw men cover thirteen miles so quickly; but as they hurried along a halt was ordered, the ranks opened, and an ambulance passed containing the dead body of the heroic General John F. Reynolds. Then the corps pushed on to within a few miles of the battle ground, where it camped that night and arrived on the field early the next morning.

## HANCOCK TO THE FRONT.

As General Hancock proceeded to the front he rode part of the way in an ambulance, so that he might examine the maps of the country, his aid, Major Mitchell, galloping ahead to announce his coming to General Howard, whom he found on Cemetery hill, and to whom he told his errand, giving him to understand that General Hancock was coming up to take command. At half-past 3 o'clock General Hancock rode up to General Howard, informed him that he had come to take command, and asked him if he wished to see his written orders. Howard answered: "No! No! Hancock, go ahead." At this moment our defeat seemed to be complete. Our troops were flowing through the streets of the town in great disorder, closely pursued by the Confederates, the retreat fast becoming a route, and in a very few minutes the enemy would have been in possession of Cemetery hill, the key to the position, and the battle of Gettysburg would have gone into history as a rebel victory. But what a change came over the scene in the next half hour. The presence of Hancock, like that of Sheridan, was magnetic. Order came out of chaos. The flying troops halt, and again face the enemy. The battalions of Howard's corps that were retreating down the Baltimore pike, are called back, and with a cheer go into position on the crest of Cemetery hill, where the division of Steinwehr had already been stationed. Wadsworth's division and a battery are sent to hold Culp's hill, and Geary, with the White Star division, goes on the double-quick to occupy the high ground toward Round Top. Confidence is restored, the enemy checked, and being deceived by these dispositions, cease their attack.

General Hancock was fully aware that General Meade had determined to fight the battle on the line of Pipe creek; but noting the topographical advantages of the ground around Gettysburg, he determined to advise General Meade to fight there. He knew that this line, the crest of Cemetery ridge, with Culp's hill on the right, Round Top on the left, and Cemetery hill in the centre, could not be bettered. So, when order had taken the place of confusion, and our lines once more intact, he sent his senior aid, Major Mitchell, back to tell General Meade that, in his judgment, Gettysburg was the place to fight our battle. Major Mitchell found General Meade in the evening near Taneytown, and communicated these views. General Meade listened attentively, and on these representations, he fortunately concluded to abandon his idea of fighting on the line of Pipe creek, and deliver the battle at Gettysburg; and turning to General Seth Williams, his adjutant general, he said: "Order up all the troops—we will fight there."

The morning of July 2, and the second day of the battle, dawned clear and bright, and found Hancock posting the Second corps on Cemetery ridge.

Soon the long lines of the Third corps are seen advancing, and how splendidly they march. It looks like a dress parade, a review. On, on they go, out towards the peach orchard, but not a shot is fired. A little while longer, and some one calls out "There!" and points to where a puff of smoke is seen arising against the dark green of the woods. Another and another cloud, until the whole face of the forest is enveloped, and the dread sound of the artillery comes loud and quick; shells are seen bursting in all directions along the lines. The bright colors of the regiment are conspicuous marks, and the shells burst around them in great numbers. The musketry begins, the infantry become engaged, and the battle extends along the whole front of Sickle's corps. Now the sounds come from Little Round Top, and the smoke rises among the trees, and all the high and wooded ground to the left of the peach orchard seems to be the scene of strife. An hour passes and our troops give way, and are falling back; but slowly, very slowly, every inch of ground is fought for. The Third corps is not in the habit of giving it up, and they hold their own well; but the odds are against them, and they are forced to retire.

Now help is called for, and Hancock tells Caldwell to have his division ready. "Fall in!" and the men run to their places. "Take arms!" and the four brigades of Zook, Cross, Brook and Kelly are ready for the fray. There is yet a few minutes to spare before starting, and the time is occupied in one of the most impressive religious ceremonies I have ever witnessed. The Irish Brigade, which had been commanded formerly by General Thomas Francis Meagher, and whose green flag had been unfurled in every battle in which the Army of the Potomac had been engaged, from the first Bull Run to Appomattox, and was now commanded by Colonel Patrick Kelly, of the Eighty-eighth New York, formed a part of this division. The brigade stood in column of regiments, closed in mass. As a large majority of its members were Catholics, the chaplain of the brigade, Rev. William Corby, proposed to give a general absolution to all the men before going into the fight.

While this is customary in the armies of Catholic countries of Europe, it was, perhaps, the first time it was ever witnessed on this continent, unless, indeed, the grim old warrior, Ponce de Leon, as he tramped through the everglades of Florida in search of the Fountain of Youth, or De Soto on his march to the Mississippi, indulged in this act of devotion. Father Corby stood upon a large rock in front of the brigade. Addressing the men, he explained what he was about to do, saying that each one could receive the benefit of the absolution by making a sincere act of contrition and firmly resolving to embrace the first opportunity of confessing their sins, urging them to do their duty well, and reminding them of the high and sacred nature of their trust as soldiers, and the noble object for which they fought, ending by saying that the Catholic Church refuses Christian burial to the soldier who turns his back upon the foe or deserts his flag.

The brigade was standing at "Order arms." As he closed his address, every man fell on his knees, with head bowed down. Then stretching his right hand toward the brigade, Father Corby pronounced the words of the absolution: "*Dominus noster Jesus Christus vos absolvat, et ego, auctoritate ipsius, vos absolvo ab omni vinculo excommunicationis et interdicti in quantum possum et vos indigetis, deinde ego absolvo vos a peccatis vestris in nomine Patris, et Filio, et Spiritus Sancto.* Amen."

The scene was more than impressive,—it was awe-inspiring. Near by stood Hancock, surrounded by a brilliant throng of officers, who had gathered to witness this very unusual occurrence, and while there was profound silence in the ranks of the Second corps, yet over to the left, out by the peach orchard and Little Round Top, where Weed and Vincent and Haslett were dying, the roar of the battle rose and swelled and re-echoed through the woods, making music more sublime than ever sounded through cathedral aisle. The act seemed to be in harmony with all the surroundings.

The fighting on the second day, July 2d, was terrible, the lines at one time being not more than thirty feet apart. At one point fourteen hundred men were lost in half an hour, including two Brigadier Commanders, General S. H. Zook and Col. E. E. Cross. On the morning of that day, General Hancock had said to Col. Cross, "this is the last day you fight as Colonel: to-day will make you a Brigadier-General," Cross with a premonition of his fate, answered: "No General, it is too late. I shall never wear a star. To-day I shall be killed."

But the great fight of all was on the 3d. Here we quote again from Gen. Mulholland:

As the day advanced the sound of artillery mingled with the musketry, and we knew that a hard fight was in progress. The men of our line almost held their breath with anxiety. About 9 o'clock the firing suddenly ceased. A tremendous cheer went up, and a minute later every man in the army knew that we were again in possession of Culp's hill. Then came a few hours of peace—a perfect calm. From Cemetery hill to Round Top not a movement had been observed or a shot fired all the morning.

About noon we could see considerable activity along Seminary ridge. Battery after battery appeared along the edge of the woods. Guns were unlimbered, placed in position and the horses taken to the rear. On our side, officers sat around in groups and, through field glasses, anxiously watched these movements in our front and wondered what it all meant. Shortly after 1 o'clock, however, we knew all about it. The headquarter wagons had just come up and General Gibbons had invited Hancock and staff to partake of some lunch. The bread that was handed around—if it ever was eaten—was consumed without butter, for as the orderly was passing the latter article to the gentlemen, a shell from Seminary ridge cut him in two. Instantly the air was filled with bursting shells; the batteries that we had been watching for the last two hours going into position in our front did not open singly or spasmodically. The whole hundred and twenty guns, which now began to play upon us, seemed to be discharged simultaneously, as though by electricity. And then for nearly two hours the storm of death went on.

I have read many accounts of this artillery duel, but the most graphic description by the most able writers falls far short of the reality. No tongue or pen can find language strong enough to convey any idea of its awfulness. Streams of screaming projectiles poured through the hot air, falling and bursting everywhere. Men and horses were torn limb from limb; caissons exploded one after another in rapid succession, blowing the gunners to pieces.

No spot within our lines was free from this frightful iron rain. The infantry hugged close the earth and sought every slight shelter that our light earth-works afforded. It was literally a storm of shot and shell that the oldest soldiers there—those who had taken part in almost every battle of the war—had not yet witnessed. That awful, rushing sound of the flying missiles, which causes the firmest hearts to quail, is everywhere.

At this tumultuous moment we witness a deed of heroism such as we are apt to attribute only to knights of the olden time. Hancock, mounted and accompanied by his staff, Major Mitchell, Captain Harry Bingham, Captain Isaac Parker and Captain E. P. Bronson, with the corps flag flying in the hands of a brave Irishman, Private James Wells, of the Sixth New York Cavalry, started at the right of his line, where it joins the Taneytown road, and slowly rode along the terrible crest to the extreme left of his position, while shot and shell roared and crashed around him, and every moment tore great gaps in the ranks at his side.

> "Storm'd at with shot and shell,
> Boldly they rode, and well."

It was a gallant deed and withal not a reckless exposure of life, for the presence and calm demeanor of the commander as he passed through the lines of his men set them an example which an hour later bore good fruit and nerved their stout hearts to win the greatest and most decisive battle ever fought on this continent. For an hour after the firing began our batteries replied vigorously and then ceased altogether, but the rebel shells came as numerously as ever. Then, for over a half hour, not a soul was seen stirring on our line—we might have been an army of dead men for all the evidence of life visible. Suddenly the enemy stopped their fire, which had been going on for nearly two hours without intermission, and then the long lines of their infantry—eighteen thousand strong—emerged from the woods and began their advance.

At this moment silence reigned along our whole line. With arms at a "right shoulder shift" the division of Longstreet's corps moved forward with a precision that was wonderfully beautiful. It is now our turn and the lines that a few moments before seemed so still now teemed with animation. Eighty of our guns open their brazen mouths; solid shot and shell are sent on their errand of destruction in quick succession. We see them fall in countless numbers among the advancing troops. The accuracy of our fire could not be excelled; the missiles strike right in the ranks, tearing and rending them in every direction. The ground over which they have passed is strewn with dead and wounded; but on they come. The gaps in the ranks are closed as soon as made. They have three-quarters of a mile to pass exposed to our fire, and half the distance is nearly passed. Our gunners now load with canister and the effect is appalling; but still they march on. Their gallantry is past all praise—it is sublime. Now they are within a hundred yards. Our infantry rise up and pour round after round into these heroic troops.

At Waterloo the Old Guard recoiled before a less severe fire; but there was no recoil in these men of the south—they marched right on as though they courted death. They concentrate in great numbers and strike on the most **advanced** part of our line. The crash of the musketry **and the** cheers of the men blend together. The Philadelphia brigade occupy this point. They are fighting on their **own** ground and for their own state, and in the bloody hand to hand engagement which ensues, the Confederates though fighting with desperate valor, find it impossible to dislodge them—they are rooted to the ground.

Seeing how utterly hopeless further effort would be and knowing the impossibility of reaching their lines should they attempt a retreat, large numbers of the rebels lay down their arms and the battle is won. To the left of the Philadelphia brigade we did not get to such close quarters. Seeing the utter annihilation of Pickett's troops, the division of Wilcox and others on their right went to pieces almost before they got within musket range. A few here and there ran away and tried to regain their lines, but many laid down their arms and came in as prisoners. At the most critical moment Hancock fell, among his men, on the line of Stannard's Vermont brigade, desperately wounded, but he continued to direct the fight until victory was assured, and then he sent Major Mitchell to announce the glad tidings to the commander of the army. Said he: "Tell General Meade that the troops under my command have repulsed the assault of the enemy, who are now flying in all directions in my front." "Say to General Hancock," said Meade, in reply, "I regret exceedingly that he is wounded, and I thank him for the country and for myself for the service he has rendered to-day." Truly, the country may thank General Hancock, as Congress afterwards did, for the great service on that field.

Five thousand prisoners were sent to the rear, and we gathered up thirty-three regimental standards in front of the Second corps. The remaining hours of daylight during this day were occupied in caring for the wounded, looking over the field and talking of the incidents of the fight.

Many noble officers and men were lost on both sides, and in the camp hospital they died in hundreds during the afternoon and night. The rebel General Armistead died in this way. As he was being carried to the rear he was met by Captain Harry Bingham, of Hancock's staff, who, getting off his horse, asked him if he could do anything for him. Armistead replied, to take his watch and spurs to General Hancock that they might be sent to his relatives. His wishes were complied with, General Hancock sending them to his friends at the first opportunity. Armistead was a brave soldier, with a chivalric presence and came forward in front of his brigade waving his sword. He was shot through the body and fell inside of our lines,

Some of the wounded rebels showed considerable animosity toward our men. One of them, who lay mortally wounded in front of the Sixty-ninth Pennsylvania, sullenly refused to be taken to the hospital, saying that he wanted to die right there on the field where he fell.

The scene after Longstreet's charge was indescribable. In front of the Philadelphia brigade the dead lay in great heaps. Dismounted guns, ruins of exploded caissons, dead and mutilated men and horses were piled up together in every direction.

On the morning of the 5th we found that the enemy had gone, and then what a scene! I think the fact was first discovered by the troops on Culp's hill, and what a cheer went up; a cheer that swelled into a roar and was taken up by the boys on Cemetery hill, rolled along the crest to Round Top and then back again. Cheers for the Philadelphia brigade that stood a living wall, against which the hosts beat in vain. Cheers for Meade, the soldier, "without fear or reproach," who here began, with a great victory, his illustrious career as commander of the army of the Potomac. Cheers for Hancock, who had stemmed the tide of defeat on the first day and selected the ground on which this glorious victory was achieved, who on the second day had again stopped the tide of rebel victory and restored our shattered lines, and on the third day had met and repulsed the final assault on which Lee's all was staked, and won the battle that was really the death-blow to the rebellion.

And then we gathered up with tender care and consigned to earth our noble dead.

When will their glory fade?

Indeed they have not died in vain. The good they have accomplished will last forever. History will record in glowing words their heroic deeds and glorious death.

Long after the granite of their monuments shall have crumbled into dust; even when the name of the battle shall have been forgotten, the Union and the blessings of civil liberty, which they died to perpetuate, shall reign throughout the land.

Three years later Congress, by joint resolution, thanked General Hancock for his gallant, meritorious and conspicuous share in that great and decisive victory.

The wound which General Hancock received at Gettysburg, barely missed being mortal. He was attended on that occasion by the distinguished New Jersey surgeon, Dr. A. N. Dougherty, of Newark, who was then upon his staff as medical director of the Second corps, to whom, as well as to General W. G. Mitchell—General Hancock's present chief of staff, the Major Mitchell of Gettysburg—the writer is indebted for much valuable material in the writing of this sketch, which he takes this occasion gratefully to acknowledge. It was Dr. Dougherty who wrote the dispatch at General Hancock's dictation, announcing the victory to General Meade.

### SUBSEQUENT BATTLES.

It was many months before General Hancock's wound healed sufficiently to enable him to again take the field; but much sooner than his physical condition warranted, he was back to his old command, its ranks made full by recruiting, and increased by the addition of one-half of the old Third corps, swelling the total to fifty thousand veterans, at the head of whom, although in constant physical pain, he fought with conspicuous ability and heroism in the battles of the Wilderness, performing in those three bloody days,—May 5th, 6th and 7th, 1864,— new prodigies of valor, throwing himself sword in hand into the midst of contest like a knight of the olden time, and thus stimulating his men to invincibility. On the 10th he led the assault at Allsops, and on the 12th performed one of the most brilliant feats of the war, which has passed into history as the assault of Spottsylvania. The enemy was strongly entrenched and possessed every advantage of ground; but early in the morning, under cover of a dense fog, he effected a partial surprise, and carried the position with a rush, capturing at one blow five thousand prisoners, twenty-two pieces of artillery, thirty stands of colors, and several thousand muskets. Among the prisoners were two general officers—Gen. Stewart and Gen. Bradley Johnson, and one entire division of the enemy. There is now in the museum at Washington, the stump of a tree, which was cut completely off by the bullets from both sides, in this engagement.

Other engagements followed, too numerous for even mention in the compass of this article. His wound re-opened, and on the march he would ride in an ambulance, mounting his horse only during action. On the 12th of August he was made Brigadier-General of the regular army. On the 25th he fought the battle of Ream's Station. On the 27th of October he gained the victory of Boydton Road, capturing one thousand prisoners.

At the battle of Hatcher's Run an incident occurred which shows the peculiar character of General Hancock's courage. Before the engagement opened, he said to the medical director: "Doctor, I want you with me to-day, and that you should keep near me. I feel that I am going to be wounded again." Fortunately the presentiment was unfulfilled. His horse fell under him, but the General was unscathed. How sublime must be the courage of that man who could thus carry himself, impressed with the belief that Death, with upraised arm, was riding invisible at his side.

Still the war went on, and the stubborn Southerners would not yield. In November, General Hancock was detached from the Army of the Potomac, and ordered to Washington. There were thousands of veterans whose terms of enlistment had expired, and whom it was desirable to bring back into the field. President Lincoln, with far-seeing sagacity, reasoned that 50,000 such men, hardened as by fire—steel-hardened in battles—would be an invaluable reliance, and bethought him of Hancock, the chief veteran general of the army, as the man to whose standard they would flock. The idea proved correct: the force was speedily raised, and with it he went to the front as Commander of the Middle Division, embracing the departments of West Virginia, Pennsylvania and Washington, with his headquarters at Winchester. His new command also included the Army of the Shenandoah, in all a force of nearly 100,000 veterans, brought thus together under the most successful fighter of the war, for the striking of a final blow. Well might Lee tremble. Hancock held himself in readiness to co-operate at one hours' notice with the Army of the Potomac, or to take transports and join Sherman in the

South; but Lee's army broke at Petersburg, and surrendered at Appomattox, and the war was at an end.

In April, 1865, Lincoln fell by the hand of an assassin, Seward was stabbed nearly to death, and everything indicated a wide-spread conspiracy to destroy the entire government by secret assassination of every prominent officer thereof. A universal feeling of fear and distrust pervaded the nation. Men cried out, "How long, O God, how long," and despair for a moment seemed to settle down upon the whole people of the North. In this emergency, Hancock was summoned to Washington. Then the nation breathed freer, and men said, "Thank God a man is in Washington who can be trusted." Andrew Johnson became President, and he kept Hancock in Washington during the trial of the conspirators, and until after their execution. There were some driveling idiots who doubted Johnson, and even accused him of being a party to the assassination of Lincoln, that he might step over his dead body to the Presidency; but none ever doubted Hancock; and those who doubted Johnson, lived to have shame crimson their faces.

It was Hancock's painful duty to superintend the execution of the prisoners convicted, one of whom, a woman—Mrs. Suratt—stoutly asserted her innocence of all complicity with the conspirators, and for her wide sympathy was aroused; but his duty was simply an executive one, and as such it was performed. Hoping and believing that the appeals of the daughter of Mrs. Suratt would touch the President's heart, he offered her every facility for gaining access to him, and on the day of the execution he planted a line of mounted sentinels from the scaffold to the White House, so that to the last moment a reprieve or any act of clemency might be swiftly and surely conveyed. The hour came; there was no reprieve. Hancock preserved the peace of the city, executioners performed their duty, and the condemned died.

In July, 1866, Hancock was made full Major-General of the regular army, having been so brevetted one year previous. He assumed command of the Department of Missouri, and conducted several campaigns against the hostile Indians of the North-west. He is, at this writing, the senior Major-General of the army, with headquarters on Governor's Island, in New York bay. His stars have been honestly won by forty years of fighting for a nation that perchance may say to him, "Well done, good and faithful servant," and with hearts swelling with gratitude, confer upon him the highest earthly honor, higher than any throne,—the Chief Magistracy of the American Union, with its fifty millions of people—its thirty-eight States—each one an empire.

In view of this contingency, let us inquire into the civil qualifications of this great soldier.

# CHAPTER XII.

## LIFE OF GEN. W. S. HANCOCK.—Continued.

### THE PEN IS MIGHTIER THAN THE SWORD.

When the Southern armies had all surrendered, and the rebellion was crushed, and the Union had been preserved, many difficulties still existed which must be settled, before the era of good feeling, contentment and reliable patriotism in the Southern States could be established. Some millions of human beings who had been held in servitude had, by the operations of the war, become free, and were entitled to the protection of the government; and in many respects the problem almost defied solution. Finally the word "reconstruction" was adopted by the party in power, with "all that the term implied," and the South was parcelled out into so-called "Military Districts," over which were placed military officers armed with extraordinary powers, and with few checks to restrain them from despotism. The military commander might at will invoke the civil law, or if not so disposed, he might establish and enforce the military code; or if a wise and patriotic man, he might adopt the former for the general government of the people, and hold the latter in reserve for any extreme emergency. Many weak and unworthy men were appointed, who appeared to consider themselves quartered upon a conquered people to rule them with a rod of iron, and not a few so-called leading statesmen believed in making the system permanent for one or two generations, or at least so long as might be expedient for the possession of political power. Andrew Johnson did not take this view, which fact brought him eventually into that collision with his party which led to his impeachment, and almost to his conviction and removal from the Presidential chair.

There having been disturbances in the 5th military district and the Department of the Gulf, exaggerated accounts of which had been widely spread at the North, the President ordered General Hancock to assume its command. Here commences his career as a statesman. His predecessor had unhesitatingly made the military arm superior to the civil law, and was ruling the great States of Louisiana and Texas—a territory comprising more than three hundred thousand square miles—with absolute and irresponsible power. Let us see what this man of camps and battle-fields did on his arrival. It was the theory of Congress that the people of the South had, by their rebellion, forfeited their constitutional liberties, and had no civil rights which a military commander was bound to respect. Years have since passed, and most men now see how erroneous was that view. From the first, General Hancock dissented, and held the belief that "*the Constitution had survived the war, and was still the rightful heritage of all the people.*" The issuing of the following order was his first official act in his new position :

HEADQUARTERS FIFTH MILITARY DISTRICT.
NEW ORLEANS, LA., November 29, 1867.

*General Orders, No. 40.*

1. In accordance with General Order No. 81, Headquarters of the Army, Adjutant-General's Office, Washington, D. C., August 27, 1867, Major-General W. S. Hancock hereby assumes command of the Fifth Military District and of the department composed of the States of Louisiana and Texas.

2. The General commanding is gratified to learn that peace and quiet reign in this department. It will be his purpose to preserve this condition of things. As a means to this great end he regards the maintenance of the civil authorities in the faithful execution of the laws as the most efficient under existing circumstances. In war it is indispensable to repel force by force and overthrow and destroy opposition to lawful authority; but when insurrectionary force has been overthrown and peace established, and the civil authorities are ready and willing to perform their duties, the military power should cease to lead and the civil administration resume its natural and rightful dominion. Solemnly impressed with these views, the General announces that the great principles of American liberty are still the lawful inheritance of this people and ever should be. The right of trial by jury, the habeas corpus, the liberty of the press, the freedom of speech, the natural rights of persons and the rights of property must be preserved. Free institutions, while they are essential to the prosperity and happiness of the people, always furnish the strongest inducements to peace and order. Crimes and offenses committed in this district must be referred to the consideration and judgment of the regular civil tribunals, and those tribunals will be supported in their lawful jurisdiction. While the General thus indicates his purpose to respect the liberties of the people, he wishes all to understand that armed in-

surrection or forcible resistance to the law will be instantly suppressed by arms.

By command of

MAJOR-GENERAL W. S. HANCOCK.

A leading journal of the north, *The Brooklyn Eagle*, said of this action :

"Probably no more astonished and delighted people could be found than the people of Louisiana and Texas when the purport of that order came to be understood. They had expected what they had before, a military dictator. They had expected to be governed by orders instead of laws. General Hancock informed them that he did not propose to rule them by military orders at all. They had looked for a Cæsar and they found in his stead an expounder and defender of the constitutional laws of the fathers of the Republic. The effect was electric," etc.

Throughout the whole of General Hancock's command of the Fifth Military District, his course was uniformly consistent with the sentiments set forth in the order above quoted. Although in supreme command, he sustained the jurisdiction of the civil courts and the purity and independence of elections by the people. He refused to organize military commission to supplant the judiciary of of the State and avoided all military interference with the administration of civil affairs. Under a rule so beneficent there was no necessity for the exercise of arbitrary power, for obedience to the laws was the homage the people voluntarily rendered to an administration so purely and wisely devoted to the public good. The following are extracts from some of his orders covering the most important cases :

### ON THE STAY OF CIVIL PROCESS.

*The Hon. E. Heath, Mayor of New Orleans.*

SIR: In answer to your communication of the 30th ult., requesting his intervention in staying proceedings in suits against the city on its notes, the Major-General commanding directs me to respectfully submit his views to you on that subject, as follows: Such a proceeding on his part would, in fact, be a stay-law in favor of the city of New Orleans, which, under the Constitution, could not be enacted by the Legislature of the State; and in his judgment such a power ought to be exercised by him, if at all, only in case of the most urgent necessity. It does not, therefore, seem to the Major-General commanding that there is an urgent necessity which would justify his interference in the manner required. Besides, the expediency of such a measure is more than questionable; for, instead of reinstating the confidence of the public in city notes, it would probably destroy it altogether.

### REVOKING A SUMMARY REMOVAL MADE BY HIS PREDECESSOR.

2. Paragraph 3 of special orders No. 188 from these headquarters, dated November 16, 1867, issued by Brevet Major-General Mower, removing P. R. O'Rourke, Clerk of Second District Court, Parish of Orleane, for malfeasance in office, and appointing R. L. Shelly in his stead, is hereby revoked, and P. R. O'Rourke is reinstated in said office. If any charges are set up against the said O'Rourke, the judicial department of the Government is sufficient to take whatever action may be necessary in the premises.

By command of

MAJOR-GENERAL HANCOCK.

December 4, 1867.

### TO PREVENT MILITARY INTERFERENCE AT THE POLLS.

\* \* \* \* \* \*

IX. Military interference with elections, "unless it shall be necessary to keep the peace at the polls," is prohibited by law, and no soldiers will be allowed to appear at any polling place, unless as citizens of the State they are registered as voters, and then only for the purpose of voting; but the commanders of posts will be prepared to act promptly if the civil authorities fail to preserve peace.
December 18, 1867.

### DISCLAIMING JUDICIAL FUNCTIONS IN CIVIL CASES.

Applications have been made at these headquarters implying an existence of arbitrary authority in the commanding general touching purely civil controversies.

One petition solicits this action, another that, and each refers to some special consideration of grace or favor which he supposes to exist and which should influence this department.

The number of such applications and the waste of time they involve, make it necessary to declare that the administration of civil justice appertans to the regular courts. The rights of litigants do not depend on the views of the general; they are to be adjudged and settled according to the laws.

By command of
MAJOR-GENERAL HANCOCK.

January 1, 1868.

### THE LETTER TO GOVERNOR PEASE, OF TEXAS.

On the great and the overshadowing question of the restoration of the southern States, General Hancock was equally specific and clear in his letter of March 9, 1868, to Governor Pease, of Texas. Governor Pease having addressed a letter to General Hancock commenting on order No. 40, the General replied in his own defense in an able state paper, of which the following are extracts:

"As respects the issue between us, any question as to what ought to have been done has no pertinence. You admit the act of Congress authorizes me to try an offender by military commission or allow the local civil tribunals to try, as I deem best; and you cannot deny the act expressly recognizes such local civil tribunals as legal authorities for the purpose specified. When you contend there are no legal local tribunals for any purpose in Texas, you must either deny the plain reading of the act of Congress or the power of Congress to pass the act.

You next remark that you dissent from my declaration 'that the country (Texas) is in a state of profound peace,' and proceed to state the grounds of your dissent. They appear to me not a little extraordinary. I quote your words: 'It is true there no longer exists here (Texas) any organized resistance to the authority of the United States; but a large majority of the white population who participated in the late rebellion are embittered against the Government and yield to it an unwilling obedience.' Nevertheless you concede they do yield it obedience. You proceed:

None of this class have any affection for the Government, and very few any respect for it. They regard the legislation of Congress on the subject of reconstruction as unconstitutional and hostile to their interests, and consider the Government now existing here under authority of the United States as an usurpation of their rights. They look on the emancipation of their late slaves and the disfranchisement of a portion of their own class as an act of insult and oppression.'

And this is all you have to present for proof that war and not peace prevails in Texas; and hence it becomes my duty—so you suppose—to set aside the local civil tribunals and enforce the penal code against citizens by means of military commissions. My dear sir, I am not a lawyer, nor has it been my business, as it may have been yours, to study the philosophy of statecraft and politics. But I may lay claim, after an experience of more than half a lifetime, to some poor knowledge of men and some appreciation of what is necessary to social order and happiness. And for the future of our common country, I could devoutly wish that no great number of our people have yet fallen in with the views you appear to entertain. Woe be to us whenever it shall come to pass that the power of the magistrate, civil or military, is permitted to deal with the mere opinions or feelings of the people. It would be difficult to show that the opponents of the Government in the days of the elder Adams, or Jefferson, or Jackson, exhibited for it either 'affection or 'respect.' You are conversant with the history of our past parties and political struggles touching the legislation on alienage, sedition, the embargo, national banks, our wars with England and Mexico, and cannot be ignorant of the fact that for one party to assert that a law or system of legislation is unconstitutional, oppressive and usurpative is not a new thing in the United States. That the people of Texas consider acts of Congress unconstitutional, oppressive or insulting to them is of no consequence to the matter in hand. The President of the United States has announced his opinion that these acts of Congress are unconstitutional. The Supreme Court, as you are aware, not long ago decided unanimously that a certain military commission was unconstitutional. Our people everywhere, in every State, without reference to the side they took during the rebellion, differ as to the constitutionality of these acts of Congress. How the matter really is, neither you or I may dogmatically affirm. I am confident you will not commit your serious judgment to the proposition that any amount of discussion, or any sort of opinions, however unwise in your judgment, or any assertion or feeling, however resentful or bitter, not resulting in a breach of law, can furnish justification for your denial that profound peace exists in Texas. You might as well deny that profound peace exists in New York, Pennsylvania, Maryland, California, Ohio and Kentucky, where a majority of the people differ with a minority on these questions; or that profound peace exists in the House of Representatives, or the Senate at Washington, or in the Supreme Court, where all these questions have been repeatedly discussed and parties respectfully and patiently heard.

You next complain that in parts of the State (Texas) it is difficult to enforce the criminal laws, that sheriffs fail to arrest, that the grand jurors will not always indict, that in some cases the military, acting in aid of the civil authorities, have not been able to execute the process of the courts; that petit jurors have acquitted persons adjudged guilty by you, and that other persons charged with offences have broke jail and fled from prosecution. I know not how these things are, but admitting your representations literally true, if for such reasons I should set aside the local civil tribunals and order a military commission, there is no place in the United States where it might not be done with equal propriety. It is rather more than hinted in your letter that there is no local State government in Texas and no local laws outside of the acts of Congress which I ought to respect, and that I should undertake to protect the rights of persons and property in my own way and in an arbitrary manner. If such be your meaning, I am compelled to differ with you. After the abolition of slavery (an event which I hope no one now regrets), the laws of Louisiana and Texas existing prior to the rebellion, and not in conflict with the acts of Congress, comprised a vast system of jurisprudence, both civil and criminal. I am satisfied, from representations of persons competent to judge, they are as perfect a system of laws as may be found elsewhere, and better suited than any other to the condition of this people, for by them they have long been governed. Why should it be supposed Congress has abolished these laws? Why should any one wish to abolish them? Let us for a moment suppose the whole civil code annulled, and that I am left, as commander of the Fifth Military District, the sole fountain of law and justice. This is the position in which you would place me.

"I am now to protect all rights and redress all wrongs. How is it possible for me to do it? Innumerable questions arise, of which I am not only ignorant, but to the solution of which a military court is entirely unfitted. One would establish a will, another a deed; or the question is one of succession, or partnership, or descent or trust; a suit of ejectment or claim to chattels; or the application may relate to robbery, theft, arson or murder. How am I to take the first step in any such matter? If I turn to the acts of Congress I find nothing on the subject. I dare not open the authors on the local code, for it has ceased to exist. And you tell me that in this perplexing condition I am to furnish, by dint of my own hasty and crude judgment, the legislation demanded by the vast and manifold interests of the people! I repeat, sir, that you and not Congress are responsible for the monstrous suggestion that there are no local laws or institutions here to be respected by me, outside the acts of Congress. I say, unhesitatingly, if it were possible that Congress should pass an act abolishing the local codes for Louisiana and Texas—which I do not believe—and it should fall to my lot to supply their places with something of my own, I do not see how I could do better than follow the laws in force here prior to the rebellion, excepting whatever therein shall relate to slavery. You are pleased to state that 'since the publication of (my) General Order No. 40 there has been a perceptible increase of crime and manifestation of hostile feeling towards the Government and its supporters,' and add that it is 'an unpleasant duty to give such a recital of the condition of the country.'

"You will permit me to say that I deem it impossible

the first of these statements can be true, and that I do very greatly doubt the correctness of the second. * * But what was Order No. 40, and how could it have the effect you attribute to it? It sets forth that 'the great principles of American liberty are still the inheritance of this people, and ever should be; that the right of trial by jury, the habeas corpus, the liberty of the press, the freedom of speech, and the natural rights of person and property must be preserved.' Will you question the truth of these declarations? Which one of these great principles of liberty are you ready to deny and repudiate? Whoever does so, avows himself the enemy of human liberty and the advocate of despotism."

General Hancock left New Orleans at his own request. The General-in-Chief of the Army having been given unconstutional control over matters in the South, superior to the prerogatives of the President, who chose to submit to that domination, Hancock applied to be relieved, desiring to avoid any futher connection with political complications. He was then, March, 1868, assigned to the command of the Military Division of the Atlantic, with headquarters at New York. In the National Democratic Convention of that year, although himself not an aspirant for the place, he received nearly a controlling vote for the nomination for President of the United States. He remained in New York until he was assigned to the Department of Dakota, with head-quarters at St. Paul, Minn., in November, 1869. After the death of General Meade he was recalled from the Northwest and placed in command of the Military Division of the Atlantic, with head-quarters at New York, in which position he now remains. At the Pennsylvania State Convention in 1869, he was tendered by his numerous friends the Democratic nomination for Governor of his native State—an honor which he then and has since declined. In the National Democratic Convention of 1872 he was again prominently mentioned for President of the United States, until it was decided to nominate a Liberal-Republican. In the Convention of 1876, on the first informal ballot, General Hancock received seventy-five votes, and was third on the list of nominees. On the 24th of June, 1880, he was unanimously nominated, by the Democratic National Convention at Cincinnati, as their Candidate for President.

His letter of acceptance, the terse periods of which, in connection with its lofty spirit of patriotism, cannot fail to add largely to his reputation as a statesman, may be found standing by itself on another page of this book.*

After the nomination at Cincinnati, the story was started and on the wings of rumor went through the country that General Hancock had written to General Sherman in 1876, a letter in regard to the action which he held should be taken by army officers in certain contingencies of a presidential election, and that the same contained treasonable sentiments. Of course such an allegation would be believed by few, but it was deemed best that the letter should be published, and it was given to the New York press by permission of General Sherman. The following is its text in full:

CARONDELET POST OFFICE,<br>ST. LOUIS, MO., Dec. 28 1876.

MY DEAR GENERAL—Your favor of the 4th inst. reached me in New York on the 5th, the day before I left for the West. I intended to reply to it before leaving, but cares incident to departure interfered. Then,

---
* See page 162.

again, since my arrival here I have been so occupied with personal affairs of a business nature, that I have deferred writing from day to day until this moment, and now I find myself in debt to you another letter in acknowledgment of your favor of the 17th, received a few days since.

I have concluded to leave here on the 29th (to-morrow) P. M., so that I may be expected in New York on the 31st inst. It has been cold and dreary since my arrival here. I have worked "like a Turk" (I presume that means hard work) in the country, in making fences, cutting down trees, repairing buildings, &c., &c., and am at least able to say that St. Louis is the coldest place in the winter, as it is the hottest in summer, of any that I have encountered in a temperate zone. I have known St. Louis in December to have genial weather throughout the month; this December has been frigid, and the river has been frozen more solid than I have ever known it.

### THE PRESIDENTIAL INAUGURAL ACTION.

When I heard the rumor that I was ordered to the Pacific coast I thought it probably true, considering the past discussion on that subject. The possibilities seemed to me to point that way. Had it been true I should, of course, have presented no complaint nor made resistance of any kind. I would have gone quickly if not prepared to go promptly. I certainly would have been relieved from the responsibilities and anxieties concerning Presidential matters which may fall to those near the throne or in authority within the next four months, as well as from other incidents or matters which I could not control and the action concerning which I might not approve. I was not exactly prepared to go to the Pacific, however, and I therefore felt relieved when I received your note informing me that there was no truth in the rumors.

Then I did not wish to appear to be escaping from responsibilities and possible dangers which may cluster around military commanders in the East, especially in the critical period fast approaching. All's well that ends well. The whole matter of the Presidency seems to me simple and to admit of a peaceful solution. The machinery for such a contingency as threatens to present itself has been all carefully prepared. It only requires lubrication, owing to disuse. The army should have nothing to do with the selection or inauguration of Presidents. The people elect the President. The Congress declares in a joint session who he is. We of the army have only to obey his mandates, and are protected in so doing only so far as they may be lawful. Our commissions express that. I like Jefferson's way of inauguration; it suits our system. He rode alone on horseback to the Capitol (I fear it was the "Old Capitol"), tied his horse to a rail fence, entered and was duly sworn, then rode to the Executive Mansion and took possession. He inaugurated himself, simply by taking the oath of office. There is no other legal inauguration in our system. The people or politicians may institute parades in honor of the event, and public officials may add to the pageant by assembling troops and banners, but all that only comes properly after the inauguration, not before; and it is not a part of it. Our system does not provide that one President should inaugurate another. There might be danger in that, and it was studiously left out of the charter. But you are placed in an exceptionally important position in connection with coming events. The Capital is in my jurisdiction also, but I am a subordinate, and not on the spot, and if I were, so also would my superior in authority, for there is the station of the Commander-in-Chief.

### WHO IS TO DECIDE.

On the principle that a regularly elected President's term of office expires with the 3d of March (of which I have not the slightest doubt), and which the laws bearing on the subject uniformly recognize, and in consideration of the possibility that the lawfully elected President may not appear until the 5th of March, a great deal of responsibility may necessarily fall upon you. You hold over! You will have power and prestige to support you. The Secretary of War, too, probably holds over; but if no President appears he may not be able to exercise functions in the name of a President, for his proper acts are those of a known superior— a lawful President. You act on your own responsibility and by virtue of a commission, only restricted by the law. The Secretary of War is the mouthpiece of a President. You are not. If neither candidate has a constitutional majority of the Electoral College, or the Senate and House on the occasion of the count do not unite in declaring some person legally elected by the people, there is a lawful machinery already provided to meet that contingency and decide the question peacefully. It has not been recently used, no occasion presenting itself; but our forefathers provided it. It has been exercised, and has been recognized and submitted to as lawful on every hand. That machinery would probably elect Mr. Tilden President and Mr. Wheeler Vice-President. That would be right enough, for the law provides that in a failure to elect duly by the people, the House shall immediately elect the President and the Senate the Vice-President. Some tribunal must decide whether the people have duly elected a President. I presume, of course, that it is the joint affirmative action of the Senate and House, or why are they present to witness the count if not to see that it is fair and just? If a failure to agree arises between the two bodies, there can be no lawful affirmative decision that the people have elected a President, and the House must then proceed to act, not the Senate. The Senate elects vice-presidents, not presidents. Doubtless in case of a failure by the House to elect a President by the 4th of March, the President of the Senate (if there be one) would be the legitimate person to exercise Presidential authority for the time being, or until the appearance of a lawful President, or for the time laid down in the Constitution. Such courses would be peaceful, and, I have a firm belief, lawful.

I have no doubt Governor Hayes would make an excellent President. I have met him and know him. For a brief period he served under my command, but as the matter stands I can't see any likelihood of his being duly declared elected by the people, unless the Senate and House come to be in accord as to that fact, and the House would, of course, not otherwise elect him. What the people want is a peaceful determination of this matter,—as fair a determination as possible, and a lawful one. No other determination could stand the test. The country, if not plunged into revolution, would become poorer day by day, business would languish, and our bonds would come home to find a depreciated market.

## TROOPS OUT OF PLACE.

I was not in favor of the military action in South Carolina recently, and if General Ruger had telegraphed to me or asked for advice, I would have advised him not under any circumstances to allow himself or his troops to determine who were the lawful members of a State Legislature. I could not have given him better advice than to refer him to the special message of the President in the case of Louisiana some time before.

But in South Carolina he had had the question settled by a decision of the Supreme Court of the State—the highest tribunal which had acted on the question—so that his line of duty seemed even to be clearer than the action in the Louisiana case. If the federal court had interfered and overruled the decision of the State court, there might have been a doubt certainly; but the federal court only interfered to complicate—not to decide or overrule.

Anyhow it is no business of the army to enter upon such questions, and even if it might be so in any event, if the civil authority is supreme, as the constitution declares it to be, the South Carolina case was one in which the army had a plain duty.

Had General Ruger asked me for advice, and if I had given it, I should of course have notified you of my action immediately, so that it could have been promptly overruled if it should have been deemed advisable by you or other superior in authority. General Ruger did not ask for my advice, and I inferred from that and other facts that he did not desire it, or that, being in direct communication with my military superiors at the seat of government, who were nearer to him in time and distance than I was—he deemed it unnecessary. As General Ruger had the ultimate responsibility of action and had really the greater danger to confront in the final action in the matter, I did not venture to embarrass him by suggestions. He was a department commander, and the lawful head of the military administration within the limits of the department; but besides, I knew that he had been called to Washington for consultation before taking command, and was probably aware of the views of the administration as to civil affairs in his command; I knew that he was in direct communication with my superiors in authority in reference to the delicate subjects presented for his consideration, or had ideas of his own which he believed to be sufficiently in accord with the views of our common superiors, to enable him to act intelligently according to his judgment and without suggestions from those not on the spot and not as fully acquainted with the facts as himself. He desired too, to be free to act, as he had the eventual greater responsibility, and so the matter was governed as between him and myself.

### ILLEGAL AND UNWISE.

As I have been writing thus freely to you, I may still further unbosom myself by stating that I have not thought it lawful or wise to use federal troops in such matters as have transpired east of the Mississippi within the last few months—save so far as they may be brought into action under the article of the constitution which contemplates meeting armed resistance, or invasion of a State, more powerful than the State authorities can subdue by the ordinary processes—and then only when requested by the Legislature, or, if it could not be convened in session, by the Governor, and when the President of the United States intervenes in that matter it is a state of war, not peace.

The army is laboring under disadvantages, and has been used unlawfully at times in the judgment of the people (in mine certainly), and we have lost a great deal of the kindly feeling which the community at large once felt for us. "It is time to stop and unload."

Officers in command of troops often find it difficult to act wisely and safely when superiors in authority have different views of the law from theirs, and when legislation has sanctioned action seemingly in conflict with the fundamental law, and they generally defer to the known judgment of their superiors. Yet the superior officers of the army are so regarded in such great crises, and are held to such responsibility, especially those at or near the head of it, that it is necessary on such momentous occasions to dare to determine for themselves what is lawful and what is not lawful under our system, if the military authorities should be invoked, as might possibly be the case in such exceptional times when there exist such divergent views as to the correct result. The army will suffer from its past action if it has acted wrongfully. Our regular army has little hold upon the affections of the people of to-day, and its superior officers should certainly, as far as lies in their power, legally and with righteous intent, aim to defend the right, which to us is THE LAW and the institution which they represent. It is a well-meaning institution, and it would be well if it should have an opportunity to be recognized as a bulwark in support of the rights of the people and of THE LAW. I am, truly yours,

WINFIELD S. HANCOCK.

To General W. T. SHERMAN, *Commanding Army of the United States, Washington, D. C.*

All these are but straws telling which way the wind blows, in the habits and character of this remarkable man.

The writing and compilation of this sketch has been a grateful task. The incidents of a long life of devotion to his country, in the field and the cabinet, would fill a volume. There has been no need of padding, to fill out the limits of the writer's space. There has been no necessity of magnifying the military achievements of its hero. The object in view, has been not to prepare a campaign document, glorifying a political candidate, but to compress into narrow limits all that was most salient and convenient for a short but accurate biography, and fortunately no space has been required for defense of personal character.

General Hancock's military and civil career has thus been briefly reviewed. It only remains to say that in personal appearance and physique, he is what the world would wish such a hero to be. Like Washington in many other respects, he is like him in stature; standing six feet and one inch in height, and weighing about two hundred and thirty-five pounds. Although in his fifty-seventh year, he bears the appearance of a man of fifty. He is in robust health, and should it be his fortune, to be elected to the Presidency in the coming campaign, it is safe to prophesy that he will fill the position with the same honor to himself, and the same benefit to his country, as has resulted from every position he has heretofore held, and that the record of his administration will contribute to American history, one of its most brilliant pages.

## CHAPTER XIII.

### LIFE OF WILLIAM H. ENGLISH.

William H. English, the nominee of the Democratic party for the Vice-Presidency, was born at Lexington, Scott County, Indiana, on August 27th, 1822.

His father, Elisha G. English, was a Kentuckian by birth, and moved to Indiana in 1818.

Young English received his early education in the common schools of the region where he lived. He showed great diligence and perseverance in the prosecution of his studies, and, under disadvantageous circumstances, succeeded in preparing himself to enter college, taking a three years' course of study at South Hanover College.

Immediately upon his graduation, he commenced the study of law, and when only eighteen years of age was admitted to practice. He however exhibited a fondness for politics, and took an active part in all the campaigns of the day. While still in his teens, he was elected a delegate from Scott County to the Democratic State Convention, at Indianapolis. He was very active as a stump-speaker, in the famous "hard-cider and log-cabin" campaign of 1840. President Tyler appointed him to his first political office—that of postmaster of his native town. In 1843 he was elected Clerk of the Indiana House of Representatives, and in 1845 President Polk gave him a position in the Treasury Department, in recognition of his services during the Presidential campaign, a position which he held for four years.

In 1850, Mr. English was made Secretary of the Indiana Constitutional Convention, and the good impression he made during its session, was instrumental in procuring his election as a Representative to the first Legislature chosen under the New Constitution. In the Democratic caucus on the Speakership, Mr. English received 22 votes, to 31 for John W. Davis, who had been Speaker of the XXIX Congress. Mr. Davis subsequently resigned, owing to a disagreement with the House, and Mr. English, although but twenty-nine years old, was at once chosen to succeed him. So well did he discharge the duties of this office, that not an appeal was taken from his decision.

In 1852, Mr. English was elected to Congress, and was re-elected in 1854, '56 and '58, each time by an increased majority. The eight years of his Congressional career occurred during a most exciting period of our history, and he did his full share of the work which Congress was called upon to perform. As a member of the Committee on Territories, at the time of the introduction of the Kansas-Nebraska bill, he submitted a minority report, containing the idea of "popular sovereignty." He was one of the few members from the Free States who survived the storm which descended on all who had sustained that bill.

Mr. English firmly opposed the admission of Kansas under the Lecompton Constitution, until that instrument had been voted upon by the people. In this he was opposed to the policy of his party upon that measure.

For several years he was a Regent of the Smithsonian Institution, and made an able speech inCongress in defence of its management.

Mr. English, though desirous of making concessions to the South, was always opposed to secession, and combatted it on the floor of Congress, assuring the South that he and his constituents would "keep step to the music of the Union."

In 1864, at the Congressional Convention, Mr. English, as Chairman of the Committee on Resolutions, prepared and submitted the following resolution, which was adopted:

"That we are now, as we ever have been, unqualifiedly in favor of the Union of the States under the Constitution, and stand ready, as we have ever stood heretofore, to do everything that loyal and true citizens should do to maintain that Union under the Constitution, and to hand it down to our children unimpaired as we received it from our fathers."

In 1863, he embarked in a banking enterprise, with J. F. D. Lanier, of New York, and Geo. W. Riggs, of Washington, establishing the First National Bank of Indianapolis, to which city he at once removed, and where he has since resided. He has proved himself a skillful financier, and has succeeded in amassing a large fortune, estimated at several millions of dollars. He has always been a consistent hard-money man, and has energetically, both in public and private, opposed inflation and unredeemable currency.

Mr. English was married to Miss Emma M. Jackson, of Virginia. Two children have been born to them: one is W. E. English, now a member of the Indiana Legislature, and the other the wife of Dr. Willoughby Walling, of Louisville, Kentucky. Mrs. English died in 1876.

In 1877, Mr. English retired from active business, and has since then lived in leisure at his elegant residence in Indianapolis.

While not a brilliant debater, Mr. English is noted for his logic and practical common sense. In personal intercourse, he is dignified and retiring. In the private and social relations of his life, he stands above reproach. He is above the average height, with an erect, well-made figure. His forehead is high, and his features regular. A man who has gained unqualified success in every position of his life, it is to be said of him that this is the result of an ability which has been equally beyond question.

# PART II.

# COMPLETE
# Political Compendium

### WITH A REVIEW OF THE
## Colonial and Constitutional Governments,
### AND
## OUR NATIONAL PROGRESS,
#### INCLUDING

BIOGRAPHICAL SKETCHES OF ALL THE PRESIDENTS; TERMS OF OFFICE; CABINETS OF EACH; EXISTING GOVERNMENT; MEMBERS OF CABINET; MEMBERS OF THE JUDICIARY; MEMBERS OF CONGRESS, MINISTERS, GOVERNORS AND OTHER OFFICIALS; THEIR DUTIES, SALARIES AND TERMS OF OFFICE; DECLARATION OF INDEPENDENCE; ARTICLES OF CONFEDERATION; CONSTITUTION U. S., WITH AMENDMENTS; IMPORTS, EXPORTS AND ANNUAL EXPENDITURES; CENSUS, WITH NUMEROUS TABLES OF STATISTICS.

#### ALSO

THE POPULAR AND ELECTORAL VOTES FOR PRESIDENT AND VICE-PRESIDENT SINCE 1789, WITH THE FULL POPULAR AND ELECTORAL VOTE BY STATES AT THE PRESIDENTIAL ELECTION IN 1876, AND THE RESULTS OF RECENT STATE ELECTIONS.

---

### By FRANK C. BLISS,
*Of the New York Bar, Author of "Citizens' Manual," &c.*

---

### WITH NUMEROUS PORTRAITS & ENGRAVINGS.

---

NEWARK, N. J.:
F. C. BLISS & COMPANY.
1880.

ENTERED according to Act of Congress, in the year 1880,

BY F. C. BLISS & COMPANY,

In the Office of the Librarian of Congress, at Washington.

# INTRODUCTION.

In the compilation of this little work, the Author has collected together the most important facts, and statistics, relating to the Political History of the country.

In its arrangement he has adopted the simplest form; that of placing events as much as possible in their chronological order, commencing with the Colonial Government, and bringing it down to the present time; introducing the Constitution, Declaration of Independence, Articles of Confederation, &c., in their appropriate places.

In preparing the Biographical Sketches of the Presidents, and of the Candidates recently nominated for the Presidency and Vice-Presidency, he has endeavored to do equal justice to all, giving the facts, without favor or prejudice, and not at all biassed by party views or interest. The Statistical matter has been obtained from reliable and official sources, and great pains has been taken to make it correct in every particular.

In presenting the work to the public, the Author trusts it will be found very useful as a book of reference to all, and especially to those, who may not have access, at all times, to large libraries, where the facts herein stated might be obtained, though not without much trouble.

It is essential to the very existence and duration of our Political Institutions, that the people take a lively interest in our public concerns. They should become thoroughly instructed in the Political History of the country; the Principles of the Government, the Character and Qualifications of the Candidates; and in this connection, we must not forget that a rumor does not prove a fact, a simple fact does not prove a theory, nor a mere *caricature*, in an illlustrated newspaper, prove a man to be either a simpleton, or a knave.

In a free government, like ours, there will naturally arise, at least two great and leading divisions. Men differently educated, and looking at questions from different standpoints, even retaining their integrity, will widely but honestly differ in their opinions on questions constantly arising; hence there ever will be Cliques, Parties, and Factions.

No Party or Faction should receive the continued confidence and support of an American Citizen, unless first, its principles are sound and correct, and second, unless it presents as its candidates to represent those principles, and to occupy its places of trust and emolument, honest, trust-worthy, and capable men.

# CONTENTS.

|  | Page. |
|---|---|
| OUR REPUBLIC | 15 |
| ITS PRESENT AREA, AND HOW ACQUIRED | 15 |
| ITS POPULATION AT EACH CENSUS PERIOD | 16 |
| TABLE OF POPULATION OF STATES AT DIFFERENT PERIODS | 17 |
| OUR REPUBLICAN GOVERNMENT | 18 |
| THE COLONIAL OR REVOLUTIONARY GOVERNMENT | 19 |
| DECLARATION OF INDEPENDENCE | 21 |
| COLONIAL GOVERNMENT UNDER THE CONFEDERATION | 27 |
| ARTICLES OF CONFEDERATION | 28 |
| SERIOUS DEFECTS IN THIS FORM OF GOVERNMENT | 39 |
| TABLE, SHOWING THE INEQUALITY OF REPRESENTATION | 40 |
| THE FOREIGN DEBT BEFORE THE CONSTITUTION | 41 |
| WHY, AND HOW THE CONSTITUTION WAS ADOPTED | 42 |
| GENERAL INDEX TO THE CONSTITUTION | 43 |
| CONSTITUTION OF THE UNITED STATES | 45 |
| AMENDMENTS TO THE CONSTITUTION | 69 |
| THE GOVERNMENT UNDER THE CONSTITUTION | 73 |
| WHEN RATIFIED BY THE ORIGINAL STATES | 73 |
| THE EXECUTIVE BRANCH OF THE GOVERNMENT | 75 |
| THE PRESIDENT AND VICE-PRESIDENT, HOW ELECTED | 75 |
| PRESIDENTIAL ELECTORS, HOW APPOINTED | 77 |
| TABLE OF APPORTIONMENT OF REPRESENTATIVES | 78 |
| ELECTORAL VOTE FOR NEXT PRESIDENTIAL ELECTION | 78 |
| THE CABINET COUNCIL | 79 |
| SECRETARIES OF DIFFERENT DEPARTMENTS | 79 |
| THEIR OFFICIAL DUTIES | 80 |
| THE LEGISLATIVE BRANCH OF THE GOVERNMENT | 81 |
| SENATE AND HOUSE OF REPRESENTATIVES | 81 |
| QUALIFICATIONS OF SENATORS AND REPRESENTATIVES | 81 |
| THE JUDICIAL DEPARTMENT OF THE GOVERNMENT | 82 |
| THE FEDERAL COURTS OF THE UNITED STATES | 82 |
| JUDGES OF FEDERAL COURTS, HOW APPOINTED | 83 |

## CONTENTS.

| | |
|---|---|
| TABLE, SHOWING SALARIES OF FEDERAL OFFICERS | 84 |
| PRESIDENTS OF THE CONTINENTAL CONGRESS | 84 |
| SIGNERS OF THE DECLARATION OF INDEPENDENCE | 85 |
| TABLE, GIVING TIME OF THEIR BIRTHS AND DEATHS | 85 |
| PRESIDENTS OF THE UNITED STATES | 86 |
| VICE-PRESIDENTS OF THE UNITED STATES | 86 |
| SECRETARIES OF STATE, AND OF THE TREASURY | 87 |
| SECRETARIES OF OTHER DEPARTMENTS | 88 |
| CHIEF JUSTICES OF THE U. S. SUPREME COURT | 89 |
| ASSOCIATE JUSTICES OF THE U. S. SUPREME COURT | 89 |
| SPEAKERS OF THE HOUSE OF REPRESENTATIVES | 90 |
| EXISTING GOVERNMENT OF THE UNITED STATES | 93 |
| NAMES OF DIFFERENT OFFICIALS | 93 |
| PRESENT SENATORS, DURATION OF TERM, &c | 95 |
| PRESENT REPRESENTATIVES, DURATION OF TERM, &c | 97 |
| GOVERNMENTS OF THE SEVERAL STATES | 101 |
| GOVERNORS OF THE SEVERAL STATES, AND THEIR SALARIES, &c | 101 |
| WHEN LEGISLATURES MEET—SESSIONS—STATE ELECTIONS | 102 |
| RESULTS AT THE LATEST STATE ELECTIONS | 103 |
| MAJORITIES ON JOINT BALLOT, IN THE SEVERAL LEGISLATURES | 107 |
| WASHINGTON'S ADMINISTRATION, CABINET, &c | 109 |
| FINANCIAL CONDITION OF THE COUNTRY | 109 |
| TABLE OF ANNUAL IMPORTS, EXPORTS, EXPENDITURES AND DEBT | 109 |
| BIOGRAPHICAL SKETCH OF GEORGE WASHINGTON | 110 |
| ADMINISTRATION OF JOHN ADAMS, AND CABINET | 114 |
| TABLE OF ANNUAL IMPORTS, EXPORTS, EXPENDITURES AND DEBT | 114 |
| BIOGRAPHICAL SKETCH OF JOHN ADAMS | 115 |
| JEFFERSON'S ADMINISTRATION, CABINET, &c | 118 |
| TABLE OF ANNUAL EXPORTS, IMPORTS, EXPENDITURES AND DEBT | 118 |
| BIOGRAPHICAL SKETCH OF THOMAS JEFFERSON | 119 |
| MADISON'S ADMINISTRATION, CABINET, &c | 122 |
| TABLE SHOWING THE FINANCIAL CONDITION OF THE COUNTRY | 122 |
| BIOGRAPHICAL SKETCH OF JAMES MADISON | 123 |
| MONROE'S ADMINISTRATION, CABINET, &c | 126 |
| TABLE SHOWING THE FINANCIAL CONDITION OF THE COUNTRY | 126 |
| BIOGRAPHICAL SKETCH OF JAMES MONROE | 127 |
| ADMINISTRATION OF JOHN QUINCY ADAMS, CABINET, &c | 130 |
| TABLE OF FINANCES, DEBT, &c | 130 |

## CONTENTS.

| | |
|---|---|
| Biographical Sketch of John Q. Adams. | 131 |
| Jackson's Administration, Cabinet, &c. | 134 |
| Table of Annual Expenditures, Debt, &c. | 134 |
| Biographical Sketch of Andrew Jackson | 135 |
| Van Buren's Aministration, Cabinet, &c | 140 |
| Table of Expenditures, Debt, &c. | 140 |
| Biographical Sketch of Martin Van Buren | 141 |
| Harrison's and Tyler's Administrations, Cabinets, &c | 144 |
| Table of Annual Expenditures, Debt, &c | 144 |
| Biographical Sketch of William H. Harrison | 145 |
| Biographical Sketch of John Tyler, | 147 |
| Administration of James K. Polk, Cabinet, &c. | 150 |
| Table of Annual Expenditures, Debt, &c. | 150 |
| Biographical Sketch of James K. Polk | 151 |
| Taylor's and Fillmore's Administrations. | 154 |
| Table of Annual Expenditures, Debt, &c | 154 |
| Biographical Sketch of Zachary Taylor | 155 |
| Biographical Sketch of Millard Fillmore | 157 |
| Administration of Franklin Pierce, Cabinet, &c. | 160 |
| Table, Showing Financial Condition of Country. | 160 |
| Biographical Sketch of Franklin Pierce. | 161 |
| Buchanan's Administration, Cabinet, &c. | 164 |
| Table of Annual Expenditures, Debt, &c | 164 |
| Biographical Sketch of James Buchanan | 165 |
| Lincoln's Administration, Cabinet, &c | 168 |
| Table of Expenditures, Debt, &c. | 168 |
| Biographical Sketch of Abraham Lincoln | 169 |
| Johnson's Administration, Cabinet, &c | 173 |
| Table of Annual Expenditures, Debt, &c | 173 |
| Biographical Sketch of Andrew Johnson | 174 |
| Grant's Administration, Cabinet, &c. | 177 |
| Financial Condition of the Country. | 177 |
| Biographical Sketch of Ulysses S. Grant | 178 |
| Electoral Vote for President and Vice-President, 1789–1797 | 184 |
| "          "          "          "          "          "          " 1797–1809 | 185 |
| "          "          "          "          "          "          " 1809–1817 | 186 |
| "          "          "          "          "          "          " 1817–1829 | 187 |
| "          "          "          "          "          "          " 1829–1841 | 188 |

ELECTORAL VOTE FOR PRESIDENT AND VICE-PRESIDENT, 1841-1853..189
      "      "    "    "    "    "    "    1853-1865..190
      "      "    "    "    "    "    "    1865-1877..191
TABLE OF THE POPULAR AND ELECTORAL VOTE OF 1876 BY STATES .192
BIOGRAPHICAL SKETCH OF RUTHERFORD B. HAYES...............193
BIOGRAPHICAL SKETCH OF WILLIAM A. WHEELER................197

# ILLUSTRATIONS.

|  | Page. |
|---|---|
| THE NATIONAL CAPITOL............FRONTISPIECE | |
| BILL OF CREDIT OR CONTINENTAL MONEY............ | 20 |
| INDEPENDENCE SQUARE—FACE PAGE............ | 21 |
| SEAL OF THE STATE DEPARTMENT............ | 80 |
| THE NATIONAL SENATE CHAMBER—FACE PAGE............ | 81 |
| HALL OF THE HOUSE OF REPRESENTATIVES—FACE PAGE............ | 100 |
| PORTRAIT OF GEORGE WASHINGTON............ | 110 |
| " " JOHN ADAMS............ | 115 |
| " " THOMAS JEFFERSON............ | 119 |
| " " JAMES MADISON............ | 123 |
| " " JAMES MONROE............ | 127 |
| " " JOHN Q. ADAMS............ | 131 |
| " " ANDREW JACKSON............ | 135 |
| " " MARTIN VAN BUREN............ | 141 |
| " " WILLIAM H. HARRISON............ | 145 |
| " " JOHN TYLER............ | 147 |
| " " JAMES K. POLK............ | 151 |
| " " ZACHARY TAYLOR............ | 155 |
| " " MILLARD FILMORE............ | 157 |
| " " FRANKLIN PIERCE............ | 161 |
| " " JAMES BUCHANAN............ | 165 |
| LINCOLN'S INAUGURATION—FACE PAGE............ | 268 |
| MEDAL FROM THE FRENCH DEMOCRATS............ | 170 |
| MEDAL TO MRS. LINCOLN............ | 171 |
| PORTRAIT OF ANDREW JOHNSON............ | 174 |
| " " ULYSSES S. GRANT............ | 178 |
| THE WHITE HOUSE FROM PENNSYLVANIA AVENUE—*Face Page*...... | 192 |
| PORTRAIT OF RUTHERFORD B. HAYES............ | 194 |
| " " WILLIAM A. WHEELER............ | 197 |

# INDEX.

## A

Area of the U. S., 15; Its growth, 16; Of the several States, 102.
Articles of Confederation, 28.
Amendments to the Constitution. 60, 71, 74.
Apportionment of Representatives 77, 78.
Attorneys—General, 80, 84, 89.
Arkansas, 17, 101, 102, 107.
Alabama, 17, 101, 102, 107.
Adams, John, Life of, 115—Cabinet, &c., 114. His Administration, 113.
Adams, John Q., Life of, 131—Cabinet &c., 130—His Administration, 129.

## B

Branches of the Government, 75, 81, 82.
Biographical Sketch of Washington, 110.
Biographical Sketch of John Adams, 115.
Biographical Sketch of Jefferson, 119.
Biographical Sketch of Madison, 123.
Biographical Sketch of Monroe, 125.
Biographical Sketch of J. Q. Adams, 131.
Biographical Sketch of Andrew Johnson, 135.
Biographical Sketch of Van Buren, 135.
Biographical Sketch of Harrison, 145.
Biographical Sketch of Tyler, 147.
Biographical Sketch of Polk, 151.
Biographical Sketch of Taylor, 155.
Biographical Sketch of Fillmore, 157.
Biographical Sketch of Pierce, 161.
Biographical Sketch of Buchanan, 165.
Biographical Sketch of Lincoln, 169.
Biographical Sketch of Johnson, 174.
Biographical Sketch of Grant, 178.
Buchanan, James, Life of. 165.

## C

Country—Its Growth and Population, 16, 17. Existing Government, 92.
Colonial Government, 19, 20.
Congress, Continental, 20. Presidents of, 84.

INDEX. xi

Confederation, Articles of, 28.
Confederate Government—Serious defects in, 39.
Convention of Delegates, to form Constitution, 42
Constitution of the United States, 43. Government under, 73. When Ratified by the States, 73. Amendments to, 45, 60, 71, 74.
Cabinet—Whom composed of, 79.
Cabinet of the Presidents, 109, 114, 118, 122, 126, 130, 134, 140, 144, 150, 154, 160, 164, 168, 173, 177.
Circuit Courts, U. S., 82. Supreme, 82, 93.
California, 17, 101, 102, 107.
Connecticut, 17, 101 102, 107.

**D**

Declaration of Independence, 21.
District Courts, U. S., 83.
District Court Judges, 83.
Delaware, 17, 101, 102, 104.

**E**

Executive branch of the Government, 75.
Electors, Presidential, 75.
Electors—How Appointed, 76.
Electoral Vote, 78, 184—191.
Existing Government, 93.
Elections, Latest State, 103—107.
Elections—When Held, 102. Presidential, 184—191.

Expenditures of the Government, 109, 114-118, 122, 126, 130, 134, 140, 144, 150, 154, 160, 164, 168, 173, 177.
Exports. See same pages as Expenditures.

**F**

Florida, 17, 101, 102, 105.

**G**

Government, Our Republican, 18.
Government, Colonial, 19. Serious Defects in, 39.
Government Under tne Constitution, 73. Existing, 93.
Government—Executive Branch, 75 Legislative Branch, 81, Judicial Branch, 82.
Government of the Several States, 101, 102.
Georgia, 17, 101, 102, 105.
Governors of States, 101 ; When Appointed, Duration of Term, Salaries, &c., 101.
Grant, Ulysses S, Life of, 178 ; Cabinet, 177.

**H**

House of Representatives, 81, 91, 97.
Harrison, Wm. H., Life of, 145.
Hayes, Rutherford B., Life of, 193

**I**

Independence, Declaration of, 21.
Indebtedness of the Country in 1787, 41 : at different periods, 109, 114, 118, 122, 126, 130, 134, 140, 144, 150, 154, 160, 164, 168, 173, 177.
Interior, Secretary of, 80, 84, 89.
Illinois, 17, 101, 102, 106.

xii  INDEX.

Indiana, 17, 101, 102, 106.
Iowa, 17, 101, 102, 106.

## J

Justices, U. S. Courts, 83, 84, 89.
Judiciary, 82, 84, 89.
Joint Ballot, Majorities on, 103.
Jefferson, Thomas, Life of, 119; Cabinet, 118.
Jackson, Andrew, Life of, 135; Cabinet, 134.
Johnson, Andrew, Life of, 174; Cabinet, 173; Impeachment, 175.

## K

Kansas, 17, 102, 102, 107.
Kentucky, 17, 101, 102, 106.

## L

Legislative Branch of Government 81.
Louisiana, 17, 101, 102, 105.
Legislatures—When they Meet, 202.
Lincoln, Abraham, Life of, 169; Cabinet, 168; Death of, 171.

## M

Ministers, 84, 93, 94.
Ministers, Table of Foreign and Resident, 93.
Maine, 17, 101, 103.
Maryland, 17, 101, 102, 104.
Massachusetts, 17, 101, 102, 103.
Michigan, 17, 101, 102, 106.
Minnesota, 17, 101, 102, 107.
Mississippi, 17, 101 102 105

Missouri, 17, 101, 102, 107.
Madison, James, Life of, 123; Cabinet, &c., 122.
Monroe, James, Life of, 127; Administration, 186.
Medal from French Democrats, to Mrs. Lincoln, 170, 171.

## N

National Constitution, 73.
Navy, Secretary of 79; Salary, 84 Table of these Officers, 88.
Nebraska, 17, 101, 102, 107.
Nevada, 17, 101, 102, 107.
New Hampshire, 17, 101, 102, 103.
New Jersey, 17, 101, 102, 104.
New York, 17, 101, 102, 103.
North Carolina, 17, 101, 102, 105.

## O

Ohio, 17, 101, 102, 106.
Oregon, 17, 101, 102, 107.

## P

Population U S., a Census Period, 16, 17.
Population of the States, 17, 102.
Powers of the Government, 72.
President, 73, 84. Presidential Electors, 75, 76, 77, 78.
Postmaster General, 80, 84, 88.
Presidents Continental Congress, 84; List of, &c., 86; Salary, 84; Electoral Votes for, 184—191.
Pennsylvania, 17, 101, 102, 104.
Polk, James K, Life of, 151; Cabinet, 150.
Pierce, Franklin, Life of 161; Cabinet, 150.

## R

Republic, Our, 15.
Republican Government, 18
Representative Table, under Confederation, 40.
Representatives, Apportionment of, 78, 82; How Elected, 81; Qualifications, 81; Salaries, 81; Names of present, 97.
Rhode Island, 17, 101, 102, 103.
Returns, State Elections, 103-107. Presidential Elections, 184-191.

## S

Secretary of State, 79, 81, 87, 93.
Secretaries, Other, 79, 81, 87, 88, 93.
Salaries of Federal Officers, 84.
Senate, 81; Present Members, 95, 96.
Senators, Qualifications of, 81.
Senators—How Classified, 81.
Supreme Court, U. S., 82, 84, 89.
Signers Declaration Independence, 85.
Speakers House Representatives, 90-92.
States, Government of, 101, 102.
State Elections, Results of, 103-107; Time of, 102.
South Carolina, 17, 101, 103, 105.

## T

Treasury, Secretary of, 79; Salary, 84.
Table of Secretaries, 87, 88, 89.
Tennessee, 17, 62, 103, 106.
Texas, 17. 101. 102, 105.
Tyler, John, 147; Cabinet, &c., 144.
Taylor, Zachary, Life of, 155.

## U

United States, Population, 16, 17.

## V

Vice-President—Qualifications and How Elected, 75; His Duties, 75; Salary, 84; Table of Vice-Presidents, 86.
Vermont, 17, 101, 102, 103.
Virginia, 17, 101, 102, 104.
Van Buren, Martin, Life of 141; Cabinet, 140.

## W

War, Secretary of, 79; Salary, 84; Table of these Officers, 88.
West Virginia, 17, 101, 102, 104.
Wisconsin, 17, 101, 102, 106.
Washington, George, Biograpical Sketch, 110; His Cabinet and Administration, 190.
Wheeler, Wm. A., Life of, 197

# OUR REPUBLIC.

The United States of America, is a Confederation of Sovereign States, and lies in the middle portion of the Western Hemisphere, extending westward to the Pacific Ocean. Its greatest breadth from east to west is about 3,000 miles, and it has a coast line of 2,163 miles on the Atlantic, 1764 miles on the Gulf of Mexico, and 1,343 miles on the Pacific, embracing an area of 3,578,372 square miles.

In 1782, the Territories of the Confederation extended westward to the Mississippi, and northward to the great Lakes, giving a total area of about 800,000 square miles, but by large acquisitions since made, it has reached its present size.

ITS PRESENT AREA HAS BEEN ACQUIRED AS FOLLOWS:

| | |
|---|---|
| Territory ceded by England in 1783, | 815,615 Square miles. |
| Louisiana, as acquired from France in 1803, | 930,928 " " |
| Florida as acquired from Spain in 1821, | 59,268 " " |
| Texas as admitted to the Union in 1845, | 237,504 " " |
| Oregon by treaty in 1846, | 280,425 " " |
| California taken from Mexico in 1847, | 649,762 " " |
| Arizona from Mexico by treaty in 1854, | 27,500 " " |
| Alaska from Russia by treaty in 1867, | 577,390 " " |
| Total present Area, | 3,578,392 Square miles. |

The increase of the population, and the rapid growth and development of the country have been truly wonderful. In 1620 there were but 300 white settlers in New England. Less than 250 years ago, New York City was made up of a dozen log-cabins, and all the land now comprising the City and County of New York, was purchased for the small pittance of twenty-four dollars.

Fifty years since, there were less than 5,000 white people in the vast region between Lake Michigan and the Pacific Ocean, while the population now exceeds 10,000,000. Chicago was then a mere trading-post of half a dozen huts.

Sixty-five years ago, those immense lakes, Ontario, Michigan, Huron, and Superior, were entirely without commerce, and an Indian's canoe was about the only craft seen upon them; but now, they are crowded thoroughfares, and the value of the traffic upon these waters, and navigable rivers, is not much less than nine hundred millions of dollars per annum.

A few years since San Francisco was Mexican territory, with a handful of wild people and almost unknown. She sprang as if by magic into existence, and in the space of two years her population increased from 1,500 to nearly 60,000. One hundred years ago, we were but thirteen feeble Colonies, with but 3,000,000 of inhabitants, while we now comprise 38 free, sovereign, and independent States, having in addition, the District of Columbia and 10 territories, with a population of about 40,000,000 of inhabitants.

THE FOLLOWING TABLE WILL SHOW THE POPULATION OF THE COUNTRY, AT THE DIFFERENT CENSUS PERIODS, SINCE, AND INCLUDING 1790.

| Census Years. | Whites. | Free Colored. | Slaves. | Total. |
|---|---|---|---|---|
| 1790 | 3,172,464 | 59,466 | 697,897 | 3,929,827 |
| 1800 | 4,304,489 | 108,395 | 893,057 | 5,305,941 |
| 1810 | 5,862,004 | 186,446 | 1,191,364 | 7,239,814 |
| 1820 | 7,866,369 | 233,524 | 1,538,008 | 9,638,191 |
| 1830 | 10,532,060 | 319,599 | 2,009,043 | 12,866,020 |
| 1840 | 14,189,705 | 386,292 | 2,487,356 | 17,069,453 |
| 1850 | 19,629,738 | 428,661 | 3,204,089 | 23,263,488 |
| 1860 | 26,957,171 | 532,000 | 3,953,790 | 31,443,521 |
| 1870 | 33,586,989 | 4,880,009 | | *38,555,983 |

*This total includes 63,254 Chinese and 25,731 Indians.

## POPULATION OF THE UNITED STATES,
ACCORDING TO THE CENSUS OF
### 1840, 1850, 1860 & 1870.

| States and Territories. | 1840. | 1850. | 1860. | 1870. |
|---|---|---|---|---|
| Alabama | 590,756 | 771,623 | 964,201 | 996,992 |
| Arkansas | 97,574 | 209,897 | 435,450 | 484,471 |
| California | ............ | 92,597 | 379,994 | 560,247 |
| Connecticut | 309,978 | 370,792 | 460,147 | 537,454 |
| Delaware | 78,085 | 91,532 | 112,216 | 125,015 |
| Florida | 54,477 | 87,445 | 140,424 | 187,748 |
| Georgia | 691,392 | 906,185 | 1,057,286 | 1,184,109 |
| Illinois | 476,183 | 851,470 | 1,711,951 | 2,539,891 |
| Indiana | 685,866 | 988,416 | 1,350,428 | 1,680,637 |
| Iowa | 43,112 | 192,214 | 674,913 | 1,191,792 |
| Kansas | ............ | ............ | 107,206 | 364,399 |
| Kentucky | 779,828 | 982,405 | 1,155,684 | 1,321,011 |
| Louisiana | 352,411 | 517,762 | 708,002 | 726,915 |
| Maine | 501,793 | 583,169 | 628,279 | 626,915 |
| Maryland | 470,019 | 583,034 | 687,049 | 780,894 |
| Massachusetts | 737,699 | 994,514 | 1,231,066 | 1,457,351 |
| Michigan | 212,267 | 397,654 | 749,113 | 1,184,059 |
| Minnesota | ............ | 6,077 | 172,023 | 439,706 |
| Mississippi | 375,651 | 606,526 | 791,305 | 827,922 |
| Missouri | 383,702 | 682,044 | 1,182,012 | 1,721,295 |
| Nebraska | ............ | ............ | 28,841 | 122,993 |
| Nevada | ............ | ............ | 6,857 | 42,491 |
| New Hampshire | 284,574 | 317,976 | 326,073 | 318,300 |
| New Jersey | 373,306 | 489,555 | 672,035 | 906,096 |
| New York | 2,428,921 | 3,097,394 | 3,880,735 | 4,382,759 |
| North Carolina | 753,419 | 869,039 | 992,622 | 1,071,361 |
| Ohio | 1,519,467 | 1,980,329 | 2,339,511 | 2,665,260 |
| Oregon | ............ | 13,294 | 52,465 | 90,923 |
| Pennsylvania | 1,724,033 | 2,311,786 | 2,906,215 | 3,521,791 |
| Rhode Island | 108,830 | 147,545 | 174,620 | 217,353 |
| South Carolina | 594,398 | 668,507 | 703,708 | 705,606 |
| Tennessee | 829,210 | 1,002,717 | 1,109,801 | 1,258,520 |
| Texas | ............ | 212,592 | 604,215 | 818,579 |
| Vermont | 291,948 | 314,120 | 315,098 | 330,551 |
| Virginia | 1,239,797 | 1,421,661 | 1,596,318 | 1,225,163 |
| West Virginia | ............ | ............ | ............ | 442,014 |
| Wisconsin | 30,945 | 305,391 | 775,881 | 1,054,670 |
| **Total States** | **17,019,641** | **23,067,262** | **31,183,744** | **38,113,253** |
| Arizona | ............ | ............ | ............ | 9,658 |
| Colorado | ............ | ............ | 34,277 | 39,864 |
| Dakota | ............ | ............ | 4,837 | 14,181 |
| District of Columbia | 43,712 | 51,687 | 75,080 | 131,700 |
| Idaho | ............ | ............ | ............ | 14,999 |
| Montana | ............ | ............ | ............ | 20,595 |
| New Mexico | ............ | 61,547 | 93,516 | 91,874 |
| Utah | ............ | 11,380 | 40,273 | 86,786 |
| Washington | ............ | ............ | 11,594 | 23,955 |
| Wyoming | ............ | ............ | ............ | 9,118 |
| Seamen in U.S. Service | 6,100 | ............ | ............ | ............ |
| **Totals** | **17,069,453** | **23,191,876** | **31,443,321** | **38,555,983** |

# OUR REPUBLICAN GOVERNMENT.

The Government of the United States is the result of deep research, cool and calm deliberation, of great wisdom and sound judgment, and is probably the best ever formed by man.

It was not brought about in a hurried manner, nor did it spring into existence, by reason of a combination of unforeseen and fortuituos circumstances, which aroused the passions of the multitude, and led them to adopt a Republican Government more tyrannical than tyranny itself.

Our government was based upon truth and justice, and the object of it was to establish justice, insure domestic tranquillity, provide for the common defence, promote the general welfare, and to secure the blessings of liberty to ourselves and posterity.

The government and constitution being purely Democratic, the People are the Sovereigns. How much is expressed in those three words, "WE, THE PEOPLE;" that is, We, the Sovereigns; We, the Rulers; We, the Law-Givers; how expressive of majesty and power, and how insignificant do they make Kings and tyrants appear. The President, Vice President, Senators, Legislators, and all other officials are the *mere agents* and *servants* of "We, the People," for they were created by, and for the people, and not the people for them. Whatever of power, whatever of authority, whatever of dignity they possess in their official stations, was delegated to them by the Sovereign People for the honor, prosperity, and happiness of the people themselves.

What government, or constitution could be devised, more perfect than that, which puts it in the power of those who suffer from an unprincipled government officer, or from the effects of a mal-administration, to remove such, or prevent their continuance, not by rash, passionate, and unlawful acts as in ancient republics, but by such as are rational, deliberate, and constitutional. This could not be done under a tyrannical, despotic, or monarchial government, because the crown and scepter are hereditary.

# THE COLONIAL
## OR
# REVOLUTIONARY GOVERNMENT.

As early as October 1765, soon after the first encroachment had been made by the British Government upon our liberties, by the passage of the Stamp Act, a congress of delegates from the Colonies of Massachusetts, Rhode Island, Connecticut, New York, New Jersey, Pennsylvania, Delaware, Maryland, and South Carolina, assembled in New York, and adopted a DECLARATION OF RIGHTS, asserting that the sole power of taxation resided in the Colonial Jegislatures, and that the restrictions imposed upon them by the late acts of Parliament, were unjust and burdensome. An address to the King, and a petition to each house of Parliament were adopted.

Subsequently, on the 4th day of September, 1774, a congress of delegates from all the Colonies excepting Georgia, assembled at Philadelphia, "with authority and direction to meet and consult together for the common welfare." Thus was organized by the people, acting in their sovereign capacity, the first general, or National Government.

The first, and most important of their acts, was a declaration, that in determining questions which should arise in this Congress, *each Colony should have one vote.* They also passed a series of resolutions declaratory of their rights, and appointed a committee to examine into their rights and grievances.

This Continental Congress was continued during the revolutionary war, but finally it was superseded by the government formed under the Articles of Confederation. It was invested by the people with large discretionary powers, such as superintending the affairs of the Union, organizing an army, regulating the land and naval forces, issuing bills of credit known as Continental money, contracting debts, and otherwise assuming all the prerogatives of an Independent Sovereignty.

A BILL OF CREDIT, OR CONTINENTAL MONEY.

INDEPENDENCE SQUARE.

# DECLARATION OF INDEPENDENCE.

[On Thursday the 4th day of July, 1776, Congress being in session in the great hall of the venerable State House, located in Independence Square, in Philadelphia, Benjamin Harrison of Virginia, reported that the committee appointed for that purpose had agreed to a declaration which they desired him to present, and which, having been read, was agreed to as follows :—]

## A DECLARATION

BY THE REPRESENTATIVES OF THE UNITED STATES OF AMERICA, IN CONGRESS ASSEMBLED.

When, in the course of human events, it becomes necessary for one people to dissolve the political bands which have connected them with another, and to assume, among the powers of the earth, the separate and equal station to which the laws of nature and of nature's God entitle them, a decent respect to the opinions of mankind requires that they should declare the causes which impel them to the separation.

We hold these truths to be self-evident, that all men are created equal; that they are endowed by their Creator with certain unalienable rights; that among these are life, liberty, and the pursuit of happiness. That to secure these rights, governments are instituted among men, deriving their just powers from the consent of the governed; that, whenever any form of government becomes destructive of these ends, it is the right of the people to alter or to abolish it, and to institute a new government, laying its foundation on such principles, and organizing its powers in such form, as to them shall seem most likely to effect their safety and happiness. Prudence, indeed, will dictate that governments long established, should not be changed for light and transient causes; and accordingly, all experience hath shown, that mankind are more disposed to suffer, while evils are sufferable, than to right themselves by abolishing the forms to which the are accustomed. But, when a long train of abuses and usurpations, pursuing invariably the same object, evinces a design to reduce them under absolute despotism, it is their right, it is their duty, to throw off such government, and to provide new guards for their future security. Such has been the patient sufferance of these colonies, and such is now the necessity which constrains them to alter their former systems of government. The history of the present King of Great Britain is a history of repeated injuries and usurpations, all having, in direct object, the establishment of an absolute tyranny over these states. To prove this, let facts be submitted to a candid world:

He has refused his assent to laws the most wholesome and necessary for the public good.

He has forbidden his Governors to pass laws of immediate and pressing importance, unless suspended in their operation till his assent should be obtained; and when so suspended, he has utterly neglected to attend to them.

He has refused to pass other laws for the accommodation of large districts of people, unless those people would relinquish the right of representation in the legislature; a right inestimable to them, and formidable to tyrants only.

He has called together legislative bodies at places unusual, uncomfortable, and distant from the depository of their public records, for the sole purpose of fatiguing them into compliance with his measures.

He has dissolved representative houses repeatedly, for opposing, with manly firmness, his invasions on the rights of the people.

He has refused, for a long time after such dissolutions, to cause others to be elected; whereby the legislative powers, incapable of annihilation, have returned to the people at large for their exercise; the state remaining, in the mean time, exposed to all the danger of invasion from without, and convulsions within.

He has endeavored to prevent the population of these states; for that purpose, obstructing the laws for naturalization of foreigners; refusing to pass others to encourage their migration hither, and raising the conditions of new appropriations of lands.

He has obstructed the administration of justice, by refusing his assent to laws for establishing judiciary powers.

He has made judges dependent on his will alone, for the tenure of their offices, and the amount and payment of their salaries.

He has erected a multitude of new offices, and sent hither swarms of officers to harass our people, and eat out their substance.

He has kept among us, in times of peace, standing armies, without the consent of our legislature.

He has affected to render the military independent of, and superior to, the civil power.

He has combined, with others, to subject us to a jurisdiction foreign to our constitution, and unacknowledged by our laws; giving his assent to their acts of pretended legislation;

For quartering large bodies of armed troops among us;

For protecting them, by a mock trial, from punishment, for any murders which they should commit on the inhabitants of these states;

For cutting off our trade with all parts of the world;

For imposing taxes on us without our consent;

For depriving us, in many cases, of the benefits of trial by jury,

For transporting us beyond seas to be tried for pretended offences;

For abolishing the free system of English laws in a neighboring province, establishing therein an arbitrary government and enlarging its boundaries, so as to render it at once an example and fit instrument for introducing the same absolute rule into these colonies;

For taking away our charters, abolishing our most valuable laws, and altering, fundamentally, the powers of our governments;

For suspending our own legislatures, and declaring themselves invested with power to legislate for us in all cases whatsoever.

He has abdicated government here, by declaring us out of his protection, and waging war against us.

He has plundered our seas, ravaged our coasts, burnt our towns, and destroyed the lives of our people.

He is, at this time, transporting large armies of foreign mercenaries to complete the works of death, desolation, and tyranny, already begun, with circumstances of cruelty and perfidy scarcely paralleled in the most barbarous ages, and totally unworthy the head of a civilized nation.

He has constrained our fellow-citizens, taken captive on the high seas, to bear arms against their country, to become the executions of their friends and brethren, or to fall themselves by their hands.

He has excited domestic insurrections amongst us, and has endeavored to bring on the inhabitants of our frontiers, the merciless Indian savages, whose known rule of warfare is an undistinguished destruction, of all ages, sexes, and conditions.

In every stage of these oppressions, we have petitioned for redress, in the most humble terms: our repeated petitions have been answered only by repeated injury. A prince, whose character is thus marked by every act which may define a tyrant, is unfit to be the ruler of a free people.

Nor have we been wanting in attention to our British brethren. We have warned them, from time to time, of attempts made by their legislature to extend an unwarrantable jurisdiction over us. We have reminded them of the circumstances of our emigration and settlement here. We have appealed to their native justice and magnanimity, and we have conjured them, by the ties of our common kindred, to disavow these usurpations, which would inevitably interrupt our connections and correspondence. They, too, have been deaf to the voice of justice and consanguinity. We must, therefore, acquiesce in the necessity, which denounces our separation, and hold them, as we hold the rest of mankind, enemies in war—in peace, friends.

We, therefore, the Representatives of the UNITED STATES OF AMERICA, in GENERAL CONGRESS assembled, appealing to the Supreme Judge of the World for the rectitude of our intentions, do, in the name, and by the authority of the good people of these Colonies, solemnly publish and declare, That these United Colonies are, and of right ought to be, FREE AND INDEPENDENT STATES; that they are absolved from all allegiance to the British crown, and that all political connection between them and the State of Great Britain, is, and ought to be, totally dissolved; and that, as *FREE AND INDEPENDENT STATES*, they have full power to levy war, conclude peace, contract alliances, establish commerce, and to do all other acts and things which INDEPENDENT STATES may of right do. And, for the support of this Declaration, with a firm reliance on the protection of DIVINE PROVIDENCE, we mutually pledge to each other, our lives, our fortunes, and our sacred honor.

The foregoing Declaration was, by order of Congress, engrossed, and signed by the following members:

JOHN HANCOCK.

*New Hampshire*
JOSIAH BARTLETT,
WILLIAM WHIPPLE,
MATTHEW THORNTON.

*Rhode Island*
STEPHEN HOPKINS,
WILLIAM ELLERY,

*Connecticut.*
ROGER SHERMAN,
SAMUEL HUNTINGTON
WILLIAM WILLIAMS,
OLIVER WOLCOTT.

*New York.*
WILLIAM FLOYD,

PHILIP LIVINGSTON,
FRANCIS LEWIS,
LEWIS MORRIS.

*New Jersey.*
RICHARD STOCKTON,
JOHN WITHERSPOON,
FRANCIS HOPKINSON,
JOHN HART,
ABRAHAM CLARK.

*Pennsylvania.*
ROBERT MORRIS,
BENJAMIN RUSH,
BENJAMIN FRANKLIN,
JOHN MORTON,
GEORGE CLYMER,
JAMES SMITH,
GEORGE TAYLOR,
JAMES WILSON,
GEORGE ROSS.

*Massachusetts Bay.*
SAMUEL ADAMS,
JOHN ADAMS,
ROBERT TREAT PAINE,
ELBRIDGE GERRY.

*Delaware.*
CÆSAR RODNEY,
GEORGE READ,
THOMAS M'KEAN.

*Maryland.*
SAMUEL CHASE,
WILLIAM PACA,
THOMAS STONE,
CHARLES CARROLL, of Carrollton.

*Virginia.*
GEORGE WYTHE,
RICHARD HENRY LEE,
THOMAS JEFFERSON,
BENJAMIN HARRISON,
THOMAS NELSON, JUN.
FRANCIS LIGHTFOOT LEE,
CARTER BRAXTON.

*North Carolina.*
WILLIAM HOOPER,
JOSEPH HEWES,
JOHN PENN.

*South Carolina.*
EDWARD RUTLEDGE,
THOMAS HEYWARD, JUN.
THOMAS LYNCH, JUN.
ARTHUR MIDDLETON.

*Georgia.*
BUTTON GWINNENT,
LYMAN HALL,
GEORGE WALTON.

[The original document containing the autographs of these venerated patriots, is carefully preserved in a glass case in the rooms of the *National Institute* at Washington. Charles Carroll, the last survivor of this noble band, departed this life in 1832 at the age of ninety years.]

# COLONIAL GOVERNMENT

## UNDER THE ARTICLES OF CONFEDERATION.

In July 1775, previous to the Declaration of Independence, Dr. Franklin submitted to the consideration of Congress, a draft of confederation between the Colonies, but no action thereon seems to have been taken.

On the 11th day of June 1776, it was resolved by Congress, that a committee should be appointed, to prepare the form of a confederation to be entered into between the Colonies, and the next day a committee was appointed, which consisted of one member from each Colony. A report was thereafter made, and the subject from time to time debated, until the 15th of November 1777 when it was finally agreed to.

These Articles however, were to be submitted to the legislatures of the States, and would not become conclusive until ratified by all the States through their delegates in Congress. Maryland for a long time positively refused the ratification, but finally was induced to do so, and her delegates signed the articles on the 1st of March 1781, more than four years after Congress had submitted the same to the States. On the 2d of March Congress assembled under its new powers.

[On the 9th of July, 1778, the Articles were signed by the delegates of New Hampshire, Massachusetts Bay, Rhode Island, Connecticut, New York, Pennsylvania, Virginia, and South Carolina. The ratification of New York was conditional that all the other States should ratify.

The delegates from North Carolina signed the Articles on the 21st of July, 1778; those of Georgia on the 24th of same month; those of New Jersey, November 26th., 1778 ; those of Delaware, on the 22d. of February and 5th. of May, 1779 ; and those of Maryland, March 1st., 1781.]

# ARTICLES OF CONFEDERATION.

ARTICLES OF CONFEDERATION AND PERPETUAL UNION

*Between the States of New Hampshire, Massachusetts Bay, Rhode Island and Providence Plantations, Connecticut, New York, New Jersey, Pennsylvania, Delaware, Maryland, Virginia, North Carolina, South Carolina, and Georgia.*

Art. 1. The style of this confederacy shall be, "*The United States of America.*"

Art. 2. Each State retains its sovereignty, freedom, and independence, and every power, jurisdiction, and right, which is not by this confederation expressly delegated to the United States in Congress assembled.

Art. 3. The said States hereby severally enter into a firm league of friendship with each other, for their common defence, the security of their liberties, and their mutual and general welfare, binding themselves to assist each other against all force offered to, or attacks made upon them, or any of them, on account of religion, sovereignty, trade, or any other pretence whatever.

Art. 4. § 1. The better to secure and perpetuate mutual friendship and intercourse among the people of the different states in this union, the free inhabitants of each of these States, —paupers, vagabonds, and fugitives from justice excepted—shall be entitled to all privileges and immunities of free citizens in the several States; and the people of each State shall have free ingress and egress to and from any other State, and shall enjoy therein all the privileges of trade and commerce, subject to the same duties, impositions, and restrictions, as the inhabitants thereof respectively; provided, that such restrictions shall not extend so far as to prevent the removal of property imported into any State, to any other state, of which the owner is an inhabitant; provided also, that no imposition, duties, or restriction, shall be laid by any State on the property of the United States, or either of them.

§ 2. If any person, guilty of, or charged with treason, felony, or other high misdemeanor, in any State, shall flee from justice, and be found in any of the United States, he shall, upon the demand of the Governor or Executive power of the State from which he fled, be delivered up and removed to the State having jurisdiction of his offence.

§ 3. Full faith and credit shall be given, in each of these States, to the records, acts, and judicial proceedings of the courts and magistrates of every other State.

Art. 5. § 1. For the more convenient management of the general interests of the United States, delegates shall be annually appointed in such manner as the legislature of each State shall direct, to meet in Congress on the first Monday in November in every year, with a power reserved to each State to recall its delegates, or any of them, at any time within the year, and to send others in their stead, for the remainder of the year.

§ 2. No State shall be represented in Congress by less than two, nor more than seven members; and no person shall be capable of being a delegate for more than three years, in any term of six years; nor shall any person, being a delegate, be capable of holding any office under the United States, for which he, or any other for his benefit, receives any salary, fees, or emolument, of any kind.

§ 3. Each State shall maintain its own delegates in a meeting of the States, and while they act as members of the committee of these States.

§ 4. In determining questions in the United States in Congress assembled, each State shall have one vote.

§ 5. Freedom of speech and debate in Congress shall not be impeached or questioned in any court or place out of Congress, and the members of Congress shall be protected in their persons from arrests and imprisonments during the time of their going to and from, and attendance on Congress, except for treason, felony, or breach of the peace.

Art. 6. § 1. No State, without the consent of the United

States in Congress assembled, shall send any embassy to, or receive any embassy from, or enter into any conference, agreement, alliance, or treaty with any king, prince, or State, nor shall any person holding any office of profit, or trust under the United States, or any of them, accept of any present, emolument, office, or title, of any kind whatever, from any king, prince, or foreign State; nor shall the United States in Congress assembled, or any of them, grant any title of nobility.

§ 2. No two or more States shall enter into any treaty, confederation, or alliance whatever, between them, without the consent of the United States in Congress assembled, specifying accurately the purposes for which the same is to be entered into, and how long it shall continue.

§ 3. No State shall lay any imposts or duties which may interfere with any stipulations in treaties entered into by the United States, in Congress assembled, with any king, prince, or State, in pursuance of any treaties already proposed by Congress to the courts of France and Spain.

§ 4. No vessels of war shall be kept up in time of peace by any State, except such number only as shall be deemed necessary by the Untied States in Congress assembled, for the defence of such State, or its trade; nor shall any body of forces be kept up by any State, in time of peace, except such number only as, in the judgment of the United States in Congress assembled, shall be deemed requisite to garrison the forts necessary for the defence of such State; but every State shall always keep up a well regulated and diciplined militia, sufficiently armed and accoutered, and shall provide and constantly have ready for use, in public stores, a due number of field-pieces and tents, and a proper quantity of arms, ammunition, and camp equipage.

§ 5. No State shall engage in any war without the consent of the United States in Congress assembled, unless such State be actually invaded by enemies, or shall have received certain advice of a resolution being formed by some nation of Indians to invade such State, and the danger is so imminent as not to admit of delay till the United States in Congress assembled can be consulted; nor shall any State grant commissions to any ships or vessels of war, nor letters of marque or reprisal, except it be after a declaration of war by the United States in Congress assembled, and then only against the kingdom or State, and the subjects thereof, against which, war has been so declared, and under such regulations as shall be established by the United States in Congress assembled, unless such State be infested by pirates, in which case vessels of war may be fitted out for that occasion, and kept so long as the danger shall continue, or until the United States in Congress assembled shall determine otherwise.

Art. 7. When land forces are raised by any State for the common defence, all officers of or under the rank of colonel, shall be appointed by the legislature of each State respectively by whom such forces shall be raised, or in such manner as such State shall direct, and all vacancies shall be filled up by the State which first made the appointment.

Art. 8. All charges of war, and all other expenses that shall be incurred for the common defence or general welfare, and allowed by the United States in Congress assembled, shall be defrayed out of a common treasury, which shall be supplied by the several States, in proportion to the value of all land within each State, granted to or surveyed for any person, as such land and the buildings and improvements thereon shall be estimated, according to such mode as the United States in Congress assembled shall, from time to time, direct and appoint. The taxes for paying that proportion shall be laid and levied by the authority and direction of the legislatures of the several States within the time agreed upon by the United States in Congress assembled.

Art. 9. § 1. The United States in Congress assembled shall have the sole and exclusive right and power of determining on peace and war, except in the cases mentioned in the sixth Article, of sending and receiving ambassadors; entering into treaties and alliances, provided that no treaty of commerce shall be made, whereby the legislative power of the respective States shall be restrained from imposing such imposts and duties on foreigners, as their own people are subjected to, or from prohibiting the exportation or importation of any species of goods or commodities whatsoever; of establishing rules for deciding in all cases what captures on land or water shall be legal, and in what manner prizes taken by land or naval forces in the service of the United States shall be divided or appropriated; of granting letters of marque and reprisal in times of peace; appointing courts for the trial of piracies and felonies committed on the high seas; and establishing courts for receiving and determining finally appeals in all cases of capture; provided that no member of Congress shall be appointed a judge of any of the said courts.

§ 2. The United States in Congress assembled shall also be the last resort on appeal in all disputes and differences now subsisting, or that may hereafter arise between two or more States concerning boundary, jurisdiction, or any other cause whatever; which authority shall always be exercised in the manner following: Whenever the legislative or executive authority or lawful agent of any State in controversy with another, shall present a petition to Congress, stating the matter in question, and praying for a hearing, notice thereof shall be given by order of Congress to the legislative or executive authority of the other State in controversy, and a day assigned for the appearance of the parties by their lawful agents, who shall then be directed to appoint, by joint consent, commissioners or judges to constitute a court for hearing and determining the matter in question; but if they cannot agree, Congress shall name three persons out of each of the United States, and from the list of such persons each party shall alternately strike out one, the petioners beginning, until the number shall be reduced to thirteen; and from that number not less than seven, nor more than nine names, as Congress shall direct, shall, in the presence of Congress, be drawn out by lot; and the persons whose names shall be so drawn, or any five of them, shall be commissioners or judges, to hear and finally determine the controversy, so always as a major part of the judges, who shall hear the cause, shall agree in the determination: and if either party shall neglect to attend at the day appointed, without showing reasons which Congress shall judge sufficient, or being present, shall refuse to strike, the Congress shall proceed to nominate three persons out of each State, and the secretary of Congress shall strike in behalf of such party absent or refusing; and the judgment and sentence of the court, to be appointed in the manner before prescribed, shall be final and conclusive; and if any of the parties shall refuse to submit to the authority of such court, or to appear or defend their claim or cause, the court shall nevertheless proceed to pronounce sentence, or judgment, which shall in like manner be final and decisive; the judgment or sentence and other proceedings being in either case transmitted to Congress, and lodged among the acts of Congress, for the security of the parties concerned: provided, that every commissioner, before he sits in judgment, shall take an oath, to be administered by one of the judges of the Supreme or Superior court of the State where the cause shall be tried, "well and truly to hear and determine the matter in question, according to the best of his judgment, without favor, affection, or hope of reward." Provided, also, that no State shall be deprived of territory for the benefit of the United States.

§ 3. All controversies concerning the private right of soil claimed under different grants of two or more States, whose jurisdiction, as they may respect such lands, and the States which passed such grants are adjusted, the said grants or either of them being at the same time claimed to have originated antecedent to such settlement of jurisdiction, shall, on the petition of either party to the Congress of the United States, be finally determined, as near as may be, in the same manner as is before prescribed for deciding disputes respecting territorial jurisdiction between different States.

§ 4. The United States in Congress assembled shall also have the sole and exclusive right and power of regulating the alloy and value of coin struck by their own authority, or by that of the respective States; fixing the standard of weights and measures throughout the United States; regulating the trade, and managing all affairs with the Indians, not members of any of the States; provided that the legislative rights of any State, within its own limits, be not infringed or violated; establishing and regulating post offices from one State to another throughout all the United States, and exacting such postage on the papers passing through the same, as may be requisite to defray the expenses of the said office; appointing all officers of the land forces in the service of the United States, excepting regimental officers; appointing all the officers of the naval forces, and commissioning all officers whatever in the service of the United States; making rules for the government and regulation of the said land and naval forces, and directing their operations.

§ 5. The United States in Congress assembled shall have authority to appoint a committee to sit in the recess of Congress, to be denominated, "*A Committee of the States,*" and to consist of one delegate from each State; and to appoint such other committees and civil officers as may be necessary for managing the general affairs of the United States under their direction; to appoint one of their number to preside; provided that no person be allowed to serve in the office of President more than one year in any term of three years; to ascertain the necessary sums of money to be raised for the service of the United States, and to appropriate and apply the same for defraying the public expenses; to borrow money or emit bills on the credit of the United States, transmitting every half-year to the respective States an account of the sums of money so borrowed or emitted; to build and equip a navy;

to agree upon the number of land forces, and to make requisitions from each State for its quota, in proportion to the number of white inhabitants in such State, which requisition shall be binding; and thereupon the legislature of each State shall appoint the regimental officers, raise the men, clothe, arm, and equip them, in a soldier-like manner, at the expense of the United States; and the officers and men so clothed, armed, and equipped, shall march to the place appointed, and within the time agreed on by the United States in Congress assembled; but if the United States in Congress assembled shall, on consideration of circumstances, judge proper that any State should not raise men, or should raise a smaller number than its quota, and that any other State should raise a greater number of men than the quota thereof, such extra number shall be raised, officered, clothed, armed, and equipped in the same manner as the quota of such State, unless the legislature of such State shall judge that such extra number cannot be safely spared out of the same, in which case they shall raise, officer, clothe, arm, and equip, as many of such extra number as they judge can be safely spared, and the officers and men so clothed, armed, and equipped, shall march to the place appointed, and within the time agreed on by the United States in Congress assembled.

§ 6. The United States in Congress assembled shall never engage in a war, nor grant letters of marque and reprisal in time of peace, nor enter into any treaties or alliances, nor coin money, nor regulate the value thereof, nor ascertain the sums and expenses necessary for the defence and welfare of the United States, or any of them, nor emit bills, nor borrow money on the credit of the United States, nor appropriate money, nor agree upon the number of vessels of war to be built or purchased, or the number of land or sea forces to be raised, nor appoint a commander-in-chief of the army or navy, unless nine States assent to the same: nor shall a question on any other point, except for adjourning from day to day, be determined, unless by the votes of a majority of the United States in Congress assembled.

§ 7. The Congress of the United States shall have power to adjourn to any time within the year, and to any place within the United States, so that no period of adjournment be for a longer duration than the space of six months, and shall publish the journal of their proceedings monthly, except such parts thereof relating to treaties, alliances, or military operations, as in their judgment require secrecy; and the yeas and nays of the delegates of each State, on any question, shall be entered on the journal, when it is desired by any delegate; and the delegates of a State, or any of them, at his or their request, shall be furnished with a transcript of the said journal, except such parts as are above excepted, to lay before the legislatures of the several States.

Art. 10. The committee of the States, or any nine of them, shall be authorized to execute, in the recess of Congress, such of the powers of Congress as the United States, in Congress assembled, by the consent of nine States, shall, from time to time, think expedient to vest them with; provided that no power be delegated to the said committee, for the exercise of which, by the Articles of Confederation, the voice of nine States, in the Congress of the United States assembled, is requisite.

Art. 11. Canada acceding to this confederation, and joining in the measures of the United States, shall be admitted into and entitled to all the advantages of this Union: But no other colony shall be admitted into the same, unless such admission be agreed to by nine States.

Art. 12. All bills of credit emitted, moneys borrowed, and debts contracted by or under the authority of Congress, before the assembling of the United States, in pursuance of the present confederation, shall be deemed and considered as a charge against the United States, for payment and satisfaction whereof the said United States and the public faith are hereby solemnly pledged.

Art. 13. Every State shall abide by the determination of the United States in Congress assembled, in all questions which by this confederation are submitted to them. And the Articles of this confederation shall be inviolably observed by every State, and the Union shall be perpetual; nor shall any alteration at any time hereafter be made in any of them; unless such alteration be agreed to in a Congress of the United States, and be afterwards confirmed by the legislature of every State.

And whereas it hath pleased the great Governor of the world, to incline the hearts of the legislatures we respectively represent in Congress to approve of, and to authorize us to ratify the said Articles of Confederation and Perpetual Union, Know ye, that we, the undersigned delegates, by virtue of the power and authority to us given for that purpose, do by these presents, in the name and in behalf of our respective constituents, fully and entirely ratify and confirm each and every of the said Articles of Confederation and Perpetual Union, and all and singular the matters and things therein contained. And we do further solemnly plight and engage the faith of our respective constituents, that they shall abide by the determinations of the United States in Congress assembled, in all questions which by the said confederation are submitted to them; and that the articles thereof shall be inviolably observed by the States we respectively represent, and that the union shall be perpetual. In witness whereof, we have hereunto set our hands in Congress.

Done at Philadelphia, in the State of Pennsylvania, the 9th day of July, in the year of our Lord 1778, and in the third year of the Independence of America.

*New Hampshire*
JOSIAH BARTLETT,
JOHN WENTWORTH, jun.

*Massachusetts Bay*
JOHN HANCOCK,
SAMUEL ADAMS,

ELBRIDGE GERRY,
FRANCIS DANA,
JAMES LOVEL,
SAMUEL HOLTEN.
   *Rhode Island, &c.*
WILLIAM ELLERY,
HENRY MARCHANT,
JOHN COLLINS.
   *Connecticut.*
ROGER SHERMAN,
SAMUEL HUNTINGTON,
OLIVER WOLCOTT,
TITUS HOSMER,
ANDREW ADAMS.
   *New York.*
JAMES DUANE,
FRA. LEWIS,
WILLIAM DUER,
GOUV. MORRIS.
   *New Jersey.*
JNO. WITHERSPOON,
NATH. SCUDDER.
   *Pennsylvania.*
ROBERT MORRIS,
DANIEL ROBERDEAU,
JONA BAYARD SMITH,
WILLIAM CLINGAN,
JOSEPH REED.

   *Delaware.*
THOMAS M'KEAN,
JOHN DICKINSON,
NICHOLAS VAN DYKE.
   *Maryland.*
JOHN HANSON,
DANIEL CARROLL.
   *Virginia.*
RICHARD HENRY LEE,
JOHN BANISTER,
THOMAS ADAMS,
JNO. HARVIE,
FRANCIS LIGHTFOOT LEE.
   *North Carolina.*
JOHN PENN,
CONS. HARNETT,
JNO. WILLIAMS.
   *South Carolina.*
HENRY LAURENS,
WM. HENRY DRAYTON,
JNO. MATTHEWS,
RICHARD HUTSON,
THOS. HEYWARD, jun.
   *Georgia.*
JNO. WALTON,
EDWARD TELFAIR,
EDWARD LANGWORTHY.

# SERIOUS DEFECTS IN THIS FORM OF GOVERNMENT.

This confederation was formed in time of war, and under very unfavorable circumstances in many respects, hence upon trial, it soon became evident that the powers conferred upon the Continental Congress were inadequate to the legitimate objects of an effective national government. More especially was this manifested, when it became necessary to legislate upon matters relating to commerce and taxes.

There was a want of, or *deficiency of coercive power in Congress*. It had not the exclusive power to regulate commerce, to issue paper money, or to enforce the laws made, the rules adopted, or the orders given, and even several of the States began to exercise the sovereign, and absolute right of treating the recommendations of Congress with contempt.

By this political compact, the United States in Congress assembled had rights and powers, *without being able to enforce them*.

Another defect was in the mode of representation, which, before the adoption of the Constitution gave to each State an *equal share of power*, although some were ten times as important as others in population and value of property. The States had each an equal voice and share in the Union. The small State of Delaware for instance, had an equal vote and an equal influence in the National Council with Virginia, although Virginia had to pay for the support of the government, by reason of the number of its inhabitants and value of its property, nearly twelve times as much as Delaware.

The population of Delaware at this time was about 50,000 and its quota of taxes in requisition of Congress was $32,475, while Virginia had a population of 650,000 and its quota of taxes was $371,136. So also Rhode Island had a population of only 59,670, and her quota of taxes was only 46,764, while Massachusetts had a population of about 400,000, and her quota of taxes was $324,746, and yet their representatives and power in Congress were equal.

## REPRESENTATIVE TABLE.

### IN 1787, UNDER CONFEDERATION.

| | Population. | Quota of taxes in requisition of Congress. | Mean proportion of votes. | Number allowed in 1787. |
|---|---|---|---|---|
| New Hampshire, | 150,000 | $76,253 | 3 | 1 |
| Massachusetts, | 400,000 | 324,743 | 11 | 1 |
| Rhode Island, | 59,670 | 46,764 | 2 | 1 |
| Connecticut, | 192,000 | 191,133 | 6 | 1 |
| New York, | 250,000 | 185,567 | 7 | 1 |
| New Jersey, | 150,000 | 120,619 | 4 | 1 |
| Pennsylvania, | 300,000 | 296,908 | 9 | 1 |
| Delaware, | 50,000 | 32,475 | 1 | 1 |
| Maryland, | 320,000 | 204,775 | 7 | 1 |
| Virginia, | 650,000 | 371,136 | 14 | 1 |
| North Carolina, | 300,000 | 157,732 | 6 | 1 |
| South Carolina, | 225,000 | 139,017 | 5 | 1 |
| Georgia, | 56,000 | 23,288 | 1 | 1 |

 The original articles of confederation were found to be insufficient, and ineffectual in many other important particulars. Public credit could not be supported, collection of taxes could not be enforced, alliances could not be obtained, nor treaties preserved, and what was still more defective, hostilities between the States could not be prevented, nor insurrections among citizens.

 In the spring of 1787 the nation seemed to be on the verge of bankruptcy. Congress had previously made a requisition upon the several States, for money to support, and carry on the government but only a few had responded. New York had paid more than her quota, Pennsylvania nearly all of hers, Connecticut and Delaware about one third of their quota, but many had paid comparatively nothing. The interest both on the foreign and domestic debt was rapidly accumulating.

 The receipts of money paid into the federal treasury from Nov. 1st, 1781, to Nov. 1st, 1784, a period of three years was only $2,025,089.34 or about $642,000 per annum. For three years previous to 1787, the whole amount in specie paid into the federal treasury, did not exceed $1,400,000, being a little more than $400,000 per annum. The amount paid in, on these requisitions to carry on the government in 1786, was less than $200,000, and this came from two or three States; thus the receipts of the treasury were constantly decreasing, while the expenditures were increasing.

The foreign debt at this time was $7,000,000 and the interest coming due, and to be paid the early part of 1787, was as follows.

| | | |
|---|---|---|
| Interest on loans of the King of France, | | $240,740 |
| " | " Spanish loans about | 48,000 |
| " | " Dutch " " | 260,000 |
| " | Certificates and foreign officers | 22,000 |

In addition, there would fall due on principal sum and interest, payable during the year 1787, on French and Dutch loans, more than $1,000,000, making in the aggregate $1,600,000 to pay in 1787, and about $1,000,000 annually thereafter, (on an average) for the next ten years on said loans, and then about $300,000 annually, for the next ten years thereafter. In addition to this, there was a large domestic debt, upon which interest was accruing, and the indebtedness increasing.

This was indeed a dark hour for the new Republic. Congress was powerless; she could make requisitions on the several States, but could not compel the payment of a farthing. "The GREAT CRISIS HAD ARRIVED when the people of these United States, by whose will, and for whose benefit, the federal government was instituted had to decide whether they would support their rank as a nation by maintaining the PUBLIC FAITH at home and abroad, or whether for want of a timely exertion in establishing a GENERAL REVENUE, and thereby giving strength to the confederacy, they would hazard not only the existence of the UNION, but of those great and invaluable privileges, for which they have so arduously and so honorably contended."

Previous to this General Washington had addressed his circular letter to the Governors of the several States, urging them in the strongest language to comply with the requisition of Congress, and to preserve the public credit. Many of the States had attempted to do this, but they were impoverished by the continued drain on the people. The war had been long and expensive, the entire cost being estimated at *one hundred and thirty millions of dollars, exclusive of certain losses of forty millions more.*

By reason of this state of affairs in Febuary 1787 a resolution was offered in Congress, that on the second Monday of May following, a convention of delegates, who should be appointed by the several States be held at Philadelphia, for the sole purpose of revising the Articles of Confederation, and reporting to Congress, and the several legislatures, such alterations and provisions therein, as the exigencies of the government required

In May 1787, the delegates from all the States presented themselves, excepting from New Hampshire and Rhode Island. They were not represented. Washington was chosen president of the convention, and for upwards of four months it continued with closed doors, and it was not till August 6th, 1787, that the committee which had been appointed for that purpose reported a rough draft of the constitution, and finally on the 15th of September 1787, after a warm and lengthy debate, and after many amendments and revisions, a Constitution was adopted.

# CONSTITUTION OF THE UNITED STATES.

## ARTICLE I.

SECTION 1. Legislative powers; in whom vested.

SEC. 2. House of Representatives, how and by whom chosen—Qualifications of a Representative—Representatives and direct taxes, how apportioned—Census—Vacancies to be filled—Power of choosing officers, and of impeachment.

SEC. 3. Senators, how and by whom chosen—How classified—State Executive to make temporary appointments, in case, etc.—Qualifications of a Senator—President of the Senate, his right to vote—President *pro tem.*, and other officers of Senate, how chosen—Power to try impeachments—When President is tried, Chief Justice to preside—Sentence.

SEC. 4. Times, etc., of holding elections, how prescribed—One Session in each year.

SEC. 5. Membership—Quorum—Adjournments—Rules—Power to punish or expel—Journal—Time of adjournments limited, unless, etc.

SEC. 6. Compensation—Privileges—Disqualification in certain cases.

SEC. 7. House to originate all revenue bills—Veto—Bill may be passed by two-thirds of each house, notwithstanding, etc.—Bill not returned in ten days—Provision as to all orders, etc., except, etc.

SEC. 8. Powers of Congress.

SEC. 9. Provision as to migration or importation of certain persons—*Habeas Corpus*—Bills of attainder, etc.—Taxes, how apportioned—No export duty—No commercial preferences—No money drawn from treasury, unless, etc.—No titular nobility—Officers not to receive presents, unless, etc.

SEC. 10. States prohibited from the exercise of certain powers.

## ARTICLE II.

SECTION 1. President; his term of office — Electors of President; number and how appointed — Electors to vote on same day — Qualification of President — on whom his duties devolve in case of his removal, death, etc. — President's compensation — His oath.

SEC. 2. President to be commander-in-chief — He may require opinion of, etc., and may pardon — Treaty-making power — Nomination of certain officers — When President may fill vacancies.

SEC. 3. President shall communicate to Congress — He may convene and adjourn Congress, in case, etc.; shall receive ambassadors, execute laws, and commission officers.

SEC. 4. All civil offices forfeited for certain crimes.

## ARTICLE III.

SECTION 1. Judicial power — Tenure — Compensation.

SEC. 2. Judicial power; to what cases it extends — Original jurisdiction of Supreme Court — Appellate — Trial by jury, except, etc. — Trial, where.

SEC. 3. Treason defined — Proof of — Punishment of.

## ARTICLE IV.

SECTION 1. Each State to give credit to the public acts, etc., of every other State.

SEC. 2. Privileges of citizens of each State — Fugitives from justice to be delivered up — Persons held to service having escaped, to be delivered up.

SEC. 3. Admission of new States — Power of Congress over territory and other property.

SEC. 4. Republican form of government guaranteed — Each State to be protected.

## ARTICLE V.

Constitution; how amended — Proviso.

## ARTICLE VI.

Certain debts, etc., adopted — Supremacy of Constitution, treaties, and laws of the United States — Oath to support Constitution, by whom taken — No religious test.

## ARTICLE VII.

What ratification shall establish Constitution.

## AMENDMENTS.

   I. Religious establishment prohibited — Freedom of speech, of the press, and right to petition.
  II. Right to keep and bear arms.
 III. No soldier to be quartered in any house, unless, etc.
  IV. Right of search and seizure regulated.
   V. Provisions concerning prosecution, trial and punishment — Private property not to be taken for public use, without, etc.
  VI. Further provision respecting criminal prosecutions.
 VII. Right of trial by jury secured.
VIII. Excessive bail or fines and cruel punishments prohibited.
  IX. Rule of construction.
   X. Same subject.
  XI. Same subject.
 XII. Manner of choosing President and Vice-President.
XIII. Slavery abolished.
 XIV. Citizenship.

We, the people of the United States, in order to form a more perfect union, establish justice, insure domestic tranquillity, provide for the common defense, promote the general welfare, and secure the blessings of liberty to ourselves and our posterity, do ordain and establish this constitution for the United States of America.

## ARTICLE I.

### Section 1.

1. All legislative powers herein granted shall be vested in a congress of the United States, which shall consist of a senate and house of representatives.

### Section 2.

1. The house of representatives shall be composed of members chosen every second year by the people of the several states; and the electors in each state shall have the qualifications requisite for electors of the most numerous branch of the state legislature.

2. No person shall be a representative who shall not have attained to the age of twenty-five years, and been seven years a citizen of the United States, and who shall not, when elected, be an inhabitant of that state in which he shall be chosen.

3. Representatives and direct taxes shall be apportioned among the several states which may be included within this Union, according to their respective numbers, which shall be determined by adding to the whole number of free persons, including those bound to service for a term of years, and excluding Indians not taxed, three-fifths of all other persons. The actual enumeration shall be made within three years after the first meeting of the congress of the United States, and within every subsequent term of ten years, in such manner as they shall by law direct. The number of representatives shall not exceed one for every thirty thousand, but each state shall have at least one representative; and until such enumeration shall be made, the state of New Hampshire shall be entitled to choose three; Massachusetts, eight; Rhode Island and Providence Plantations, one; Connecticut, five; New-York, six; New Jersey, four; Pennsylvania, eight; Delaware, one; Maryland, six; Virginia, ten; North Carolina five; South Carolina, five; and Georgia, three.

4. When vacancies happen in the representation from any state, the executive authority thereof shall issue writs of election to fill such vacancies.

5. The house of representatives shall choose their speaker and other officers, and shall have the sole power of impeachment.

## SECTION 3.

1. The senate of the United States shall be composed of two senators from each state, chosen by the legislature thereof, for six years; and each senator shall have one vote.

2. Immediately after they shall be assembled in conse-

quence of the first election, they shall be divided as equally as may be into three classes. The seats of the senators of the first class shall be vacated at the expiration of the second year, of the second class at the expiration of the fourth year, and of the third class at the expiration of the sixth year, so that one-third may be chosen every second year; and if vacancies happen, by resignation or otherwise, during the recess of the legislature of any state, the executive thereof may make temporary appointments until the next meeting of the legislature, which shall then fill such vacancies.

3. No person shall be a senator who shall not have attained the age of thirty years, and been nine years a citizen of the United States, and who shall not, when elected, be an inhabitant of that state for which he shall be chosen.

4. The vice-president of the United States shall be president of the senate, but shall have no vote unless they be equally divided

5. The senate shall choose their other officers, and also a president *pro tempore* in the absence of the vice-president, or when he shall exercise the office of president of the United States.

6. The senate shall have the sole power to try all impeachments. When sitting for that purpose, they shall be on oath or affirmation. When the president of the United States is tried, the chief justice shall preside; and no person shall be convicted without the concurrence of two-thirds of the members present.

7. Judgment in cases of impeachment shall not extend further than to removal from office, and disqualification to hold and enjoy any office of honor, trust or profit under the United States; but the party convicted shall, nevertheless, be liable and subject to indictment, trial, judgment and punishment, according to law.

## Section 4.

1. The times, places and manner of holding elections for senators and representatives shall be prescribed in each state by the legislature thereof; but the congress may at any time by law make or alter such regulations, except as to the place of choosing senators.

2. The congress shall assemble at least once in every year; and such meeting shall be on the first Monday in December, unless they shall by law appoint a different day.

## Section 5.

1. Each house shall be the judge of the elections, returns and qualifications of its own members, and a majority of each shall constitute a quorum to do business; but a smaller number may adjourn from day to day, and may be authorized to compel the attendance of absent members, in such manner and under such penalties as each house may provide.

2. Each house may determine the rule of its proceedings, punish its members for disorderly behavior, and with the concurrence of two-thirds, expel a member.

3. Each house shall keep a journal of its proceedings, and from time to time publish the same, excepting such parts as may, in their judgment, require secrecy, and the yeas and nays of the members of either house on any question shall, at the desire of one-fifth of those present, be entered on the journal.

4. Neither house, during the session of congress, shall, without the consent of the other, adjourn for more than three days, nor to any other place than that in which the two houses shall be sitting.

## Section 6.

1. The senators and representatives shall receive a compensation for their services, to be ascertained by law, and

paid out of the treasury of the United States. They shall, in all cases except treason, felony and breach of the peace, be privileged from arrest during their attendance at the session of their respective houses, and in going to and returning from the same; and for any speech or debate in either house they shall not be questioned in any other place.

2. No senator or representative shall, during the time for which he was elected, be appointed to any civil office under the authority of the United States, which shall have been created, or the emoluments wherof shall have been increased, during such time; and no person holding any office under the United States shall be a member of either house during his continuance in office.

## Section 7.

1. All bills for raising revenue shall originate in the house of representatives; but the senate may propose or concur with amendments as on other bills.

2. Every bill which shall have passed the house of representatives and the senate shall, before it becomes a law, be presented to the president of the United States; if he approve, he shall sign it; but if not, he shall return it, with his objections, to that house in which it shall have originated; who shall enter the objections at large on their journal, and proceed to reconsider it. If, after such reconsideration, two-thirds of that house shall agree to pass the bill, it shall be sent, together with the objections, to the other house, by which it shall likewise be reconsidered; and, if approved by two-thirds of that house, it shall become a law. But in all cases, the votes of both houses shall be determined by yeas and nays, and the names of the persons voting for and against the bill shall be entered on the journal of each house repectively. If any bill shall not be returned by the president within ten days (Sundays excepted) after it shall have been presented to him, the

same shall be a law in like manner as if he had signed it, unless the congress, by their adjournment, prevent its return, in which case it shall not be a law.

3. Every order, resolution or vote, to which the concurrence of the senate and house of representatives may be necessary (except on a question of adjournment), shall be presented to the president of the United States; and, before the same shall take effect, shall be approved by him; or, being disapproved by him, shall be repassed by two-thirds of the senate and house of representatives, according to the rules and limitations prescribed in the case of a bill.

## Section 8.

The congress shall have power:

1. To lay and collect taxes, duties, imposts, and excises; to pay the debts and provide for the common defense and general welfare of the United States; but all duties, imposts and excises shall be uniform throughout the United States.

2. To borrow money on the credit of the United States.

3. To regulate commerce with foreign nations, and among the several states, and with the Indian tribes.

4. To establish an uniform rule of naturalization, and uniform laws on the subject of bankruptcies throughout the United States.

5. To coin money, regulate the value thereof, and of foreign coin, and fix the standard of weights and measures.

6. To provide for the punishment of counterfeiting the securities and current coin of the United States.

7. To establish post-offices and post-roads.

8. To promote the progress of science and useful arts, by securing for limited times, to authors and inventors, the exclusive right to their respective writings and discoveries.

9. To constitute tribunals inferior to the supreme court; to define and punish piracies and felonies committed on the high seas, and offenses against the law of nations.

10. To declare war, grant letters of marque and reprisal, and make rules concerning captures on land and water.

11. To raise and support armies; but no appropriation of money to that use shall be for a longer term than two years.

12. To provide and maintain a navy.

13. To make rules for the government and regulation of the land and naval forces.

14. To provide for calling forth the militia to execute the laws of the Union, suppress insurrections, and repel invasions.

15. To provide for organizing, arming and disciplining the militia, and for governing such part of them as may be employed in the service of the United States; reserving to the states respectively the appointment of the officers and the authority of training the militia according to the discipline prescribed by congress.

16. To exercise exclusive legislation in all cases whatsoever, over such district (not exceeding ten miles square) as may, by cession of particular states, and the acceptance of congress, become the seat of government of the United States; and to exercise like authority over all places purchased, by the consent of the legislature of the state in which the same shall be, for the erection of forts, magazines, arsenals, dockyards, and other needful buildings; and

17. To make all laws which shall be necessary and proper for carrying into execution the foregoing powers, and all other powers vested by this constitution in the government of the United States, or in any department or officer thereof.

## Section 9.

1. The migration or importation of such persons as any of the states now existing shall think proper to admit, shall not be prohibited by the congress prior to the year one thousand eight hundred and eight; but a tax or duty

may be imposed on such importation not exceeding ten dollars for each person.

2. The privilege of the writ of *habeas corpus* shall not be suspended, unless when, in cases of rebellion or invasion, the public safety may require it.

3. No bill of attainder, or *ex post facto* law shall be passed.

4. No capitation or other direct tax shall be laid, unless in proportion to the census or enumeration herein before directed to be taken.

5. No tax or duty shall be laid on any articles exported from any state. No preference shall be given by any regulation of commerce or revenue to the ports of one state over those of another; nor shall vessels bound to or from one state be obliged to enter, clear or pay duties in another.

6. No money shall be drawn from the treasury but in consequence of appropriations made by law; and a regular statement and account of the receipts and expenditures of all public money shall be published from time to time.

7. No title of nobility shall be granted by the United States; and no person holding any office of profit or trust under them shall, without the consent of the congress, accept of any present, emolument, office, or title of any kind whatever, from any king, prince, or foreign state.

## Section 10.

1. No state shall enter into any treaty, alliance or confederation; grant letters of marque and reprisal; coin money; emit bills of credit; make any thing but gold and silver coin a tender in payment of debts; pass any bill of attainder, *ex post facto* law, or law impairing the obligation of contracts; or grant any title of nobility.

2. No state shall, without the consent of the congress, lay any imposts or duties on imports or exports, except what may be absolutely necessary for executing its inspection laws, and the net produce of all duties and imposts laid

by any state on imports or exports shall be for the use of the treasury of the United States, and all such laws shall be subject to the revision and control of the congress. No state shall, without the consent of the congress, lay any duty of tonnage, keep troops or ships of war in time of peace, enter into any agreement or compact with another state, or with a foreign power, or engage in war, unless actually invaded, or in such imminent danger as will not admit of delay.

## ARTICLE II.

### Section I.

1. The executive power shall be vested in a president of the United States of America. He shall hold his office during the term of four years; and, together with the vice-president chosen for the same term, be elected as follows:

2. Each state shall appoint, in such manner as the legislature thereof may direct, a number of electors equal to the whole number of senators and representatives to which the state may be entitled in the congress; but no senator or representative, or person holding an office of trust or profit under the United States, shall be appointed an elector.

3. The electors shall meet in their respective states, and vote by ballot for two persons, of whom one at least shall not be an inhabitant of the same state with themselves. And they shall make a list of all the persons voted for, and of the number of votes for each; which list they shall sign and certify, and transmit sealed to the seat of government of the United States, directed to the president of the senate. The president of the senate shall, in the presence of the senate and house of representatives, open all the certificates, and the votes shall then be counted. The person having the greatest number of votes shall be the president, if such number be a majority of the whole number of electors appointed: and if there be more than one who

have such majority, and have an equal number of votes, then the house of representatives shall immediately choose, by ballot, one of them for president; and if no person have a majority, then, from the five highest on the list, the said house shall, in like manner, choose the president. But in choosing the president, the vote shall be taken by states, the representation from each state having one vote; a quorum for this purpose shall consist of a member or members from two-thirds of the states, and a majority of all the states shall be necessary to a choice. In every case, after the choice of the president, the person having the greatest number of votes of the electors shall be the vice-president. But if there should remain two or more who have equal votes, the senate shall choose from them, by ballot, the vice-president.

4. The congress may determine the time of choosing the electors, and the day on which they shall give their votes, which day shall be the same throughout the United States.

5. No person, except a natural born citizen, or a citizen of the United States at the time of the adoption of this constitution, shall be eligible to the office of president; neither shall any person be eligible to that office who shall not have attained to the age of thirty-five years, and been fourteen years a resident within the United States.

6. In case of the removal of the president from office, or of his death, resignation, or inability to discharge the powers and duties of the said office, the same shall devolve on the vice-president; and the congress may, by law, provide for the case of removal, death, resignation or inability, both of the president and vice-president, declaring what officer shall then act as president; and such officer shall act accordingly, until the disability be removed, or a president shall be elected.

7. The president shall, at stated times, receive for his services a compensation which shall neither be increased nor diminished during the period for which he shall

have been elected; and he shall not receive within that period any other emolument from the United States, or any of them.

8. Before he enter on the execution of his office, he shall take the following oath of affirmation:

"I do solemnly swear (or affirm) that I will faithfully execute the office of president of the United States; and will, to the best of my ability, preserve, protect and defend the constitution of the United States."

### Section 2.

1. The president shall be commander-in-chief of the army and navy of the United States, and of the militia of the several states, when called into the actual service of the United States. He may require the opinion, in writing, of the principal officer in each of the executive departments, upon any subject relating to the duties of their respective offices; and he shall have power to grant reprieves and pardons for offenses against the United States, except in cases of impeachment.

2. He shall have power, by and with the advice and consent of the senate, to make treaties, provided two-thirds of the senators present occur; and he shall nominate, and by and with the advice and consent of the senate shall appoint, ambassadors, other public ministers and consuls, judges of the supreme court, and all other officers of the United States whose appointments are not herein otherwise provided for, and which shall be established by law. But the congress may, by law, vest the appointment of such inferior officers as they think proper, in the president alone, in the courts of law, or in the heads of departments.

3. The president shall have power to fill up all vacancies that may happen during the recess of the senate, by granting commissions which shall expire at the end of their next session.

### Section 3.

1. He shall, from time to time, give to the congress information of the state of the Union, and recommend to their consideration such measures as he shall judge necessary and expedient. He may, on extraordinary occasions, convene both houses, or either of them; and in case of disagreement between them, with respect to the time of adjournment, he may adjourn them to such time as he shall think proper. He shall receive ambassadors and other public ministers. He shall take care that the laws be faithfully executed; and shall commission all the officers of the United States.

### Section 4.

1. The president, vice-president and all civil officers of the United States, shall be removed from office on impeachment for, and conviction of treason, bribery or other high crimes and misdemeanors.

## ARTICLE III.

### Section 1.

1. The judicial power of the United States shall be vested in one supreme court, and in such inferior courts as the congress may, from time to time, ordain and establish. The judges, both of the supreme and inferior courts, shall hold their offices during good behavior; and shall, at stated times, receive for their services a compensation, which shall not be diminished during their continuance in office.

### Section 2.

1. The judicial power shall extend to all cases in law and equity arising under this constitution, the laws of the United States, and treaties made, or which shall be made, under their authority; to all cases affecting ambassadors, other public ministers and consuls; to all cases of admiralty

and maritime jurisdiction; to controversies to which the United States shall be a party; to controversies between two or more states; between a state and citizens of another state; between citizens of different states, between citizens of the same state claiming lands under grants of different states, and between a state, or the citizens thereof, and foreign states, citizens or subjects.

2. In all cases affecting ambassadors, other public ministers and consuls, and those in which a state shall be party, the supreme court shall have original jurisdiction. In all the other cases before mentioned, the supreme court shall have appellate jurisdiction, both as to law and fact, with such exceptions and under such regulations as the congress shall make.

3. The trial of all crimes, except in cases of impeachment, shall be by jury, and such trial shall be held in the state where the said crimes shall have been committed; but when not committed within any state, the trial shall be at such place or places as the congress may by law have directed.

## Section 3.

1. Treason against the United States shall consist only in levying war against them or in adhering to their enemies, giving them aid and comfort. No person shall be convicted of treason, unless on the testimony of two witnesses to the same overt act, or on confession in open court.

2. The congress shall have power to declare the punishment of treason; but no attainder of treason shall work corruption of blood, or forfeiture, except during the life of the person attainted.

## ARTICLE IV.

### Section 1.

1. Full faith and credit shall be given in each state to the public acts, records and judicial proceedings of every

other state ; and the congress may, by general laws, prescribe the manner in which such acts, records and proceedings shall be proved, and the effect thereof.

## Section 2.

1. The citizens of each state shall be entitled to all privileges and immunities of citizens in the several states.

2. A person charged in any state with treason, felony or other crime, who shall flee from justice, and be found in another state, shall, on demand of the executive authority of the state from which he fled, be delivered up, to be removed to the state having jurisdiction of the crime.

3. No person held to service or labor in one state under the laws thereof, escaping into another, shall, in consequence of any law or regulation therein, be discharged from such service or labor ; but shall be delivered up on claim of the party to whom such service or labor may be due.

## Section 3.

1. New states may be admitted by the congress into this Union ; but no new state shall be formed or erected within the jurisdiction of any other state, nor any state be formed by the junction of two or more states or parts of states, without the consent of the legislatures of the states concerned, as well as of the congress.

2. The congress shall have power to dispose of, and make all needful rules and regulations respecting, the territory or other property belonging to the United States; and nothing in this constitution shall be so construed as to prejudice any claims of the United States, or of any particular state.

## Section 4.

1. The United States shall guarantee to every state in this Union a republican form of government, and shall protect each of them against invasion ; and, on application

of the legislature, or of the executive (when the legislature cannot be convened), against domestic violence.

## ARTICLE V.

1. The congress, whenever two-thirds of both houses shall deem it necessary, shall propose amendments to this constitution; or, on the application of the legislatures of two-thirds of the several states, shall call a convention for proposing amendments, which, in either case, shall be valid to all intents and purposes, as part of this constitution, when ratified by the legislatures of three-fourths of the several states, or by conventions in three-fourths thereof, as the one or the other mode of ratification may be proposed by the congress; provided that no amendment, which may be made prior to the year one thousand eight hundred and eight, shall in any manner affect the first and fourth clauses in the ninth section of the first article; and that no state, without its consent, shall be deprived of its equal suffrage in the senate.

## ARTICLE VI.

1. All debts contracted and engagements entered into before the adoption of this constitution shall be as valid against the United States under this constitution, as under the confederation.

2. This constitution, and the laws of the United States which shall be made in pursuance thereof, and all treaties made, or which shall be made, under the authority of the United States, shall be the supreme law of the land; and the judges in every state shall be bound thereby, any thing in the constitution or laws of any state to the contrary notwithstanding.

3. The senators and representatives before mentioned, and the members of the several state legislatures, and all executive and judicial officers, both of the United States and of the several states, shall be bound by oath or affir-

mation to support this constitution; but no religious test shall ever be required as a qualification to any office or public trust under the United States.

## ARTICLE VII.

1. The ratification of the conventions of nine states shall be sufficient for the establishment of this constitution between the states so ratifying the same.

> Done in convention by the unanimous consent of the states present, the seventeenth day of September, in the year of our Lord one thousand seven hundred and eighty-seven, and of the Independence of the United States of America the twelfth. In witness whereof we have hereunto subscribed our names.
>
> GEORGE WASHINGTON,
> *President, and Deputy from Virginia.*

AMENDMENTS TO THE CONSTITUTION OF THE UNITED STATES.

[The following amendments were proposed at the first session of the first congress of the United States, which was begun and held at the city of New York on the 4th of March, 1789, and were adopted by the requisite number of states. Laws of the U. S., vol. 1, page 82.]

[The following preamble and resolution preceded the original proposition of the amendments, and as they have been supposed by a high equity judge (8th Wendell's Reports, p. 100) to have an important bearing on the construction of those amendments, they are here inserted. They will be found in the journals of the first session of he first congress.

## CONGRESS OF THE UNITED STATES.

*Begun and held at the city of New York, on Wednesday, the 4th day of March, 1789.*

The conventions of a number of the states having, at the time of their adopting the constitution, expressed a desire, in order to prevent misconstruction or abuse of its powers, that further declaratory and restrictive clauses should be added, and as extending the ground of public confidence in the government will best insure the beneficent ends of its institution:

*Resolved*, By the Senate and House of Representatives of the United States of America, in congress assembled, two-thirds of both houses concurring, that the following articles be proposed to the legislatures of the several states, as amendments to the constitution of the United States; all or any of which articles, when ratified by three-fourths of the said legislatures, to be valid to all intents and purposes, as part of the said constitution, namely:]

## ARTICLE I.

Congress shall make no law respecting an establishment of religion, or prohibiting the free exercise thereof; or abridging the freedom of speech or of the press; or the right of the people peaceably to assemble, and to petition the government for a redress of grievances.

## ARTICLE II.

A well regulated militia being necessary to the security of a free state, the right of the people to keep and bear arms shall not be infringed.

## ARTICLE III.

No soldier shall, in time of peace, be quartered in any house without the consent of the owner, nor in time of war but in a manner to be prescribed by law.

## ARTICLE IV.

The right of the people to be secure in their persons, houses, paper and effects, against unreasonable searches and seizures, shall not be violated; and no warrants shall issue but upon probable cause, supported by oath or affirmation, and particularly describing the place to be searched, and the persons or things to be seized.

## ARTICLE V.

No person shall be held to answer for a capital or otherwise infamous crime, unless on a presentment or indictment of a grand jury, except in cases arising in the land or naval forces, or in the militia, when in actual service in time of war or public danger; nor shall any person be subject for the same offense to be twice put in jeopardy of life or limb; nor shall be compelled, in any criminal case, to be a witness against himself, nor be deprived of life, liberty or property, without due process of law; nor shall private property be taken for public use without just compensation.

## ARTICLE VI.

In all criminal prosecutions, the accused shall enjoy the right to a speedy and public trial, by an impartial jury of the state and district wherein the crime shall have been committed, which district shall have been previously ascertained by law; and to be informed of the nature and cause of the accusation; to be confronted with the witnesses against him; to have compulsory process for obtaining witnesses in his favor, and to have the assistance of counsel for his defense.

## ARTICLE VII.

In suits at common law, where the value in controversy shall exceed twenty dollars, the right of trial by jury shall be preserved; and no fact tried by a jury shall be otherwise re-examined in any court of the United States, than according to the rules of the common law.

## ARTICLE VIII.

Excessive bail shall not be required, nor excessive fines imposed, nor cruel and unusual punishments inflicted.

## ARTICLE IX.

The enumeration in the constitution of certain rights shall not be construed to deny or disparage others retained by the people.

## ARTICLE X.

The powers not delegated to the United States by the constitution, nor prohibited to it by the states, are reserved to the states respectively, or to the people.

[The following amendment was proposed at the second session of the third congress. It is printed in the Laws of the United States, vol. 1, p. 73, as article 11.]

## ARTICLE XI.

The judicial power of the United States shall not be construed to extend to any suit in law or equity, commenced or prosecuted against one of the United States by citizens of another state, or by citizens or subjects of any foreign state.

[The three following sections were proposed as amendments at the first session of the eighth congress. They are printed in the Laws of the United States as article 12.]

## ARTICLE XII.

1 The electors shall meet in their respective states, and vote by ballot for president and vice-president, one of whom at least shall not be an inhabitant of the same state with themselves. They shall name in their ballots the person voted for as president, and in distinct ballots the person voted for as vice-president; and they shall make distinct lists of all persons voted for as president, and of all persons voted for as vice-president, and of the number of votes for each; which lists they shall sign and certify, and transmit sealed to the seat of the government of the United States, directed to the president of the senate. The presi-

dent of the senate shall, in the presence of the senate and house of representatives, open all the certificates, and the votes shall then be counted. The person having the greatest number of votes for president shall be the president, if such number be a majority of the whole number of electors appointed; and if no person have such majority, then from the persons having the highest numbers, not exceeding three, on the list of those voted for as president, the house of representatives shall choose immediately, by ballot, the president. But in choosing the president, the votes shall be taken by states, the representation from each state having one vote; a quorum for this purpose shall consist of a member or members from two-thirds of the states, and a majority of all the states shall be necessary to a choice. And if the house of representatives shall not choose a president, whenever the right of choice shall devolve upon them, before the fourth day of March next following, then the vice-president shall act as president, as in the case of the death or other constitutional disability of the president.

2. The person having the greatest number of votes as vice-president shall be the vice-president, if such number be a majority of the whole number of electors appointed, and if no person have a majority, then from the two highest numbers on the list the senate shall choose the vice-president. A quorum for the purpose shall consist of two-thirds of the whole number of senators, and a majority of the whole number shall be necessary to a choice.

3. But no person constitutionally ineligible to the office of president shall be eligible to that of vice-president of the United States.

## ARTICLE XIII.

### Section 1.

Neither slavery nor involuntary servitude, except as a punishment for crime, whereof the party shall have been duly convicted, shall exist within the United States, or any place subject to their jurisdiction.

### SECTION 2.

Congress shall have power to enforce this article by appropriate legislation.

---

The following is the certificate of the secretary of state of the United States, announcing the ratification of the foregoing article:

WILLIAM H. SEWARD, *Secretary of State of the United States:*

TO ALL TO WHOM THESE PRESENTS MAY COME, GREETING:

KNOW YE, That, whereas the congress of the United States, on the first of February last, passed a resolution, which is in the words following, namely: "A Resolution submitting to the legislatures of the several states a proposition to amend the constitution of the United States.

"*Resolved*, By the senate and house of representatives of the United States of America in congress assembled (two-thirds of both houses concurring), that the following article be proposed to the legislatures of the several states as an amendment to the constitution of the United States, which, when ratified by three-fourths of said legislatures, shall be valid, to all intents and purposes, as a part of the said constitution, namely:"

(See Article XIII, above.)

And whereas it appears from official documents on file in this department, that the amendment to the constitution of the United States proposed as aforesaid, has been ratified by the legislatures of the states of Illinois, Rhode Island, Michigan, Maryland, New York, West Virginia, Maine, Kansas, Massachusetts, Pennsylvania, Virginia, Ohio, Missouri, Nevada, Indiana, Louisiana, Minnesota, Wisconsin, Vermont, Tennessee, Arkansas, Connecticut, New Hampshire, South Carolina, Alabama, North Carolina and Georgia; in all twenty-seven states.

And whereas, the whole number of states in the United States is thirty-six; and whereas, the before specially-named states, whose legislatures have ratified the said proposed amendment, constitute three-fourths of the whole number of states in the United States:

Now, therefore, be it known, that I, WILLIAM H. SEWARD, secretary of state of the United States, by virtue and in pursuance of the second section of the act of congress, approved the twentieth of April, eighteen hundred and eighteen, entitled, "An act to provide for the publication of the laws of the United States, and for other purposes," do hereby certify, that the amendment aforesaid has become valid, to all intents and purposes, as a part of the constitution of the United States.

In testimony whereof, I have hereunto set my hand, and caused the seal of the department of state to be affixed.

Done at the city of Washington, this eighteenth day of December, in the year of our Lord one thousand eight hundred [L. S.] and sixty-five, and of the Independence of the United States of America the ninetieth.

WILLIAM H. SEWARD,
*Secretary of State.*

## ARTICLE XIV.

### Section 1.

All persons born or naturalized in the United States, and subject to the jurisdiction thereof, are citizens of the United States and of the state wherein they reside. No state shall make or enforce any law which shall abridge the privileges or immunities of citizens of the United States; nor shall any state deprive any person of life, liberty or property, without due process of law, nor deny to any person within its jurisdiction the equal protection of the laws.

### Section 2.

Representatives shall be apportioned among the several states according to their respective numbers, counting the whole number of persons in each state, excluding Indians not taxed. But when the right to vote at any election for the choice of electors for president and vice-president of the United States, representatives in congress, the executive and judicial officers of a state, or the members of the legislature thereof, is denied to any of the male inhabitants of such state, being twenty-one years of age, and citizens of the United States, or in any way abridged, except for participation in rebellion or other crime, the basis of representation therein shall be reduced in the proportion which the number of such male citizens shall bear to the whole number of male citizens twenty-one years of age in such state.

### Section 3.

No person shall be a senator or representative in congress, or elector of president and vice-president, or hold any office, civil or military, under the United States, or under any state, who, having previously taken an oath as a member of congress, or as an officer of the United States, or as a member of any state legislature, or as an executive or judicial officer of any state, to support the constitution of the United States, shall have engaged in insurrection or rebellion against the same, or given aid or comfort to the enemies thereof. But congress may, by a vote of two-thirds of each house, remove such disability.

## SECTION 4.

The validity of the public debt of the United States authorized by law, including debts incurred for payment of pensions and bounties for services in suppressing insurrection or rebellion, shall not be questioned. But neither the United States nor any state shall assume or pay any debt or obligation incurred in aid of insurrection or rebellion against the United States, or any claim for the loss or emancipation of any slave; but all such debts, obligations, and claims shall be held illegal and void.

## SECTION 5.

The congress shall have power to enforce, by appropriate legislation, the provisions of this article.

---

The following are the certificates or the secretary of state of the United States, announcing the ratification of the foregoing article:

WILLIAM H. SEWARD, *Secretary of State of the United States:*

TO ALL TO WHOM THESE PRESENTS MAY COME, GREETING:

WHEREAS, the congress of the United States, on or about the sixteenth of June, in the year one thousand eight hundred and sixty-six, passed a resolution, which is in the words and figures following, to wit:

"Joint Resolution proposing an Amendment to the Constitution of the United States.

"*Be it Resolved,* by the senate and house of representatives of the United States of America in congress assembled (two-thirds fo both houses concurring), That the following article be proposed to the legislatures of the several states as an amendment to the constitution of the United States, which, when ratified by three-fourths of said legislatures, shall be valid as part of the constitution, namely:"

(See Article XIV, above.)

And whereas, by the second section of the act of congress, approved the twentieth of April, one thousand eight hundred and eighteen, entitled "An act to provide for the publication of the laws of the United States, and for other purposes," it is made the duty of the secretary of state forthwith to cause any amendment to the constitution of the United States, which has been adopted according to the provisions of the said constitution, to be published in the newspapers authorized to promulgate the laws, with his certificate specifying the states by which the same may have been adopted, and that the same has become valid, to all intents and purposes, as a part of the constitution of the United States;

And whereas, neither the act just quoted from, nor any other law, expressly or by conclusive implication, authorizes the secretary of state to determine and decide doubtful questions as to the authenticity of the organization of state legislatures, or as to the power of any state legislature to recall a previous act or resolution of ratification of any amendment proposed to the constitution;

And whereas, it appears from official documents on file in this department, that the amendment to the constitution of the United States, proposed as aforesaid, has been ratified by the legislatures of the states of Connecticut, New Hampshire, Tennessee, New Jersey, Oregon, Vermont, New York, Ohio, Illinois, West Virginia, Kansas, Maine, Nevada, Missouri, Indiana, Minnesota, Rhode Island, Wisconsin, Pennsylvania, Michigan, Massachusetts, Nebraska, and Iowa;

And whereas, it further appears, from documents on file in this department, that the amendment to the constitution of the United States, proposed as aforesaid, has also been ratified by newly constituted and newly established bodies, avowing themselves to be, and acting as, the legislatures, respectively, of the states of Arkansas, Florida, North Carolina, Louisiana, South Carolina, and Alabama;

And whereas, it further appears, from official documents on file in this department, that the legislatures of two of the states first above enumerated, to wit: Ohio and New Jersey, have since passed resolutions, respectively, withdrawing the consent of each of said states to the aforesaid amendment;

And whereas, it is deemed a matter of doubt and uncertainty whether such resolutions are not irregular, invalid, and, therefore, ineffectual, for withdrawing the consent of the said two states, or of either of them, to the aforesaid amendment;

And whereas, the whole number of states in the United States is thirty-seven, to wit: New Hampshire, Massachusetts, Rhode Island, Connecticut, New York, New Jersey, Pennsylvania, Delaware, Maryland, Virginia, North Carolina, South Carolina, Georgia, Vermont, Kentucky, Tennessee, Ohio, Louisiana, Indiana, Mississippi, Illinois, Alabama, Maine, Missouri, Arkansas, Michigan, Florida, Texas, Iowa, Wisconsin, Minnesota, California, Oregon, Kansas, West Virginia, Nevada and Nebraska;

And whereas, the twenty-three states first hereinbefore named, whose legislatures have ratified the said proposed amendment, and the six states next thereafter named, as having ratified the said proposed amendment by newly constituted and established legislative bodies, together constitute three-fourths of the whole number of states in the United States.

Now, therefore, be it known, that I, WILLIAM H. SEWARD, secretary of state of the United States, by virtue and in pursuance of the second section of the act of congress, approved the twentieth of April, eighteen hundred and eighteen, hereinbefore cited, do hereby certify, that, if the resolutions of the legislatures of Ohio and New Jersey, ratifying the aforesaid amendment, are to be deemed as remaining of full force and effect, notwithstanding the subsequent resolutions of the legislatures of those states, which purport to withdraw the consent of said states from such ratification, then the aforesaid amendment has been ratified in the manner hereinbefore mentioned, and so has become valid, to all intents and purposes, as a part of the constitution of the United States.

In testimony whereof, I have hereunto set my hand, and caused the seal of the department of state to be affixed.

Done at the city of Washington, this twentieth day of July, in the year of our Lord one thousand eight hundred and [L. S.] sixty-eight, and of the Independence of the United States of America the ninety-third.

WILLIAM H. SEWARD,
*Secretary of State.*

---

WILLIAM H. SEWARD, *Secretary of State of the United States:*

TO ALL TO WHOM THESE PRESENTS MAY COME, GREETING.

WHEREAS, by an act of congress, passed on the twentieth of April, one thousand eight hundred and eighteen, entitled "An act to provide for the publication of the laws of the United States, and for other purposes," it is declared that, whenever official notice shall have been received at the department of state that any amendment which heretofore has been and hereafter may be proposed to the constitution of the United States has been adopted according to the provisions of the constitution, it shall be the duty of the said secretary of state, forthwith, to cause the said amendment to be published in the newspapers authorized to promulgate the laws, with his certificate, specifying the states by which the same may have been adopted, and that the same has become valid, to all intents and purposes, as a part of the constitution of the United States;

And whereas, the congress of the United States, on or about the sixteenth day of June, one thousand eight hundred and sixty-six, submitted to the legislatures of the several states a proposed amendment to the constitution, in the following words, to wit:

"Joint Resolution proposing an Amendment to the Constitution of the United States.

"*Be it Resolved*, by the senate and house of representatives of the United States of America, in congress assembled (two-thirds of both houses concurring), That the following article be proposed to the legislatures of the several states as an amendment to the constitution of the United States, which, when ratified by three-fourths of said legislatures, shall be valid as part of the constitution, namely:"

(See Article XIV, above.)

And whereas, the senate and house of representatives of the congress of the United States, on the twenty-first day of July, one thousand eight hundred and sixty-eight, adopted and transmitted to the department of state a concurrent resolution, which concurrent resolution is in the words and figures following, to wit:

"IN SENATE OF THE UNITED STATES,
"*July* 21, 1868.

"WHEREAS, the legislatures of the states of Connecticut, Tennessee, New Jersey, Oregon, Vermont, West Virginia, Kansas, Missouri, Indiana, Ohio, Illinois, Minnesota, New York, Wisconsin, Pennsylvania, Rhode Island, Michigan, Nevada, New Hampshire, Massachusetts, Nebraska, Maine, Iowa, Arkansas, Florida,

North Carolina, Alabama, South Carolina and Louisiana, being three-fourths and more of the several states of the Union, have ratified the fourteenth article of amendment to the constitution of the United States, duly proposed by two-thirds of each house of the thirty-ninth congress; therefore,

"*Resolved*, by the senate (the house of representatives concurring), That said fourteenth article is hereby declared to be a part of the constitution of the United States, and it shall be duly promulgated as such by the secretary of state.

"Attest: GEO. C. GORHAM, *Secretary*."

"IN THE HOUSE OF REPRESENTATIVES,
"*July* 21, 1868.

"*Resolved*, That the house of representatives concur in the foregoing concurrent resolution of the senate, 'declaring the ratification of the fourteenth article of amendment of the constitution of the United States.'

"Attest: EDWD. McPHERSON, *Clerk*."

And whereas, official notice has been received at the department of state that the legislatures of the several states next hereinafter named, have, at the times respectively herein mentioned, taken the proceedings hereinafter recited, upon or in relation to the ratification of the said proposed amendment, called article fourteenth, namely: The legislature of Connecticut ratified the amendment June 30th, 1866; the legislature of New Hampshire ratified it July 7th, 1866; the legislature of Tennessee ratified it July 19th, 1866; the legislature of New Jersey ratified it September 11th, 1866, and the legislature of the same state passed a resolution in April, 1868, to withdraw its consent to it; the legislature of Oregon ratified it September 19th, 1866; the legislature of Texas rejected it November 1st, 1866; the legislature of Vermont ratified it on or previous to November 9th, 1866; the legislature of Georgia rejected it November 13th, 1866, and the legislature of the same state ratified it July 21st, 1868; the legislature of North Carolina rejected it December 4th, 1866, and the legislature of the same state ratified it July 4th, 1868; the legislature of South Carolina rejected it December 20th, 1866, and the legislature of the same state ratified it July 9th, 1868; the legislature of Virginia rejected it January 9th, 1867; the legislature of Kentucky rejected it January 10th, 1867; the legislature of New York ratified it January 10th, 1867; the legislature of Ohio ratified it January 11th, 1867, and the legislature of the same state passed a resolution in January, 1868, to withdraw its consent to it; the legislature of Illinois ratified it January 15th, 1867; the legislature of West Virginia ratified it January 16th, 1867; the legislature of Kansas ratified it January 18th, 1867; the legislature of Maine ratified it January 19th, 1867; the legislature of Nevada ratified it January 22d, 1867; the legislature of Missouri ratified it on or previous to January 26th, 1867; the legislature of Indiana ratified it January 29th, 1867; the legislature of Minnesota ratified it February 1st, 1867; the legislature of Rhode Island ratified it February 7th, 1867; the legislature of Delaware rejected it February 7th, 1867; the legislature of Wisconsin ratified it February 13th, 1867; the legislature of Pennsylvania ratified it February 13th, 1867; the legislature of Michigan ratified it February 15th, 1867; the legislature of Massachusetts ratified it March 20th, 1867; the legislature of Maryland rejected it March 23d, 1867; the legislature of Nebraska ratified it June 15th, 1867; the legislature of Iowa ratified it April 3d, 1868; the legislature of Arkansas ratified it April 6th, 1868; the legislature of Florida ratified it June 9th, 1868; the legislature of Louisiana ratified it July 9th, 1868; and the legislature of Alabama ratified it July 13th, 1868;

Now, therefore, be it known, that I, WILLIAM H. SEWARD, secretary of state of the United States, in execution of the aforesaid act, and of the aforesaid concurrent resolution of the 21st of July, 1868, and in conformance thereto, do hereby direct the said proposed amendment to the constitution of the United States to be published in the newspapers authorized to promulgate the laws of the United States, and I do hereby certify, that the said proposed amendment has been adopted in the manner hereinbefore mentioned by the states specified in the said concurrent resolution, namely: The states of Connecticut, New Hampshire, Tennessee, New Jersey, Oregon, Vermont, New York, Ohio, Illinois, West Virginia, Kansas, Maine, Nevada, Missouri, Indiana, Minnesota, Rhode Island, Wisconsin, Pennsylvania, Michigan, Massachusetts, Nebraska, Iowa, Arkansas, Florida, North Carolina, Louisiana, South Carolina, Alabama, and also by the legislature of the state of Georgia; the states thus specified being more than three-fourths of the states of the United States.

And I do further certify, that the said amendment has become valid to all intents and purposes, as a part of the constitution of the United States.

In testimony whereof, I have hereunto set my hand, and caused the seal of the department of state to be affixed.

Done at the city of Washington this twenty-eighth day of July, in the year of our Lord one thousand eight hundred and [L. S.] sixty-eight, and of the Independence of the United States of America the ninety-third.

WILLIAM H. SEWARD,
*Secretary of State.*

## ARTICLE XV.

### SECTION 1.

The right of citizens of the United States to vote shall not be denied or abridged by the United States or by any state on account of race, color, or previous condition of servitude.

### SECTION 2.

The congress shall have power to enforce this article by appropriate legislation.

---

The following is the certificate of the secretary of state of the United States, announcing the ratification of the foregoing article:

HAMILTON FISH, *Secretary of State of the United States:*

TO ALL TO WHOM THESE PRESENTS MAY COME, GREETING:

KNOW YE, That the congress of the United States, on or about the twenty-seventh day of February, in the year one thousand eight hundred and sixty-nine, passed a resolution in the words and figures following, to wit:

"A Resolution proposing an Amendment to the Constitution of the United States.

"*Resolved*, By the senate and house of representatives of the United States of America, in congress assembled (two-thirds of both houses concurring), That the following article be proposed to the legislatures of the several states as an amendment to the constitution of the United States, which, when ratified by three-fourths of said legislatures, shall be valid as part of the constitution, namely:"

(See Article XV, above.)

And, further, that it appears from official documents on file in this department, that the amendment to the constitution of the United States, proposed as aforesaid, has been ratified by the legislatures of the states of North Carolina, West Virginia, Massachusetts, Wisconsin, Maine, Louisiana, Michigan, South Carolina, Pennsylvania, Arkansas, Connecticut, Florida, Illinois, Indiana, New York, New Hampshire, Nevada, Vermont, Virginia, Alabama, Missouri, Mississippi, Ohio, Iowa, Kansas, Minnesota, Rhode Island, Nebraska, and Texas; in all, twenty-nine states:

And, further, that the states whose legislatures have so ratified the said proposed amendment constitute three-fourths of the whole number of states in the United States;

And, further, that it appears, from an official document on file in this department, that the legislature of the state of New York has since passed resolutions claiming to withdraw the said ratification of the said amendment which had been made by the legislature of that state, and of which official notice had been filed in this department;

And, further, that it appears, from an official document on file in this department, that the legislature of Georgia has, by resolution, ratified the said proposed amendment:

Now, therefore, be it known, that I, HAMILTON FISH, secretary of state of the United States, by virtue and in pursuance of the second section of the act of congress approved the twentieth day of April, in the year eighteen hundred and eighteen, entitled "An act to provide for the publication of the laws of the United States, and for other purposes," do hereby certify, that the amendment aforesaid has become valid to all intents and purposes as part of the constitution of the United States.

In testimony whereof, I have hereunto set my hand, and caused the seal of the department of state to be affixed.

Done at the city of Washington, this thirtieth day of March, in the year of our Lord one thousand eight hundred and
[L. S.]   seventy, and of the Independence of the United States the ninety-fourth.

HAMILTON FISH.

# THE GOVERNMENT UNDER THE CONSTITUTION.

### TIME OF RATIFICATION BY THE ORIGINAL STATES.

After copies of the Constitution had been sent to the State Legislatures, more than a year elapsed, before the requisite number of States had ratified it.

| | | | |
|---|---|---|---|
| By Convention of | Delaware, | ............... | December 7th., 1787. |
| " | " | Pennsylvania, ......... | December 12th., 1787. |
| " | " | New Jersey............ | December 18th., 1787. |
| " | " | Georgia,................. | January 2d, 1788. |
| " | " | Connecticut,............. | January 9th., 1788. |
| " | " | Massachusetts.......... | February 6th., 1788 |
| " | " | Maryland,................. | April 28th., 1788. |
| " | " | South Carolina,........... | May 23d., 1788. |
| " | " | New Hampshire,........... | June 21st., 1788. |
| " | " | Virginia,................ | June 26th., 1788. |
| " | " | New York, :............. | July 26th., 1788. |
| " | " | North Carolina,....... | November 21st., 1788. |
| " | " | Rhode Island,............ | May 29th., 1790. |

On the 4th of March 1789, the NATIONAL CONSTITUTION went into effect, and became the organic law of the land. The first Congress thereafter, met in the city of New York, and a quorum was formed on the 6th of April, 1789.

The three most important powers of a government are—1st. That of making laws, or the Legislative power. 2nd. That of executing them, or the Executive power. 3rd. That of interpreting the laws, and applying them to individual cases, or the Judicial power. The first is vested in Congress, the second is vested in the President, and the third is vested in one Supreme Court, and such other courts as Congress may establish. The government therefore is divided into three independent branches, to wit—the *Legislative*—the *Executive*, and the *Judiciary*.

After the organization of the new goverment, the first matters brought before Congress were those pertaining to the financial affairs of the country, and forming a system of revenues, and also the business of organizing the different branches.

There were three departments arranged for the executive, to wit, The *Treasury*, The *War*, and of *Foreign Affairs*, the heads of which were to be styled Secretaries, and were to constitute a Cabinet Council.

A national Judiciary was also established, consisting of a Supreme Court of the United States, having one Chief Justice and five Associate Justices. District Courts were also established, and each State was made a district, and also three Circuit Courts—the States being formed into three circuits. The question as to *amendments* to the Constitution was then brought forward, and also the Bills of Rights proposed by Virginia and New York. Twelve amendments were agreed to by Congress, but only ten of them subsequently ratified by the States.

[These ten amendments were ratified by the constitutional number of States on the 15th of December 1791. Another the *Eleventh* was proposed on the 5th of March 1794, and ratified on the 8th of January 1798. The *Twelfth* was proposed in December 1803, and ratified on the 25th of September 1804. The *Thirteenth* was ratified in 1865, the *Fourteenth* in 1868, and the *Fifteenth* in 1870, all now being a part of the National Constitution.]

# THE EXECUTIVE BRANCH OF THE GOVERNMENT.

## THE PRESIDENT.

The executive power is vested in a President of the United States of America. He must be a natural born citizen, a resident of the United States for fourteen years, and of the age of thirty-five years or upwards. He holds his office during the the term of four years, and may be re-elected for a second term.

He is the Commander-in-Chief of the army and navy, and with the consent of the Senate, appoints all cabinet, judicial and executive officers; has power to grant pardons and reprieves for offences against the United States, and it is his duty to see that the laws are faithfully executed.

## THE VICE-PRESIDENT.

The Vice-President is elected at the same time, in the same manner, and for the same term as the President, and must have the same qualifications. In case of the death or disability of the President, the duties of the office devolve upon the Vice-President during the term. In case of the death or disability of the Vice-President, the president of the Senate, *pro tempore* takes his place.

## PRESIDENTIAL ELECTORS.

The present mode of election of the President and Vice-President of the United States, is not, by the the *direct vote of the people*, but through the machinery of an "Electoral College." Each State has as many Electors, as it has Senators and Representatives in Congress, who must be chosen within thirty-four days preceding the first Wednesday of December of the year in which an election of President and Vice-President takes place.

By an Act of Congress, approved January 23rd, 1845, the uniform time for holding elections for Electors in all the States of the Union, was fixed for the Tuesday next after the first Monday, in the month of November of the year in which they are to be appointed. Each State may also by law provide for the filling of any vacancy or vacancies which may occur in its College of Electors, when such College meets to give its electoral vote, and if any State having held an election for the purpose of choosing electors, should fail to make a choice on the day appointed, then the Electors may be appointed on a subsequent day, in such manner as the State shall by law provide

The Electors must meet at the capitol of their respective States, on the first Wednesday of December, and vote by distinct ballots for President and Vice-President, one of whom shall not be an inhabitant of the same State with themselves.

Having made lists of the number of votes cast and for whom given, they must sign, certify, seal up, and transmit them by a special messenger to the President of the Senate, at Washington. These are opened by the President of the Senate, and the votes are counted in the presence of the Senate and House of Representatives, who have convened on a day fixed for that purpose.

The person having the greatest number of votes for President is duly elected, if such a number be a *majority of the whole number of electors appointed.* If no person has such a majority, then from the persons having the highest number, not exceeding three, in the list of those voted for, the House of Representatives shall choose immediately, and by ballot, the President. In case they neglect to do this before the 4th of March following, then the Vice-President shall act as President, as he would in case of the death or other constitutional disability of the President.

## PRESIDENTIAL ELECTORS—HOW APPOINTED

After each decennial enumeration, the aggregate representative population of the United States is ascertained by the Secretary of the Interior.

This was *formerly* done by adding to the whole number of free persons in all the States, including those bound to service for a term of years, excluding the Indians not taxed, and three-fifths of all other persons. As the Members of the House of Representatives were limited by Act of May 23d, 1850, to 233, this aggregate representative population was divided by that number, and the quotient, rejecting fractions, if any, was the ratio of apportionment for the several States.

The loss by fractions was made up by assigning to as many States, having the largest fractions, as may be necessary to make the whole number of Representatives 233, one additional Member each, for its fraction. When new States were admitted, Representatives were assigned to such States on the above basis, in addition to the number limited, till the next census. Thus under the census of 1860 the ratio was found to be 126,823.

By a subsequent Act in March 1862, this ratio was changed, and the number of Representatives after March 1863 was increased from 233 to 241, and subsequently increased by addition of new States and an additional Representative to some of the States to 243.

Now add to this 243, (the number of Representatives,) 74, (the number of Senators,) and we have the number of Presidential Electors of 1868, provided the Electoral College had been full, and all the States (37) had been represented; but as Virginia, Mississippi, and Texas had no vote, only 34 States were represented.

# APPORTIONMENT OF REPRESENTATIVES.

| Prior to 1863 under Census 1860 | New Apportionment, Census 1870 |
|---|---|
| Alabama..........6 | Alabama..........8 |
| Arkansas..........3 | Arkansas..........4 |
| California..........3 | California..........4 |
| Connecticut..........4 | Connecticut..........4 |
| Delaware..........1 | Delaware..........1 |
| Florida..........1 | Florida..........2 |
| Georgia..........7 | Georgia..........9 |
| Illinois..........14 | Illinois..........19 |
| Indiana..........11 | Indiana..........13 |
| Iowa..........6 | Iowa..........9 |
| Kansas..........1 | Kansas..........3 |
| Kentucky..........9 | Kentucky..........10 |
| Louisiana..........5 | Louisiana..........6 |
| Maine..........5 | Maine..........5 |
| Maryland..........5 | Maryland..........6 |
| Massachusetts..........10 | Massachusetts..........11 |
| Michigan..........6 | Michigan..........9 |
| Minnesota..........2 | Minnesota..........3 |
| Mississippi..........5 | Mississippi..........6 |
| Missouri..........9 | Missouri..........13 |
| Nebraska..........1 | Nebraska..........1 |
| Nevada..........1 | Nevada..........1 |
| New Hampshire..........3 | New Hampshire..........3 |
| New Jersey..........5 | New Jersey..........7 |
| New York..........31 | New York..........33 |
| North Carolina..........7 | North Carolina..........8 |
| Ohio..........19 | Ohio..........20 |
| Oregon..........1 | Oregon..........1 |
| Pennsylvania..........24 | Pennsylvania..........27 |
| Rhode Island..........2 | Rhode Island..........2 |
| South Carolina..........4 | South Carolina..........5 |
| Tennessee..........8 | Tennessee..........10 |
| Texas..........4 | Texas..........6 |
| Virginia..........8 | Virginia..........9 |
| Vermont..........3 | Vermont..........3 |
| West Virginia..........3 | West Virginia..........3 |
| Wisconsin..........6 | Wisconsin..........8 |
| Total..........243 | Total..........292 |

## THE CABINET.

The Administrative business of the Country is attended to by several officers, having the titles of Secretaries &c. &c., who together form the Cabinet, and they are appointed by the President. It is now composed of the Secretary of State, Secretary of the Treasury, Secretary of War, Secretary of the Navy, Secretary of the Interior, Postmaster-General, and the Attorney-General, who is the legal adviser of the Administration, and the Official law authority. Each of these Secretaries has charge of a separate department.

### THE SECRETARY OF STATE

has charge of the *great seal* of the United States, but cannot affix it to any instrument in writing, without authority from the President. He conducts all treaties we make with other powers, attends to the correspondence with our Ministers at foreign courts, and with Ministers of foreign courts residing here; grants passports, &c.

### THE SECRETARY OF THE TREASURY

superintends all the financial matters of the Government; the settling of all the public accounts, and recommends to Congress any measure he may deem advisable for the condition of the revenue.

### THE SECRETARY OF WAR

has the exclusive control of the military affairs of the Nation, and superintends every department of the same; attends to the making of public surveys; erection of fortifications, &c. The Adjutant-General's office; Quartermaster-General's Bureau; the Ordinance, Typographical, Medical, Engineer, and Subsistence Bureaus, all come under his supervision.

### THE SECRETARY OF THE NAVY

superintends generally all naval affairs, and directs the naval forces. The several Bureaus, such as of Docks, of Navy Yards, of Construction, Equipment, and repairs of Ordinance and Hydrography are all under his supervision.

## THE SECRETARY OF THE INTERIOR

superintends all matters connected with the public domain, Indian Affairs, Patents, Public Buildings, Pensions, the Census, and the Expenditures of the Federal Judiciary.

## THE POSTMASTER-GENERAL

has the charge of all postal arrangements within the United States, as well as with all Foreign States. The Contract Office, the Appointment Office, and the Inspection Office, all come under his supervision.

## THE ATTORNEY-GENERAL

is the Law Counsel for the President, and other officers of the Government. He is the Constitutional Adviser of the Government, and defends the same when necessary.

SEAL OF THE STATE DEPARTMEMT.

THE NATIONAL SENATE CHAMBER.

# THE LEGISLATIVE BRANCH OF THE GOVERNMENT.

All Legislative powers are vested in Congress, which consists of a Senate and House of Representatives, analagous to Parliament in Great Britain, which consists of a House of Lords and a House of Commons.

## SENATE.

The Senate consists of two members from each State, elected by the Legislature thereof respectively for six years. They are divided into three classes, each one-third, which is renewed biennially. No person can be a Senator, who has not attained the age of *thirty years*, and been nine years a citizen of the United States, and who shall not, when elected, be an inhabitant of the State for which he shall be chosen.

The Vice-President of the United States is *Ex-Officio*, the President of the Senate. Besides its Legislative prerogatives, the Senate is vested with judicial functions, and its members may constitute a High Court of Impeachment; but the sole power of impeachment belongs to the Representatives.

## HOUSE OF REPRESENTATIVES.

The members of the House of Representatives are elected by the people, to seats therein for two years, and the number of such members is in accordance with the population of the several States. In order to ascertain the number, each State is entitled to a census, which is taken every ten years, and heretofore in this computation, two-thirds of the Slaves, and Indians not taxed have been excluded. Each State, however, is entitled to one Representative.

To be *qualified* for this office, the person must be at least *twenty-five* years of age, at least seven years a citizen of the United States, and an inhabitant of the State in which he is chosen.

The ratio based on the census of 1790, was one Representative for every 33,500 inhabitants. The ratio according to the census of 1860, was one for every 126,823 persons, the whole number being limited to 233, but subsequently, by Act of March 4th, 1862, and by additional Act of March 3d, 1863, the ratio was changed; the whole number after March 3d 1863 being made 243. The representative ratio under the census of 1870, is 135,239. (Vide page 77.)

---

# THE JUDICIAL DEPARTMENT OF THE GOVERNMENT.

The Judicial powers of the country are vested in the Supreme, Circuit and District Courts of the United States. These are called the *Federal* Courts. Congress however, may from time to time establish such other and inferior courts, as may be considered advisable.

### THE SUPREME COURT OF THE UNITED STATES.

This is the highest Judicial Tribunal in the land. It has a Chief Justice and eight associate Justices. It has *exclusive jurisdiction* in matters between the States, and *appellate jurisdiction* from final decrees and judgments of the Circuit Courts, in cases where the matters in dispute exclusive of costs exceed the sum of $2,000, and from final judgments and decrees of the highest courts of the several States in certain cases. It has also power to issue writs of *prohibition* and *mandamus* in certain cases.

### THE CIRCUIT COURTS OF THE UNITED STATES.

They are held by a Justice of the Supreme Court assigned to the Circuit, and by the Judge of the District in which the Court sits, conjointly. They have original jurisdiction concurrent with the courts of the several States, of all suits at Common Law, or in Equity, when the matter in dispute exclusive of costs, *exceeds the sum of five hundred dollars* and the United States are plaintiff, or an alien is a party, or where the suit is between a citizen of the State where the suit is brought and another State.

They have also exclusive cognizance of most of the crimes and offences cognizable under the authority of the United States, and concurrent jurisdiction with the District Court of offences cognizable therein. They have also appellate jurisdiction from judgments and final decrees of the District Courts of the United States, in all cases where the matter in dispute exceeds the sum, or value of fifty dollars.

The trial of *issues of fact* in all suits, excepting those of equity, and admiralty and maritime jurisdiction, is by a jury.

## THE DISTRICT COURTS OF THE UNITED STATES.

They have exclusive original jurisdiction of all civil cases of Admiralty and Maritime jurisdiction, including all seizures under the navigation laws, or of impost, or trade of the United States, where they are made upon tide waters, saving however to suitors, the right of a common law remedy where the common law gives it, also of all crimes and offences cognizable under the authority of the United States, committed within their respective Districts, or upon the high seas in certain cases. They have also concurrent jurisdiction with the State Courts in certain cases. The trial is by jury, except in civil cases of Admiralty and Maritime jurisdiction.

## JUDGES HOW APPOINTED.

The appointment of all Judges of the Federal Courts is made by the President, by, and with the approval and consent of the Senate, and they hold their offices during good behavior, and can be removed only on impeachment.

## SALARIES OF FEDERAL OFFICERS.

| | |
|---|---:|
| President of the United States, per annum, | $50,000.00 |
| Vice President " " " " " | 8,000.00 |
| Secretary of State and other Cabinet Ministers, each " " | 8,000.00 |
| Chief Justice Supreme Court, " " | 10,500.00 |
| Each Associate Justice Supreme Court " " | 10,000.00 |
| Senators and Representatives,* " " | 5,000.00 |
| Speaker House of Representatives, " " | 8,000.00 |
| Secretary of the Senate, " " | 3,600.00 |
| Clerk House of Representatives, " " | 3,600.00 |
| Superintendent Coast Survey, " " | 6,000.00 |
| Ministers Plenipotentiary to Great Britain and France, " " | 17,500.00 |
| Ministers Plenipotentiary to Russia, Prussia, Spain, Austria, Italy, China, Brazil and Mexico, " " | 12,000.00 |
| Ministers Resident to Portugal and other States, " " | 7,500.00 |
| Consul Generals, Per Annum, from | $3,000.00 to 6,000.00 |
| Consuls, " " | 1,000.00 to 7,000.00 |
| Secretaries of Legation, " " | 1,500.00 to 2,700.00 |

*Senators and Representatives also receive twenty cents per mile as mileage. There is deducted from their salaries $8.00 per diem for each day's absence, unless caused by sickness.

## PRESIDENTS OF THE CONTINENTAL CONGRESS.

*From 1774 to 1789.*

| Name. | From what Colony. | When Elected | Born | Died |
|---|---|---|---|---|
| Peyton Randolph, | Virginia, | Sept 5, 1774 | 1723 | 1775 |
| Henry Middleton, | South Carolina, | Oct 22, 1774 | .... | .... |
| Peyton Randolph, | Virginia, | May 10, 1775 | 1723 | 1775 |
| John Hancock, | Massachusetts, | May 24, 1775 | 1737 | 1793 |
| Henry Laurens, | South Carolina, | Nov 1, 1777 | 1724 | 1792 |
| John Jay, | New York, | Dec 10, 1778 | 1745 | 1829 |
| Samuel Huntington, | Connecticut, | Sept 28, 1779 | 1732 | 1796 |
| Thomas McKean, | Delaware, | July 10, 1781 | 1734 | 1817 |
| John Hanson, | Maryland, | Nov 5, 1781 | .... | 1783 |
| Elias Boudinot, | New Jersey, | Nov 4, 1782 | 1740 | 1824 |
| Thomas Mifflin, | Pennsylvania, | Nov 3, 1783 | 1744 | 1800 |
| Richard Henry Lee, | Virginia, | Nov 30, 1784 | 1732 | 1794 |
| John Hancock, | Massachusetts, | Nov 23, 1785 | 1737 | 1775 |
| Nathaniel Gorham, | Massachusetts, | June 6, 1786 | 1738 | 1796 |
| Arthur St. Clair, | Pennsylvania, | Feb 2, 1787 | .... | 1818 |
| Cyrus Griffin, | Virginia. | Jan 22, 1788 | 1748 | 1810 |

# SIGNERS OF THE DECLARATION OF INDEPENDENCE.

| Names | Time and place of birth. | | Died. |
|---|---|---|---|
| Adams, John | Braintree, Mass. ........Oct. | 19, 1735 | July 4, 1826 |
| Adams, Samuel | Boston, Mass. ........Sept. | 27, 1722 | Oct. 2, 1803 |
| Bartlett, Josiah | Amesbury, Mass.......in Nov. | 1729 | May 19, 1795 |
| Braxton, Carter | Newington, Va. ........Sept. | 10, 1736 | Oct. 10, 1797 |
| Carroll, Charles | Annapolis, Md. ........ept. | 20, 1737 | Nov. 14, 1832 |
| Chase, Samuel | Somerset Co., Md. ....Apr. | 17, 1741 | June 19, 1811 |
| Clark, Abraham | Elizabethtown, N. J....Feb. | 15, 1726 | Sept., 1794 |
| Clymer, George | Philadelphia, Pa. ........in | 1739 | Jan. 23, 1813 |
| Ellery, William | Newport, R. I. ........Dec. | 22, 1727 | Feb. 15, 1820 |
| Floyd, William | Suffolk Co., N. Y. ....Dec. | 17, 1734 | Aug. 4, 1821 |
| Franklin, Benjamin | Boston, Mass. ........Jan. | 17, 1706 | April 17, 1790 |
| Gerry, Elbridge | Marblehead, Mass. ....July | 17, 1744 | Nov. 23, 1814 |
| Gwinnett, Button | England ........in | 1732 | May 27, 1777 |
| Hall, Lyman | Connecticut ........in | 1731 | Feb., 1790 |
| Hancock, John | Braintree, Mass. ........in | 1737 | Oct. 8, 1793 |
| Harrison, Benjamin | Berkely, Va. | | April, 1791 |
| Hart, John | Hopewell, N. J. ........about | 1715 | 1780 |
| Heyward, Thomas, Jr. | St. Luke's, S. C. ........in | 1746 | March, 1809 |
| Hewes, Joseph | Kingston, N. J. ........in | 1730 | Nov. 10, 1779 |
| Hooper, William | Boston, Mass. ........June | 17, 1742 | Oct., 1790 |
| Hopkins, Stephen | Scituate, R. I. ........March | 7, 1707 | July 13, 1785 |
| Hopkinson, Francis | Philadelphia, Penn...in | 1737 | May 9, 1790 |
| Huntington, Samuel | Windham, Conn. ........July | 3, 1732 | Jan. 5, 1796 |
| Jefferson, Thomas | Shadwell, Va. ........April | 13, 1743 | July 4, 1826 |
| Lee, Francis Lightfoot | Stratford, Va. ........Oct. | 14, 1734 | April, 1797 |
| Lee, Richard Henry | Stratford, Va. ........Jan. | 20, 1732 | June 19, 1794 |
| Lewis, Francis | Landaff, Wales ........in Mar., | 1713 | Dec. 30, 1803 |
| Livingston, Philip | Albany, N. Y. ........Jan. | 15, 1716 | June 12, 1778 |
| Lynch, Thomas, Jr. | St. George's, S. C. ....Aug. | 5, 1749 | Lost at sea, 1779 |
| McKean, Thomas | Chester Co., Pa. ........Mar. | 19, 1734 | June 24, 1817 |
| Middleton, Arthur | Middleton Place, S. C.In | 1743 | Jan. 1, 1787 |
| Morris, Lewis | Morrisania, N. Y. ....In | 1726 | Jan. 22, 1798 |
| Morris, Robert | Lancashire, Eng. ....Jan., | 1733-'4 | May 8, 1806 |
| Morton, John | Ridley, Pa. ........in | 1724 | April, 1777 |
| Nelson, Thomas, Jr. | York, Va. ........Dec. | 26, 1738 | Jan. 4, 1789 |
| Paca, William | Wye Hill, Md. ........Oct. | 31, 1740 | 1799 |
| Paine, Robert Treat | Boston, Mass. ........in | 1731 | May 11, 1814 |
| Penn, John | Caroline Co., Va. ....May | 17, 1741 | Oct. 26, 1800 |
| Read, George | Cecil Co., Md. ........in | 1734 | 1796 |
| Rodney, Cæsar | Dover, Del. ........in | 1730 | 1783 |
| Ross, George | New Castle, Del. ....in | 1730 | July, 1779 |
| Rush, Benjamin, M.D. | Byberry, Pa. ........Dec. | 24, 1745 | April 19, 1813 |
| Rutledge, Edward | Charleston, S. C. ....in Nov., | 1749 | Jan. 23, 1800 |
| Sherman, Roger | Newton, Mass. ........April | 19, 1721 | July 23, 1793 |
| Smith, James | Ireland | | July 11, 1806 |
| Stockton, Richard | Princeton, N. J. ........Oct. | 1, 1730 | Feb. 28, 1781 |
| Stone, Thomas | Charles Co., Md. ........in | 1742 | Oct. 5, 1787 |
| Taylor, George | Ireland ........in | 1716 | Feb. 28, 1787 |
| Thornton, Matthew | Ireland ........in | 1714 | June 24, 1803 |
| Walton, George | Frederick Co., Va. ....In | 1740 | Feb. 2, 1805 |
| Whipple, William | Kittery, Me. ........in | 1730 | Nov. 28, 1785 |
| Williams, William | Lebanon, Conn. ........April | 8, 1731 | Aug. 2, 1811 |
| Wilson, James | Scotland ........about | 1742 | Aug. 28, 1798 |
| Witherspoon, John | Yester, Scotland ....Feb. | 5, 1722 | Nov. 15, 1794 |
| Wolcott, Oliver | Windsor, Conn. ........Nov. | 26, 1726 | Dec. 1, 1797 |
| Wythe, George | Elizabeth City Co.,Va.In | 1726 | June 8, 1806 |

# PRESIDENTS AND VICE-PRESIDENTS OF UNITED STATES.

## PRESIDENTS.

| Year of qualific'n. | Name. | Where from. | Term of office. |
|---|---|---|---|
| 1789 | George Washington | Virginia | 8 years. |
| 1797 | John Adams | Massachusetts | 4 years. |
| 1801 | Thomas Jefferson | Virginia | 8 years. |
| 1809 | James Madison | Virginia | 8 years. |
| 1817 | James Monroe | Virginia | 8 years. |
| 1824 | John Quincy Adams | Massachusetts | 4 years. |
| 1829 | Andrew Jackson | Tennessee | 8 years. |
| 1837 | Martin Van Buren | New York | 4 years. |
| 1841 | Wm. Henry Harrison* | Ohio | 1 month. |
| 1841 | John Tyler | Virginia | 3 yrs., 11 mos. |
| 1845 | James Knox Polk | Tennessee | 4 years. |
| 1849 | Zachary Taylor* | Louisiana | 1 yr., 4 m., 5 d. |
| 1850 | Millard Fillmore | New York | 2 yr., 7 m., 26 d. |
| 1853 | Franklin Pierce | New Hampshire | 4 years. |
| 1857 | James Buchanan | Pennsylvania | 4 years. |
| 1861 | Abraham Lincoln* | Illinois | 4 yr., 1 m., 10 d. |
| 1865 | Andrew Johnson | Tennessee | 3 yr. 10 m., 20 d. |
| 1869 | Ulysses S. Grant | Illinois | 8 years. |

## VICE-PRESIDENTS.

| Year of qualification. | Name. | Where from. |
|---|---|---|
| 1789 | John Adams | Massachusetts. |
| 1797 | Thomas Jefferson | Virginia. |
| 1801 | Aaron Burr | New York. |
| 1804 | George Clinton | New York. |
| 1813 | Elbridge Gerry | Massachusetts. |
| 1817 | Daniel D. Tompkins | New York. |
| 1824 | John C. Calhoun | South Carolina. |
| 1833 | Martin Van Buren | New York. |
| 1837 | Richard M. Johnson | Kentucky. |
| 1841 | John Tyler | Virginia. |
| 1842 | Samuel L. Southard§ | New Jersey. |
| 1845 | George M. Dallas | Pennsylvania. |
| 1849 | Millard Fillmore | New York. |
| 1851 | William R. King§ | Alabama. |
| 1853 | David R. Atchison§ | Missouri. |
| 1855 | Jesse D. Bright§ | Indiana. |
| 1857 | John C. Breckinridge | Kentucky. |
| 1861 | Hannibal Hamlin | Maine. |
| 1865 | Andrew Johnson | Tennessee. |
| 1865 | Lafayette C. Foster§ | Connecticut. |
| 1869 | Schuyler Colfax | Indiana. |
| 1873 | Henry Wilson* | Massachusetts. |
| 1875 | Thomas W. Ferre§ | Michigan. |

\* Died in office.
§ *Ex-officio* as President *pro tem.* of the Senate.

## SECRETARIES OF STATE.

| Names. | State. | Term of Service. | Born | Died |
|---|---|---|---|---|
| Thomas Jefferson, | Virginia | 1789-1794 | 1743 | 1826 |
| Edmund Randolph, | Virginia | 1794-1795 | .... | 1813 |
| Timothy Pickering, | Massachusetts | 1795-1800 | 1745 | 1829 |
| John Marshall, | Virginia | 1800-1801 | 1755 | 1835 |
| James Madison, | Virginia | 1801-1809 | 1751 | 1857 |
| Robert Smith, | Massachusetts | 1809-1811 | .... | .... |
| James Monroe, | Virginia | 1811-1817 | 1759 | 1831 |
| John Quincy Adams, | Massachusetts | 1817-1825 | 1767 | 1848 |
| Henry Clay, | Kentucky | 1825-1829 | 1777 | 1852 |
| Martin Van Buren, | New York | 1829-1831 | 1782 | 1862 |
| Edward Livingston, | Louisiana | 1831-1833 | 1764 | 1836 |
| Louis McLane, | Delaware | 1833-1835 | 1786 | 1857 |
| John Forsyth, | Georgia | 1835-1841 | 1780 | 1841 |
| Daniel Webster, | Massachusetts | 1841-1843 | 1782 | 1852 |
| Hugh S. Legare, | South Carolina | 1843-1843 | 1797 | 1843 |
| Abel P. Upshur, | Virginia | 1843-1844 | 1790 | 1844 |
| John C. Calhoun, | South Carolina | 1844-1845 | 1782 | 1850 |
| James Buchanan, | Pennsylvania | 1845-1849 | 1791 | 1868 |
| John M. Clayton, | Delaware | 1849-1850 | 1796 | 1856 |
| Daniel Webster, | Massachusetts | 1850-1852 | 1782 | 1852 |
| Edward Everett, | Massachusetts | 1852-1853 | 1794 | 1865 |
| William L. Marcy, | New York | 1853-1857 | 1786 | 1860 |
| Lewis Cass, | Michigan | 1857-1861 | 1782 | .... |
| Jeremiah S. Black, | Pennsylvania | 1861-1861 | 1810 | .... |
| William H. Seward, | New York | 1861-1869 | 1801 | .... |
| Elihu B. Washburne, | Illinois | 1869 | .... | .... |
| Hamilton Fish, | New York | 1869 | .... | .... |

## SECRETARIES OF THE TREASURY.

| Names. | State | When app'd | Names. | State | When app'd |
|---|---|---|---|---|---|
| Alexander Hamilton | N. Y | 1789 | Walter Forward | Penn | 1841 |
| Oliver Wolcott | Conn | 1795 | John C. Spencer | N. Y | 1843 |
| Samuel Dexter | Mass | 1801 | George M. Bibb | Ky | 1844 |
| Albert Gallatin | Penn | 1802 | Robert J. Walker | Miss | 1845 |
| George W. Campbell | Tenn | 1814 | William M. Meredith | Penn | 1849 |
| Alexander J. Dallas | Penn | 1814 | Thomas Corwin | Ohio | 1850 |
| William H. Crawford | Ga | 1817 | James Guthrie | Ky | 1853 |
| Richard Rush | Penn | 1825 | Howell Cobb | Ga | 1857 |
| Samuel D. Ingham | Penn | 1829 | Philip F. Thomas | Md | 1860 |
| Louis McLane | Del | 1831 | John A. Dix | N. Y | 1861 |
| William S. Duane | Penn | 1833 | Salmon P. Chase | Ohio | 1861 |
| Roger B. Taney | Md | 1833 | Wm P. Fessenden | Me | 1864 |
| Levi Woodbury | N. H | 1834 | Hugh McCulloch | Ind | 1865 |
| Thomas Ewing | Ohio | 1841 | George S. Boutwell | Mass | 1869 |
| | | | Wm. A. Richardson | Mass | 1873 |
| | | | Benj. H. Bristow | Ky. | 1874 |

## CABINET OFFICERS.

## SECRETARIES OF WAR.

| Names. | State | When app'd | Names | State | When app'd |
|---|---|---|---|---|---|
| Henry Knox | Mass | 1789 | Joel R. Poinsett | S. C | 1837 |
| Timothy Pickering | Penn | 1795 | John Bell | Tenn | 1841 |
| James McHenry | Md | 1796 | John C. Spencer | N. Y | 1841 |
| Samuel Dexter | Mass | 1800 | James M. Porter | Penn | 1843 |
| Roger Griswold | Conn | 1801 | William Wilkins | Penn | 1844 |
| Henry Dearborn | Mass | 1801 | William L. Marcy | N. Y | 1845 |
| William Eustis | Mass | 1809 | George W. Crawford | Ga | 1849 |
| John Armstrong | N. Y | 1813 | Charles M. Conrad | La | 1850 |
| James Monroe | Va | 1814 | Jefferson Davis | Miss | 1853 |
| William H. Crawford | Ga | 1815 | John B. Floyd | Va | 1857 |
| George Graham | Va | 1817 | Joseph Holt | Ky | 1860 |
| John C. Calhoun | S. C | 1817 | Simon Cameron | Penn | 1861 |
| James Barbour | Va | 1825 | Edwin M. Stanton | Penn | 1862 |
| Peter B. Porter | N. Y | 1828 | John M. Schofield | N. Y | 1868 |
| John H. Eaton | Tenn | 1829 | John A. Rawlins | Ill | 1869 |
| Lewis Cass | Mich | 1831 | William W. Belknap | Iowa | |
| Benjamin F. Butler | N. Y | 1837 | Alphonso Taft | Ohio | 1876 |

## SECRETARIES OF THE NAVY.

| Names. | State. | When app'd. | Names | State | When app'd |
|---|---|---|---|---|---|
| George Cabot | Mass | 1798 | Abel P. Upshur | Va | 1841 |
| Benjamin Stoddert | Md | 1798 | David Henshaw | Mass | 1843 |
| Robert Smith | Md | 1801 | Thomas W. Gilmer | Va | 1844 |
| Jacob Crowninshield | Mass | 1805 | John Y. Mason | Va | 1844 |
| Paul Hamilton | S. C | 1809 | George Bancroft | Mass | 1845 |
| William Jones | Penn | 1813 | John Y. Mason | Va | 1846 |
| B. W. Crowninshield | Mass | 1814 | William B. Preston | Va | 1849 |
| Smith Thompson | N. Y | 1818 | William A. Graham | N. C | 1850 |
| John Rodgers | | 1823 | John P. Kennedy | Md | 1852 |
| Samuel L. Southard | N. J | 1823 | James C. Dobbin | N. C | 1853 |
| John Branch | N. C | 1829 | Isaac Toucey | Conn | 1857 |
| Levi Woodbury | N. H | 1831 | Gideon Wells | Conn | 1861 |
| Mahlon Dickerson | N. J | 1834 | Adolph E. Borie | Penn | 1869 |
| James K. Paulding | N. Y | 1838 | George M. Robeson | N. J | 1869 |
| George E. Badger | N. C | 1841 | | | |

## POST MASTERS—GENERAL.

| Names. | State | When app'd. | Names | State | When app'd |
|---|---|---|---|---|---|
| Samuel Osgood | Mass | 1789 | Jacob Collamer | Vt | 1849 |
| Timothy Pickering | Penn | 1791 | Nathan K. Hall | N. Y | 1850 |
| Joseph Habersham | Ga | 1795 | Samuel D. Hubbard | Conn | 1852 |
| Gideon Granger | Conn | 1801 | James Campbell | Penn | 1853 |
| Return Meigs, Jr. | Ohio | 1811 | Aaron V. Brown | Tenn | 1857 |
| John McLean | Ohio | 1823 | Joseph Holt | Ky | 1860 |
| William T. Barry | Ky | 1829 | Horatio King | | 1860 |
| Amos Kendall | Ky | 1835 | Montgomery Blair | Md | 1861 |
| John M. Niles | Conn | 1840 | William Dennison | Ohio | 1865 |
| Francis Granger | N. Y | 1841 | Alex. W. Randall | Wis | 1866 |
| Charles A. Wickliffe | Ky | 1841 | John A. J. Creswell | Md. | 1869 |
| Cave Johnston | Tenn | 1845 | Marshall Jewell | Conn | 1874 |

## ATTORNEYS-GENERAL.

| Names. | State | When app'd | Names | State | When app'd |
|---|---|---|---|---|---|
| Edmund Randolph | Va | 1789 | Hugh S. Legare | S. C | 1841 |
| William Bradford | Penn | 1794 | John Nelson | Md | 1843 |
| Charles Lee | Va | 1795 | John Y. Mason | Va | 1845 |
| Levi Lincoln | Mass | 1801 | Nathan Clifford | Me | 1846 |
| Robert Smith | Md | 1805 | Isaac Toucey | Conn | 1848 |
| John Breckenridge | Ky | 1805 | Reverdy Johnson | Md | 2849 |
| Cæsar A. Rodney | Del | 1807 | John J. Crittenden | Ky | 1850 |
| William Pinkney | Md | 1811 | Caleb Cushing | Mass | 1853 |
| Richard Rush | Penn | 1814 | Jeremiah S. Black | Penn | 1857 |
| William Wirt | Va | 1817 | Edwin M. Stanton | Penn | 1860 |
| John M. Berrien | Ga | 1829 | Edward Bates | Mo | 1861 |
| Roger B. Taney | Md | 1831 | James Speed | Ky | 1864 |
| Benjamin F. Butler | N. Y | 1833 | Henry Stanberry | Ohio | 1866 |
| Felix Grundy | Tenn | 1838 | William M. Evarts | N. Y | 1868 |
| Henry D. Gilpin | Penn | 1840 | E Rockwood Hoar | Mass | 1869 |
| John J. Crittenden | Ky | 1841 | George H. Williams | Ore'n | 1869 |
|  |  |  | Edward Pierrepont | N. Y. | 1875 |

## SECRETARIES OF THE INTERIOR.

| | | | | | |
|---|---|---|---|---|---|
| Thomas Ewing | Ohio | 1849 | John P. Usher | Ind | 1862 |
| T. M. T. McKennan | Penn | 1850 | James Harlan | Iowa | 1865 |
| Alex'r H. H. Stewart | Va | 1850 | O. H. Browning | Ill | 1866 |
| Robert McClelland | Mich | 1853 | Jacob D. Cox | Ohio | 1869 |
| Jacob Thompson | Miss | 1857 | Columbus Delano | Ohio | 1869 |
| Caleb B. Smith | Ind | 1861 | Zachariah Chandler | Mich | 1875 |

## CHIEF JUSTICES U. S. SUPREME COURT.

| | | | | | |
|---|---|---|---|---|---|
| John Jay | N. Y. | 1789 | Roger B. Taney | Md | 1836 |
| John Rutledge | S. C. | 1795 | Salmon P. Chase | Ohio | 1864 |
| Oliver Ellsworth | Conn | 1796 | Morrison R. Waite | Ohio | 1874 |
| John Marshall | Va | 1801 | | | |

## ASSOCIATE JUSTICES U. S. SUPREME COURT.

| | | | | | |
|---|---|---|---|---|---|
| John Rutledge | S. C | 1789 | Henry Baldwin | Penn | 1830 |
| William Cushing | Mass | 1789 | James M. Wayne | Ga | 1835 |
| James Wilson | Penn | 1789 | Philip P. Barbour | Va | 1836 |
| John Blair | Va | 1789 | John Catron | Tenn | 1837 |
| Robert H. Harrison | Md | 1789 | William Smith | Ala | 1837 |
| James Iredell | N. C | 1790 | John McKinley | Ala | 1837 |
| Thomas Johnson | Md | 1791 | Peter V. Daniel | Va | 1841 |
| William Patterson | N. J | 1793 | Samuel Nelson | N. Y | 1845 |
| Samuel Chase | Md | 1796 | Levi Woodbury | N. H | 1845 |
| Bushrod Washington | Va | 1798 | Robert C. Grier | Penn | 1846 |
| Alfred Moore | N. C | 1799 | Benjamin R. Curtis | Mass | 1851 |
| William Johnson | S. C | 1804 | James A. Campbell | Ala | 1853 |
| Brock Livingston | N. Y | 1806 | Nathan Clifford | Me | 1858 |
| Thomas Todd | Ky | 1807 | Noah H. Swayne | Ohio | 1862 |
| Joseph Story | Mass | 1811 | Samuel F. Miller | Iowa | 1862 |
| Gabriel Duval | Md | 1811 | David Davis | Ill | 1862 |
| Smith Thompson | N. Y | 1823 | Stephen J. Field | Cal | 1863 |
| Robert Trimble | Ky | 1826 | William M. Strong | Pa | 1870 |
| John McLean | Ohio | 1829 | Joseph P. Bradley | N. J | 1870 |
| Ward Hunt | N. Y. | 1872 | | | |

# NAMES OF THE SPEAKERS

## OF THE

# HOUSE OF REPRESENTATIVES.

### From 1789 to 1872.

*1st Congress.*—FREDERICK AUGUSTUS MUHLENBURGH, of Pennsylvania, was elected speaker of the house of representatives, April 1, 1789, and served to March 3, 1791.

*2d Congress.*—JONATHAN TRUMBULL, of Connecticut, was elected speaker, and served from the 24th of October, 1791, to March 3, 1793.

*3d Congress.*—FREDERICK AUGUSTUS MUHLENBURGH, of Pennsylvania, was elected speaker, and served from December 2, 1793, to 3d of March, 1795.

*4th and 5th Congresses.*—JONATHAN DAYTON, of New Jersey, was elected speaker, and served from 7th of December, 1795, to 3d of March, 1799.

*6th Congress.*—THEODORE SEDGWICK, of Massachusetts, was elected speaker, and served from 2d December. 1799, to 3d March, 1801.

*7th, 8th and 9th Congresses.*—NATHANIEL MACON, of North Carolina, was elected speaker, and served from 7th December, 1801, to March 3, 1807.

*10th and 11th Congresses.*—JOSEPH B. VARNUM, of Massachusetts, was elected speaker, and served from October 26, 1807, to 3d March, 1811.

*12th, 13th, 14th, 15th and 16th Congresses.*—HENRY CLAY, of Kentucky, was elected speaker, and served from 4th November, 1811, to 3d March, 1821.

*17th Congress.*—PHILIP P. BARBOUR, of Virginia, was elected speaker, and served from 3d December, 1821, to 3d of March, 1823.

18*th Congress.*—HENRY CLAY, of Kentucky, was elected speaker, and served from 1st of December, 1823, to March 3, 1825.

19*th Congress.*—JOHN W. TAYLOR, of New York, was elected speaker, and served from December 5, 1825, to March 3, 1827.

20*th, 21st, 22d and 23d Congresses.*—ANDREW STEPHENSON, of Virginia, was elected speaker, and served from 3d December, 1827, to 3d of June, 1834; and JOHN BELL, of Tennessee, was, on the 4th of June, 1834, elected to serve out the balance of the 23d Congress, which ended on the 3d of March, 1835.

24*th and 25th Congresses.*—JAMES K. POLK, of Tennessee, was elected speaker, and served from 7th December, 1835, to March 3, 1839.

26*th Congress.*—ROBERT M. T. HUNTER, of Virginia, was elected speaker, and served from the 16th of December, 1839, to March 3, 1841.

27*th Congress.*—JOHN WHITE, of Kentucky, was elected speaker, and served from 31st May, 1841, to March 3, 1843.

28*th Congress.*—JOHN W. JONES, of Virginia, was elected speaker, and served from 4th December 1843, to March 3, 1845.

29*th Congress.*—JOHN W. DAVIS, of Indiana, was elected speaker, and served from 1st December 1845, to March 3, 1847.

30*th Congress.*—ROBERT C. WINTHROP, of Massachusetts, was elected speaker, and served from the 6th of December, 1847, to March 3, 1849.

31*st Congress.*—HOWELL COBB, of Georgia, was elected speaker, and served from 24th December, 1849, to March 3, 1851.

32*d and 33d Congresses.*—LINN BOYD, of Kentucky, was elected speaker, and served from 4th December, 1851, to March 3, 1855.

*34th Congress.*—NATHANIEL P. BANKS, Jr., of Massachusetts, was elected speaker, and served from February 2, 1856, to March 3, 1857.

*35th Congress.*—JAMES L. ORR, of South Carolina, was elected speaker, and served from December 7, 1857, to March 3, 1859.

*36th Congress.*—WILLIAM PENNINGTON, of New Jersey, was elected speaker, February 1, 1860, and served to March 3, 1861.

*37th Congress.*—GALUSHA A. GROW, of Pennsylvania, was elected speaker, July 4, 1861, and served to March 3, 1863.

*38th Congress.*—SCHUYLER COLFAX, of Indiana, was elected speaker, December 7, 1863, and served to March 4, 1865.

*39th Congress.*—SCHUYLER COLFAX, of Indiana, was elected speaker December 4, 1865, and served to March 4, 1867.

*40th Congress.*—SCHUYLER COLFAX, of Indiana, was elected speaker March 4, 1867, and served to March 4, 1869.

*41st Congress.*—JAMES G. BLAINE, of Maine, was elected speaker, March 4, 1869, to serve to March 4, 1871.

*42d. Congress.*—JAMES G. BLAINE, of Maine, was elected speaker, March 4, 1871, to serve to March 4, 1873.

*43d. Congress.*—JAMES G. BLAINE, of Maine, was elected speaker, March 4, 1873, to serve to March 4, 1875.

*44th Congress.*—Michael C. Kerr, of Indiana, was elected speaker, March 4, 1875, to serve to March 4, 1877.

*45th Congress.*—SAMUEL J. RANDALL, of Pennsylvania.

# EXISTING GOVERNMENT OF THE UNITED STATES,

AND THE PRINCIPAL OFFICERS THEREOF.

1879.

## THE EXECUTIVE.

RUTHERFORD B. HAYES, of Ohio, *President of the U. S.*
WILLIAM A. WHEELER, of New York, *Vice-President, U. S.*

## THE CABINET.

WILLIAM M. EVARTS, of New York, *Secretary of State.*
JOHN SHERMAN, of Ohio, *Secretary of the Treasury.*
ALEXANDER RAMSEY, of Minn., *Secretary of War.*
RICHARD M. THOMPSON, of Indiana, *Sec. of the Navy.*
CARL SCHURZ, of Missouri, *Secretary of the Interior.*
HORACE MAYNARD, of Tennessee, *Postmaster General.*
CHARLES DEVENS, of Massachusetts, *Attorney General.*

## THE JUDICIARY.

MORRISON R. WAITE, of Ohio, *Chief Justice.*
NATHAN CLIFFORD, of Maine, - - *Associate Justice.*
NOAH H. SWAYNE, of Ohio, - - - " "
SAMUEL F. MILLER, of Iowa, - - - " "
JOHN M. HARLAN, of Kentucky, - - " "
STEPHEN J. FIELD, of California, - - " "
WILLIAM M. STRONG, of Pennsylvania, " "
JOSEPH P. BRADLEY, of New Jersey, - " "
WARD HUNT, of New York, - - - " "

## MINISTERS TO FOREIGN COUNTRIES.

*ENVOYS EXTRAORDINARY AND MINISTERS PLENI-POTENTIARY.*

| Country. | Capital. | Minister. | State. |
|---|---|---|---|
| Austria-Hungary | Vienna | John A. Kasson | Iowa. |
| Brazil | Rio Janeiro | Henry W. Hilliard | Ga. |
| Chili | Santiago | Cornelius A. Logan | Kan. |
| China | Pekin | George F. Seward | N. Y. |
| France | Paris | Edward F. Noyes | Ohio. |
| Great Britain | London | John Welsh | Pa. |
| Italy | Rome | George P. Marsh | Vt. |
| Japan | Yeddo | John A. Bingham | Ohio. |
| Mexico | Mexico | John W. Foster | Ind. |
| Peru | Lima | Richard Gibbs | N. Y. |
| Germany | Berlin | Bayard Taylor * | Pa. |
| Russia | St. Petersburg | Edwin W. Stoughton | N. Y. |
| Spain | Madrid | James R. Lowell | Mass. |

*Deceased. Succeeded by Andrew D. White, of New York.

## MINISTERS RESIDENT.

| Country. | Capital. | Minister. | State. |
|---|---|---|---|
| Argentine Republic | Buenos Ayres | Thomas O. Osborn | Ill. |
| Belgium | Brussels | William C. Goodloe | Ky. |
| Central American States | Guatemala | Geo. Williamson | La. |
| Hawaiian Islands | Honolulu | Jas. M. Comly | Ohio. |
| Hayti | Port-au-Prince | John M. Langston | Ohio. |
| Liberia | Monrovia | John H. Smythe | Ga. |
| Netherlands | The Hague | James Birney | Mich. |
| Sweden and Norway | Stockholm | John L. Stevens | Me. |
| Turkey | Constantinople | Horace Maynard | Tenn. |
| Venezuela | Caracas | Elihu Baker | Ill. |

## CHARGES D' AFFAIRES.

| Denmark | Copenhagen | M. J. Cramer | Ky. |
|---|---|---|---|
| Greece | Athens | John M. Read | Pa. |
| Portugal | Lisbon | Benjamin Moran | Pa. |
| Switzerland | Berne | Nicholas Fish | N. Y. |
| Uruguay & Paraguay | Montevideo | John C. Caldwell | Me. |

## CONSULS GENERAL.

| Austria-Hungary | Vienna | P. Sidney Post | Pa. |
|---|---|---|---|
| Brazil | Rio Janeiro | Thomas Adamson | Pa. |
| China | Shanghai | | |
| France | Paris | Lucius Fairchild | Minn. |
| Germany | Berlin | H. Kreismann | Ill. |
| " | Frankfort | Alfred E. Lee | Ohio. |
| Italy | Rome | Charles McMillan | N. Y. |
| Great Britain | Calcutta | A. C. Litchfield | Mich. |
| " " | London | Adam Badeau | N.Y. |
| " " | Melbourne | O. M. Spencer | |
| " " | Montreal | John Q. Smith | Ohio. |
| Japan | Kanagawa | Thos. B. Van Buren | N. J. |
| Mexico | Mexico | Justin E. Colburn | Vt. |
| Russia | St. Petersburg | Wm. H. Edwards | Ohio. |
| Spain | Havana | Henry C. Hall | Conn. |
| Turkey | Constantinople | G. Harris Heap | |
| " | Cairo | E. E. Farman | N. Y. |

## THE FORTY-SIXTH CONGRESS.

Term extends from March 4th, 1879, to March 4th, 1881.

### LIST OF MEMBERS.

## SENATE.

**PRESIDENT OF THE SENATE,** WILLIAM A. WHEELER, *of New York.*
**SECRETARY,** - - GEORGE C. GORHAM, *of California.*

| | Term Expires. | | Term Expires. |
|---|---|---|---|
| *Alabama.* | | *Indiana.* | |
| John T. Morgan | 1883 | Joseph E. McDonald | 1881 |
| Luke Pryor | 1885 | Daniel W. Voorhees | 1885 |
| *Arkansas.* | | *Iowa.* | |
| Augustus H. Garland | 1883 | Samuel J. Kirkwood | 1883 |
| James D. Walker | 1885 | William B. Allison | 1885 |
| *California.* | | *Kansas.* | |
| Newton Booth | 1881 | Preston B. Plumb | 1883 |
| James T. Farley | 1885 | John J. Ingalls | 1885 |
| *Colorado.* | | *Kentucky.* | |
| Henry M. Teller | 1883 | James B. Beck | 1883 |
| Nathaniel P. Hill | 1885 | John G. Williams | 1885 |
| *Connecticut.* | | *Louisiana.* | |
| William W. Eaton | 1881 | William Pitt Kellogg | 1883 |
| Orville H. Platt | 1885 | B. F. Jonas | 1885 |
| *Delaware.* | | *Maine.* | |
| Thomas F. Bayard | 1881 | Hannibal Hamlin | 1881 |
| Eli Saulsbury | 1883 | James G. Blaine | 1883 |
| *Florida.* | | *Maryland.* | |
| Charles W. Jones | 1881 | William P. Whyte | 1881 |
| Wilkinson Call | 1885 | James B. Groome | 1885 |
| *Georgia.* | | *Massachusetts.* | |
| Benjamin H. Hill | 1883 | Henry L. Dawes | 1881 |
| John P. Gordon | 1885 | George F. Hoar | 1883 |
| *Illinois.* | | *Michigan.* | |
| David Davis | 1883 | H. P. Baldwin | 1881 |
| John A. Logan | 1885 | Thomas W. Ferry | 1883 |

## FORTY-SIXTH CONGRESS.

### Minnesota.
| | Term Expires. |
|---|---|
| S. J. R. McMillan | 1881 |
| William Windom | 1883 |

### Mississippi.
| | |
|---|---|
| Blanche K. Bruce | 1881 |
| *L. Q. C. Lamar* | 1883 |

### Missouri.
| | |
|---|---|
| *Francis M. Cockrell* | 1881 |
| George G. Best | 1885 |

### Nebraska.
| | |
|---|---|
| Algernon S. Paddock | 1881 |
| Alvin Saunders | 1883 |

### Nevada.
| | |
|---|---|
| William Sharon | 1881 |
| John P. Jones | 1885 |

### New Hampshire.
| | |
|---|---|
| Edward H. Rollins | 1883 |
| Henry W. Blair | 1885 |

### New Jersey.
| | |
|---|---|
| *Theodore F. Randolph* | 1881 |
| *John R. McPherson* | 1883 |

### New York.
| | |
|---|---|
| *Francis Kernan* | 1881 |
| Roscoe Conkling | 1885 |

### North Carolina.
| | |
|---|---|
| *Matt. W. Ransom* | 1883 |
| *Zebulon B. Vance* | 1885 |

### Ohio.
| | |
|---|---|
| *Allen G. Thurman* | 1881 |
| *George H Pendleton* | 1885 |

### Oregon.
| | Term Expires. |
|---|---|
| *Lafayette Grover* | 1883 |
| *James H. Slater* | 1885 |

### Pennsylvania.
| | |
|---|---|
| *William A. Wallace* | 1881 |
| James D. Cameron | 1885 |

### Rhode Island.
| | |
|---|---|
| Ambrose E. Burnside | 1881 |
| Henry B. Anthony | 1883 |

### South Carolina.
| | |
|---|---|
| *Manning C. Butler* | 1883 |
| *Wade Hampton* | 1885 |

### Tennessee.
| | |
|---|---|
| *James E. Bailey* | 1881 |
| *Isham G. Harris* | 1883 |

### Texas.
| | |
|---|---|
| *Samuel B. Maxey* | 1881 |
| *Richard Coke* | 1883 |

### Vermont.
| | |
|---|---|
| George F. Edmunds | 1881 |
| Justin S. Morrill | 1885 |

### Virginia.
| | |
|---|---|
| *Robert E. Withers* | 1881 |
| *John W. Johnston* | 1883 |

### West Virginia.
| | |
|---|---|
| *Frank Hereford* | 1881 |
| *Henry G. Davis* | 1883 |

### Wisconsin.
| | |
|---|---|
| Angus Cameron | 1881 |
| Matt. W. Carpenter | 1885 |

Republicans (in Roman) 33.—Democrats (in *Italics*) 41.—Independent (in SMALL CAPS) 1.—Doubtful 1.—Total 76.

## HOUSE OF REPRESENTATIVES.

SPEAKER,....SAMUEL J. RANDALL, *of Pennsylvania.*
CLERK,......GEORGE M. ADAMS, *of Kentucky.*

*Alabama*—8.
1. Thomas H. Herndon.
2. Hilary A. Herbert.
3. Wm. J. Stamford.
4. Charles M. Shelly.
5. Thomas Williams.
6. Burwell B. Lewis.
7. Wm. H. Forney.
8. Wm. M. Lowe.

*Arkansas*—4.
1. Poindexter Dunn.
2. William F. Slemons.
3. Jordan E. Cravens.
4. Thomas M. Gunter.

*California*—4.*
1. Horace Davis.
2. Horace F. Page.
3. C. P. Berry.
4. R. Pacheco.

*Colorado*—1.
1. J. B. Belford.

*Connecticut*—4.
1. Joseph R. Hawley.
2. James Phelps.
3. John T. Wait.
4. Frederick Miles.

*Delaware*—1.
1. Edward L. Martin.

*Florida*—2.
1. Robert H. M. Davidson.
2. Noble A. Hull.

*Georgia*—9.
1. John E. Nichols.
2. William E. Smith.
3. Philip Cook.
4. Henry Persons.
5. N. J. Hammond.
6. James H. Blount.
7. William H. Felton.
8. Alexander H. Stephens.
9. Emery Speer.

*Illinois*—19.
1. William Aldrich.
2. George R. Davis.
3. Hiram Barber Jr.
4. John C. Sherwin.
5. R. M. A. Hawk.
6. Thomas J. Henderson.
7. Philip C. Hayes.
8. Greenbury L. Fort.
9. Thomas A. Boyd.
10. Benjamin F. Marsh.
11. James W. Singleton.
12. William M. Springer.
13. A. E. Stevenson.
14. Joseph G. Cannon.
15. Albert S. Forsythe.
16. William A. J. Sparks.
17. William R Morrison.
18. John R. Thomas.
19. Richard W. Townsend.

*Indiana*—13.
1. William Hellman.
2. Thomas R. Cobb.
3. George A Bicknell.
4. Jeptha D. New.
5. Thomas M. Browne.
6. William R. Myers.
7. Gilbert DeLaMatyr.
8. Andrew J. Hastetter.
9. Godlove S. Orth.
10. William H. Calkins.
11. Calvin Cowgill.

* Elects new members in Sept. 1879.

12. Walpole G. Colerick.
13. John H. Baker.

### Iowa—9.
1. Moses A. McCoid.
2. Hiram Price.
3. Thomas Updegraff.
4. Nathaniel C. Deering.
5. W. G. Thompson.
6. J. B. Weaver.
7. E. H. Gillette.
8. William F. Sapp.
9. Cyrus C. Carpenter.

### Kansas—3.
1. John A. Anderson.
2. Dudley C. Haskell.
3. Thomas Ryan.

### Kentucky—10.
1. Oscar Turner.
2. James A. McKenzie.
3. John W. Caldwell.
4. J. Proctor Knott.
5. Albert G. Willis.
6. John G. Carlisle.
7. Joseph C. S. Blackburn.
8. Philip B. Thompson Jr.
9. Thomas Turner.
10. Elijah C. Phister.

### Louisiana—6.
1. Randall L. Gibson.
2. E. John Ellis.
3. Joseph H. Acklen.
4. Joseph B. Elam.
5. J. Floyd King.
6. Edward W. Robertson.

### Maine—5.
1. Thomas B. Reed.
2. William P. Frye.
3. Stephen D. Lindsey.
4. George W. Ladd.
5. Thompson H. Murch.

### Maryland—6.
1. Daniel M. Henry.
2. J. F. C. Talbott.
3. William Kimmell.
4. Robert M. McLane.
5. Eli J. Henkle.
6. Milton G. Urner.

### Massachusetts—11.
1. William W. Crape.
2. Benjamin W. Harris.
3. Walbridge A. Field.
4. Leopold Morse.
5. S. Z. Bowman.
6. George B. Loring.
7. Wm. A. Russell.
8. William Claflin.
9. William W. Rice.
10. Amasa Norcross.
11. George D. Robinson.

### Michigan—9.
1. John S. Newberry.
2. Edwin Willits.
3. Jonas H. McGowan.
4. Julius C. Burrows.
5. John W. Stone.
6. Mark S. Brewer.
7. Omar D. Conger.
8. Roswell G. Horr.
9. Jay A. Hubbell.

### Minnesota—3.
1. Mark H. Dunnell.
2. Henry Poehler.
3. William D. Washburn.

### Mississippi—6.
1. Henry L. Muldrow.
2. Van H. Manning.
3. Hernando D. Money.
4. Otho R. Singleton.
5. Charles E. Hooker.
6. James R. Chalmers.

### Missouri—13.
1. Martin L. Clardy.
2. Erastus Wells.
3. Richard G. Frost.
4. Lowndes H. Davis.
5. Richard P. Bland.
6. James R. Waddill.
7. John F. Phillips.
8. Samuel L. Sawyer.
9. Nicholas Ford.
10. Gideon F. Rothwell.

11. John B. Clarke Jr.
12. William H. Hatch.
13. Aylett H. Buckner.

*Nebraska*—1.

1. Edward K. Valentine.

*Nevada*—1.

1. Rollin M. Daggett.

*New Hampshire*—3.

1. Joshua G. Hall.
2. James F. Briggs.
3. Evarts W. Farr.

*New Jersey*—7.

1. George M. Robeson.
2. Hezekiah B. Smith.
3. Miles Ross.
4. Alvah A. Clark.
5. Charles H. Voorhis.
6. John L. Blake.
7. Lewis A. Brigham.

*New York*—33.

1. James W. Covert.
2. Daniel O'Reilly.
3. Simeon B. Chittenden.
4. Archibald M. Bliss.
5. Nicholas Muller.
6. Samuel S. Cox.
7. Edwin Einstein.
8. Anson G. McCook.
9. Fernando Wood.
10. James O'Brien.
11. Levi P. Morton.
12. Waldo Hutchins.
13. John H. Ketcham.
14. John W. Ferdon.
15. William Lounsberry.
16. John M. Bailey.
17. Walter A. Wood.
18. John Hammond.
19. Amaziah B. James.
20. John H. Starin.
21. David Wilbur.
22. Warner Miller.
23. Cyrus D. Prescott.
24. Joseph Mason.

25. Frank Hiscock.
26. John H. Camp.
27. Elbridge G. Lapham.
28. Jeremiah W. Dwight.
29. David P. Richardson.
30. John Van Voorhis.
31. Richard Crowley.
32. Ray V. Pierce.
33. Henry Van Aernam.

*North Carolina*—8.

1. Joseph J. Martin.
2. W. H. Kitchen.
3. Daniel L. Russell.
4. Joseph J. Davis.
5. Alfred M. Scales.
6. Walter L. Steele.
7. Robert F. Armfield.
8. Robert B. Vance.

*Ohio*—20.

1. Benjamin Butterworth.
2. Thomas L. Young.
3. John A. McMahon.
4. J. Warren Keifer.
5. Benjamin Lefevre.
6. W. D. Hill.
7. Frank Hurd.
8. Ebenezer B. Finley.
9. George L. Converse.
10. Thomas Ewing.
11. Henry L. Dickey.
12. Henry S. Neal.
13. A. J. Warner.
14. Gibson Atherton.
15. George W. Geddes.
16. William McKinley Jr.
17. James Monroe.
18. John T. Updegraff.
19. James A. Garfield.
20. Amos Townsend.

*Oregon*—1.

1. John Whitaker.

*Pennsylvania*—27.

1. Henry H. Bingham.
2. Charles O'Neill.
3. Samuel J. Randall.

4. William D. Kelley.
5. Alfred C. Harmer.
6. William Ward.
7. Wm. Godshalk.
8. Hiester Clymer.
9. A. Herr Smith.
10. Reuben K. Bachman.
11. Robert Klotz.
12. Hendrick B. Wright.
13. John W. Ryan.
14. John W. Killinger.
15. Edward Overton Jr.
16. John J. Mitchell.
17. A. H. Coffroth.
18. Horatio G. Fisher.
19. Frank E. Beltzhoover.
20. Seth H. Yocum.
21. Morgan R. Wise.
22. Russell Errett.
23. Thomas M. Bayne.
24. William S. Shallenberger.
25. Harry White.
26. Samuel B. Dick.
27. J. H. Osmer.

*Rhode Island*—2.

1. Nelson W. Aldrich.
2. Lattimer W. Ballou.

*South Carolina*—5.

1. John S. Richardson.
2. M. P. O'Connor.
3. D. Wyatt Aiken.
4. John H. Evins.
5. G. D. Tillman.

*Tennessee*—10.

1. R. L. Taylor.
2. L. C. Houck.
3. George C. Dibrell.
4. Benton McMillan.
5. John M. Bright.
6. John F. House.
7. Wash. C. Whitthorne.
8. John D. C. Atkins.
9. C. B. Simonton.
10. H. Casey Young.

*Texas*—6.

1. John H. Reagan.
2. David B. Culberson.
3. Olin Wellborn.
4. Roger Q. Mills.
5. George W. Jones.
6. C. Upson.

*Vermont*—3.

1. Charles H. Joyce.
2. James M. Tyler.
3. Bradley Barlow.

*Virginia*—9.

1. R. L. T. Beale.
2. John Goode Jr.
3. Joseph E. Johnston.
4. Joseph Jorgensen.
5. George C. Cabell.
6. J. Randolph Tucker.
7. John T. Harris.
8. Eppa Hunton.
9. James B. Richmond.

*West Virginia*—3.

1. Benjamin Wilson.
2. Benjamin F. Martin.
3. John E. Kenna.

*Wisconsin*—8.

1. Charles G. Williams.
2. Lucien B. Caswell.
3. George C. Hazleton.
4. Peter V. Deuster.
5. Edward S. Bragg.
6. Gabriel Bouk.
7. Herman L. Humphrey.
8. Thaddeus C. Pound.

STATE GOVERNMENTS.

# GOVERNORS OF THE SEVERAL STATES.
## 1879.

| States. | Capitals. | Governors. | Terms Expire. | Salaries. |
|---|---|---|---|---|
| Alabama | Montgomery | *Rufus W. Cobb* | Nov 1881 | $3,000 |
| Arkansas | Little Rock | *William R. Miller* | Jan 1883 | 3,500 |
| California | Sacramento | *William Irwin* | Dec 1879 | 7,000 |
| Connecticut | Hartford | Charles B. Andrews | Jan 1881 | 2,000 |
| Colorado | Denver | F. W. Pitkin | Jan 1881 | 3,000 |
| Delaware | Dover | *John W. Hall* | Jan 1883 | 2,000 |
| Florida | Tallahassee | *George F. Drew* | Jan 1881 | 3,500 |
| Georgia | Atlanta | *Alfred H. Colquitt* | Jan 1881 | 4,000 |
| Illinois | Springfield | Shelby W. Cullom | Jan 1881 | 5,000 |
| Indiana | Indianapolis | *James D. Williams* | Jan 1881 | 3,000 |
| Iowa | Des Moines | John H. Gear | Jan 1882 | 2,500 |
| Kansas | Topeka | John P. St. John | Jan 1883 | 3,000 |
| Kentucky | Frankfort | *James B. McCreary* | Sept 1879 | 5,000 |
| Louisiana | New Orleans | *Francis T. Nichols.* | Jan 1881 | 8,000 |
| Maine | Augusta | *Alonzo Garcelon* | Jan 1880 | 2,500 |
| Maryland | Annapolis | *John Lee Carroll* | Jan 1880 | 4,500 |
| Massachusetts | Boston | Thomas Talbot | Jan 1880 | 5,000 |
| Michigan | Lansing | Charles M. Croswell | Jan 1881 | 1,000 |
| Minnesota | St. Paul | John S. Pillsbury. | Jan 1880 | 3,000 |
| Mississippi | Jackson | *John M. Stone* | Jan 1881 | 3,000 |
| Missouri | Jefferson City | *John S. Phelps* | Jan 1881 | 5,000 |
| Nebraska | Lincoln | Albinus Nance | Jan 1881 | 1,000 |
| Nevada | Carson City | John H. Kinkead. | Jan 1880 | 6,000 |
| New Hampshire | Concord | Benjamin F. Prescott | June 1879 | 1,000 |
| New Jersey | Trenton | *George B. McClellan* | Jan 1881 | 5,000 |
| New York | Albany | *Lucius Robinson* | Jan 1880 | 10,000 |
| North Carolina | Raleigh | *Zebulon B. Vance* * | Jan 1881 | 4,000 |
| Ohio | Columbus | *Richard M. Bishop* | Jan 1880 | 4,000 |
| Oregon | Salem | *Wm. Wallace Thayer* | June 1882 | 1,500 |
| Pennsylvania | Harrisburg | Henry M. Hoyt | Jan 1883 | 10,000 |
| Rhode Island | Prov. & Npt. | Charles C. VanZandt | May 1879 | 1,000 |
| South Carolina | Columbia | *Wade Hampton* * | Jan 1881 | 3,500 |
| Tennessee | Nashville | *Albert L. Marks* | Jan 1881 | 4,000 |
| Texas | Austin | *Oran M. Roberts* | Jan 1883 | 5,000 |
| Vermont | Montpelier | Redfield Proctor | Oct 1880 | 1,000 |
| Virginia | Richmond | *F. W. M. Holliday* | Jan 1882 | 5,000 |
| West Virginia | Wheeling | *Henry M. Matthews* | Mar 1881 | 2,700 |
| Wisconsin | Madison | William E. Smith | Jan 1880 | 5,000 |

**Republicans in Roman. Democrats in *Italics*. * Elected U. S. Senator.**

# GOVERNMENTS OF THE SEVERAL STATES.
## (CONTINUED.)

| States | Area, sq miles | Population 1870 | Legislatures Meet | State Elections |
|---|---|---|---|---|
| Alabama | 50,722 | 996,992 | 3 M Nov | Tu aft 1 M Nov |
| Arkansas | 52,198 | 484,471 | 1 M Jan | 1 Monday Nov |
| California | 188,981 | 560,247 | *1 M Dec | 1 Wed Sept |
| Connecticut | 4,750 | 537,454 | | |
| Delaware | 2,120 | 125,015 | *1 Tu Jan | 1 Tuesday Aug |
| Florida | 59,248 | 187,748 | T a 1 M Jan | Tu aft 1 M Nov |
| Georgia | 58,000 | 1,184,109 | *1 W Jan | Tu aft 1 M Nov |
| Illinois | 55,410 | 2,539,891 | *1 M Jan | Tu aft 1 M Nov |
| Indiana | 33,809 | 1,680,637 | *1 W Jan | 2 Tuesday Oct |
| Iowa | 55,045 | 1,194,792 | *2 M Jan | 2 Tuesday Oct |
| Kansas | 81,318 | 364,399 | 2 Tu Jan | Tu aft 1 M Nov |
| Kentucky | 37,680 | 1,321,011 | *1 M Dec | 1 Monday Aug |
| Louisiana | 41,346 | 726,915 | 1 M Jan | 1 Monday Nov |
| Maine | 35,000 | 626,915 | 1 W Jan | 2 Monday Sept |
| Maryland | 11,124 | 780,894 | *1 W Jan | Tu aft 1 M Nov |
| Massachusetts | 7,800 | 1,457,351 | W Jan | Tu aft 1 M Nov |
| Michigan | 56,451 | 1,184,059 | *1 W Jan | Tu aft 1 M Nov |
| Minnesota | 83,531 | 439,706 | T a 1 M Jan | Tu aft 1 M Nov |
| Mississippi | 47,156 | 827,922 | T a 1 M Jan | Tu aft 1 M Nov |
| Missouri | 65,350 | 1,721,295 | *Last M Dec | Tu aft 1 M Nov |
| Nebraska | 75,995 | 122,993 | *Th a 1 M Jan | 2 Tuesday Oct |
| Nevada | 81,531 | 42,491 | *1 M Jan | Tu aft 1 M Nov |
| New Hampshire | 9,280 | 318,300 | 1 M June | 2 Tuesday Mar |
| New Jersey | 8,320 | 906,096 | 2 Tu Jan | Tu aft 1 M Nov |
| New York | 47,000 | 4,382,758 | 1 Tu Jan | Tu aft 1 M Nov |
| North Carolina | 50,704 | 1,071,361 | 1 Th Nov | 1 Thursday Aug |
| Ohio | 39,964 | 2,665,260 | *1 M Jan | 2 Tuesday Oct |
| Oregon | 95,274 | 90,923 | 2 M Sept | 2 Monday June |
| Pennsylvania | 46,000 | 3,521,791 | 1 Tu Jan | 2 Tuesday Oct |
| Rhode Island | 1,306 | 217,353 | May & Jan | 1 Wed April |
| South Carolina | 34,000 | 705,606 | 3 W Oct | 4 Monday Nov |
| Tennessee | 45,600 | 1,258,520 | *1 M Oct | 1 Monday Aug |
| Texas | 274,356 | 818,579 | 2 Tu Jan | 1 Tuesday Nov |
| Vermont | 10,212 | 330,051 | *2 Th Oct | 1 Tuesday Sept |
| Virginia | 38,352 | 1,225,163 | 1 M Dec | Tu aft 1 M Nov |
| West Virginia | 23,000 | 442,014 | 2 Tu Jan | 4 Thursday Oct |
| Wisconsin | 53,924 | 1,054,670 | 1 W Jan | Tu aft 1 M Nov |

*Biennial Sessions and Elections.

# RESULTS AT STATE ELECTIONS.

MAINE.—In 1879, total vote for Governor, 138,335, viz.: Daniel F. Davis, Rep. 68,766; Smith, Gr. 47,590; Garcelon, Dem. 21,668. Republican over Democrat, 47,098; over Greenback, 21,176. Democrat and Greenback over Republican, 492.
*Republican majority on Joint Ballot in Legislature*, 44.

NEW HAMPSHIRE.—In 1878, total vote for Governor, 75,959, viz.: Natt Head, Rep. 38,175; Dem. 31,135; rest were scattering. Republican plurality, 7,040.
*Republican majority on Joint Ballot in Legislature*, 72.

VERMONT.—In 1878, total vote for Governor, 57,957, viz.: Redfield Proctor, Rep. 37,312; Dem. 17,247; Greenback, 2,635. Republican plurality, 20,065.
*Republican majority on Joint Ballot in Legislature*, 146.

MASSACHUSETTS.—In 1879, total vote for Governor, 243,534, viz.: John D. Long, Rep. 122,751; Butler, Dem.-Gr. 109,149; Adams, Dem. 9,989; rest were scattering. Republican plurality, 13,602.
*Republican majority on Joint Ballot in Legislature*, 158.

CONNECTICUT.—In 1878, total vote for Governor, 104,645, viz.: Charles B. Andrews, Rep. 48,867; Hubbard, Dem. 46,385; Gr. 8,314; rest were scattering. Republican plurality, 2,482.
*Republican majority on Joint Ballot in Legislature*, 88.

RHODE ISLAND.—In 1879, total vote for Governor, 15,653, viz.: Charles C. Van Zandt, Rep. 9,717; Segar, Dem. 5,936. Republican majority, 3,871.
*Republican majority on Joint Ballot in Legislature*, 57.

## STATE ELECTIONS.

NEW YORK.—In 1879, total vote for Governor, 901,535, viz.: Alonzo B. Cornell, Rep. 418,567; Robinson, Dem. 375,790; Kelly, Tam. 77,566; Lewis, Gr. 20,286; rest were scattering. Republican plurality, 42,777.
*Republican majority on Joint Ballot in Legislature, 75.*

NEW JERSEY.—In 1877, total vote for Governor, 189,427, viz.: George B. McClellan, Dem. 97,837; Newell, Rep. 85,094; Hoxsey, Gr. 5,058. Dem. plurality, 12,743.
*Republican majority on Joint Ballot in Legislature, 13.*

PENNSYLVANIA.—In 1878, total vote for Governor, 702,144, viz.: Henry M. Hoyt, Rep. 319,490; Dill, Dem. 297,137; Gr. 81,758. Republican plurality, 22,353.
*Republican majority on Joint Ballot in Legislature, 27.*

DELAWARE.—In 1878, total vote for Governor, 13,565, viz.: John W. Hall, Dem. 10,730; Stewart, Gr. 2,835. Democratic majority, 7,895.
*Legislature, unanimously Democratic.*

MARYLAND.—In 1879, total vote for Governor, 159,380, viz.: William T. Hamilton, Dem. 90,771; Garey, Rep. 68,609. Democratic majority, 22,162.
*Democratic majority on Joint Ballot in Legislature, 58.*

VIRGINIA.—In 1877, total vote for Governor, 106,329, viz.: Fred. W. M. Holliday, Dem. 101,940; scattering, 4,389. Democratic majority, 97,551.
*Legislature, on Joint Ballot: Conservative Debtpayers, 56; Conservative Readjusters, 56; Republicans, 26; doubtful, 2.*

WEST VIRGINIA.—In 1878, total vote for Congress, 94,905, viz.: Dem. 50,318; Gr. 24,531; Rep. 20,056. Dem. plurality, 25,787.
*Democratic majority on Joint Ballot in Legislature, 33.*

NORTH CAROLINA.—In 1878, total vote for Congress, 128,921, viz.: Dem. 68,263; Rep. 53,369; Ind. 7,289. Democratic plurality, 14,894.
*Democratic majority on Joint Ballot in Legislature, 56.*

SOUTH CAROLINA.—In 1878, total vote for Congress, 161,998, viz.: Dem. 116,917; Rep. 45,081. Dem. majority, 71,836.
*Legislature almost entirely Democratic.*

GEORGIA.—In 1878, total vote for Congress, 125,282, viz.: Dem. 69,788; Opposition, 55,494. Dem. majority, 14,294.
*Legislature largely Democratic in both branches.*

FLORIDA.—In 1878, total vote for Congress, 39,562, viz.: Dem. 21,169; Rep. 18,393. Dem. majority, 2,776.
*Democratic majority on Joint Ballot in Legislature, 52.*

ALABAMA.—In 1878, total vote for Congress, 87,794, viz: Dem. 54,775; Opp. 33,019 Dem. majority, 21,756.
*Democratic majority on Joint Ballot in Legislature, 109.*
Election for State officers held Aug. 2, 1880. No full returns yet received, but the Democratic majority will range from 50,000 to 60,000.

MISSISSIPPI.—In 1878, total vote for Congress, 51,583, viz.: Dem. 36,128; Rep., Ind. and Gr. 15,455. Dem. majority, 20,673.
*Democratic majority on Joint Ballot in Legislature, 106.*

LOUISIANA.—In 1879, total vote for Governor, 115,533, viz.: Louis A. Wiltz, Dem. 74,769; Beattie, Rep. 40,764. Dem. majority, 34,005.
*Democratic majority on Joint Ballot in Legislature, 81.*

TEXAS.—In 1878, total vote for Governor, 237,337, viz: Abram M. Roberts, Dem. 158,933; Hammau, Gr. 55,002; Norton, Rep. 23,402. Dem. majority, 80,529.
*Democratic majority on Joint Ballot in Legislature, 68.*

OHIO.—In 1879, total vote for Governor, 668,610, viz.: Charles Foster, Rep. 336,261; Ewing, Dem. 319,132; Pratt, Gr. 9,072; Stewart, Pro. 4,145. Rep. plurality, 17,129.
*Republican majority on Joint Ballot in Legislature, 30.*

INDIANA.—In 1878, total vote for Secretary of State, 414,842, viz.: Dem. 194,770; Rep. 180,657; Gr. 39,415. Dem. plurality, 14,113.
*Democratic majority on Joint Ballot in Legislature,* 10.

ILLINOIS.—In 1878, total vote for State Treasurer, 451,675, viz.: Rep. 206,458; Dem. 170,085; Gr. 65,689. Rep. plurality, 36,373.
*Republican majority on Joint Ballot in Legislature,* 4.

KENTUCKY.—In 1879, total vote for Governor, 226,635, viz.: Luke P. Blackburn, Dem. 125,799; Evans, Rep. 81,882; Cook, Gr. 18,954. Dem. plurality, 43,917.
*Legislature largely Democratic.*

TENNESSEE.—In 1878, total vote for Governor, 146,542, viz.: Albert S. Marks, Dem. 89,018; Rep. 42,328; Gr. 15,196. Dem. plurality, 46,690.
*Democratic majority on Joint Ballot in Legislature,* 52.

MICHIGAN.—In 1879, total vote for Judge of Supreme Court, 258,583, viz.: Rep. 132,313; Dem. and Gr. 126,270. Rep. majority, 6,043.
*Republican majority on Joint Ballot in Legislature,* 46.

WISCONSIN.—In 1879, total vote for Governor, 188,948, viz.: William E. Smith, Rep. 100,535; Jenkins, Dem. 75,030; May, Gr. 12,996. Rep. plurality, 25,505.
*Republican majority on Joint Ballot in Legislature,* 57.

IOWA.—In 1879, total vote for Governor, 291,314. viz.: John H. Gear, Rep. 157,571; Trimble, Dem. 85,056; Campbell, Gr. 45,429. Rep. plurality, 72,515.
*Republican majority on Joint Ballot in Legislature,* 94.

MISSOURI.—In 1878, total vote for Congress, 320,077, viz.: Dem. 167,036; Gr. 85,261; Rep. 54,214; Ind. 13,566. Dem. plurality, 81,775.
*Democratic majority on Joint Ballot in Legislature,* 97.

## STATE ELECTIONS.

**ARKANSAS.**—In 1878, total vote for Congress, 51,619, viz.: Dem. 32,652; Gr. 18,967. Dem. majority, 13,685.
*Democratic majority on Joint Ballot in Legislature, 96.*

**CALIFORNIA.**—In 1879, total vote for Governor, 160,213, viz.: Geo. C. Perkins, Rep. 67,965; Glenn, Dem. 47,647; White, Work's 44,482. Rep. plurality, 20,318.
*Anti-Republican majority on Joint Ballot in Legislature, 2.*

**MINNESOTA.**—In 1879, total vote for Governor, 105,663, viz.: John S. Pilsbury, Rep. 56,918; Rice, Dem. 41,583. Rep. majority, 15,335.
*Legislature largely Republican.*

**OREGON.**—In 1878, total vote for Secretary of State, 33,882, viz.: Rep. 16,333; Dem. 16,042. Rep. majority, 291.
*Democratic majority on Joint Ballot in Legislature, 12.*

**KANSAS.**—In 1878, total vote for Governor, 138,285, viz.: John P. St. John, Rep. 74,020; Dem. 37,028. Rep. majority, 36,812.
*Republican majority on Joint Ballot in Legislature, 93.*

**NEVADA.**—In 1878, total vote for Governor, 18,999, viz.: J. H. Kinkead, Rep. 9,811; Dem. 9,148. Rep. majority, 663.
*Republican majority on Joint Ballot in Legislature, 37.*

**NEBRASKA.**—In 1879, total vote for Judge of Supreme Court, 71,665, viz.: Rep. 46,113; Dem. 20,827. Rep. majority, 25,286.
*Republican majority on Joint Ballot in Legislature, 48.*

**COLORADO.**—In 1879, total vote for Judge of Supreme Court, 30,868, viz.: Rep. 16,920; Dem. 12,702. Rep. majority, 4,218.
*Republican majority on Joint Ballot in Legislature, 37.*

# WASHINGTON'S ADMINISTRATION,

## WITH

## BIOGRAPHICAL SKETCH.
## 1789–1797.

### TWO TERMS—EIGHT YEARS.

#### ELECTED BY THE UNANIMOUS VOTE OF THE ELECTORS.

# CABINET.

### PRESIDENT:
George Washington, Virginia.

### VICE-PRESIDENT:
John Adams, Massachusetts.

### SECRETARIES OF STATE:
Thomas Jefferson, Virginia.     1789.
Edmund Randolph, Virginia.      1794.
Timothy Pickering, Massachusetts. 1795.

### SECRETARIES OF THE TREASURY:
Alexander Hamilton, New York.   1789.
Oliver Wolcott, Connecticut.    1795.

### SECRETARIES OF WAR AND NAVY:
Henry Knox, Massachusetts.      1789.
Timothy Pickering, Massachusetts. 1794.
James McHenry, Maryland.        1796.

### POSTMASTERS-GENERAL:
Samuel Osgood, Massachusetts.   1789.
Timothy Pickering, Massachusetts. 1794.
Joseph Habersham, Georgia.      1795.

### ATTORNEYS-GENERAL:
Edmund Randolph, Virginia.      1789.
William Bradford, Pennsylvania. 1794.
Charles Lee, Virginia.          1795.

---

## FINANCIAL CONDITION OF THE COUNTRY.

| Year | Imports | Exports | Expenditures | Debt |
|---|---|---|---|---|
| 1790 | $23,000,000 | $20,205,156 | .......... | $75,463,476 |
| 1791 | 29,200,000 | 19,012,041 | $7,207,539 | 77,227,924 |
| 1792 | 31,500,000 | 20,753,098 | 9,141,569 | 80,352,634 |
| 1793 | 31,000,000 | 26,109,572 | 7,529,575 | 78,427,404 |
| 1794 | 34,600,000 | 33,026,233 | 9,302,124 | 80,747,587 |
| 1795 | 69,756,268 | 47,989,472 | 10,105,069 | 80,747,587 |
| 1796 | 81,436,164 | 67,064,097 | 8,367,776 | 83,762,172 |

# GEORGE WASHINGTON.

## BIOGRAPHICAL SKETCH.

The twenty-second day of February 1732, will ever be memorable, as the birthday of that great and good man who has been justly styled the "Father of his country." Descended from English ancestors, who emigrated to this country, and settled in Virginia as early as 1657, he was born in a plain farm-house upon the banks of the Potomac, in the County of Westmoreland, Va., on the day above mentioned.

GEORGE WASHINGTON.

His father, Augustine Washington, died in 1743, when George —who was his eldest son by his second wife, Mary Ball—was but ten years of age. He was blessed with a kind, affectionate and intelligent mother, by whom he was instructed in sound principles and correct habits.

At the early age of fifteen, an opportunity was afforded him of entering the British Navy as a midshipman, which position he strongly desired as a path to honorable distinction, but the evident reluctance of his mother to the separation induced him to abandon the project.

He received a good English, but not a thorough literary or scientific education. Having a mind naturally philosophical and mathematical, his attention was given to surveying, and to the science of arms; and of athletic exercises he was passionately fond. At the age of nineteen, he was appointed one of the Adjutant-Generals of Virginia with the rank of Major.

In October 1753, he was commissioned by Governor Dinwidde of Virginia to convey important dispatches to the French on the Ohio, which hazardous undertaking, after suffering great hardships and escaping many dangers, he accomplished to the great satisfaction of the Governor. Subsequently, in 1754, he was appointed Lieutenant-Colonel, and under Colonel Fry was sent with a regiment of troops against the French, and having received permission to march with two companies in advance, on the dark and rainy night of May 24th, 1754, he surrounded and surprised a detachment of French troops, who were compelled to surrender.

This was the commencement of his glorious military career, the history of which is familiar to every American citizen. After his return from the successful expedition against the French in 1758, and the close of the Campaign, he left the army, and was married to a Mrs. Martha Custis, a widow lady of Virginia, who was highly esteemed for her amiable disposition and womanly virtues.

During the subsequent sixteen years, he devoted his time principally in the cultivation of his estate, and in the enjoyment of domestic life at Mount Vernon. In 1774, he represented Virginia as a delegate in the Continental Congress, and on the 15th of June, 1775, was unanimously appointed Commander-in Chief of the American forces, which position he held till the close of the war.

In May 1787, he was a delegate to the Convention which met at Philadelphia, and was appointed to preside over the same, and exerted his influence to cause the adoption of the Constitution.

Having been unanimously elected the first President of the United States, the inauguration ceremonies took place on the 30th of April, 1789, in the City Hall in the city of New York. The first session of the first Congress, held at New York, occupied a period of six months, the adjournment taking place on the 29th of September 1789. In 1793, he was unanimously re-elected to the presidency for another term by the two great political parties, who united only on the name of Washington. Having determined to retire from office, he issued in 1796 his farewell address to the people of the United States, so full of love, and wisdom, and anxiety for the future welfare of his country, and in 1797, after witnessing the inauguration of his successor, he retired to Mount Vernon to spend the rest of his days in retirement.

His administration was a wise and successful one; all disputes with foreign nations had been adjusted, excepting those of France. Ample provision had been made for the security and ultimate payment of the public debt; public and private credit had been restored, and the affairs of the country were prosperous.

On Thursday, the 12th of December, 1799, he was seized with an inflammation in his throat, and on the 14th of the same month, he died, in the sixty-eighth year of his age.

# ADAMS'S ADMINISTRATION,

## WITH

## BIOGRAPHICAL SKETCH.
## 1797—1801.

### ONE TERM—FOUR YEARS.

ELECTED BY THE FEDERALISTS.

# CABINET.

### PRESIDENT:
JOHN ADAMS, Massachusetts.

### VICE-PRESIDENT:
THOMAS JEFFERSON, Virginia.

### SECRETARIES OF STATE:
| | |
|---|---|
| TIMOTHY PICKERING, Massachusetts. | 1797. |
| JOHN MARSHALL, Virginia. | 1797. |

### SECRETARIES OF THE TREASURY:
| | |
|---|---|
| OLIVER WOLCOTT, Connecticut. | 1797. |
| SAMUEL DEXTER, Massachusetts. | 1800. |

### SECRETARIES OF WAR:
| | |
|---|---|
| JAMES MCHENRY, Maryland. | 1797. |
| SAMUEL DEXTER, Massachusetts. | 1800. |
| ROGER GRISWOLD, Connecticut. | 1801. |

### SECRETARIES OF THE NAVY:
| | |
|---|---|
| GEORGE CABOT, Massachusetts. | 1798. |
| BENJAMIN STODDERT, Maryland. | 1798. |

### POST MASTER GENERAL:
JOSEPH HABERSHAM, Georgia.        1797.

### ATTORNEY-GENERAL:
CHARLES LEE, Virginia.        1797.

---

## FINANCIAL CONDITION OF THE COUNTRY.

| Year | Imports | Exports | Expenditures | Debt |
|---|---|---|---|---|
| 1797 | $75,379,406 | $56,850,206 | $8,626,012 | $82,064,479 |
| 1798 | 68,551,700 | 61,527,097 | 8,613,507 | 79,228,529 |
| 1799 | 79,069,148 | 78,665,522 | 11,077,043 | 78,408,669 |
| 1800 | 91,252,768 | 70,970,780 | 11,989,739 | 82,976,291 |

# JOHN ADAMS.

## BIOGRAPHICAL SKETCH.

John Adams, the second President of the United States, was the fourth in descent from Henry Adams, who fled from persecution in England, and settled in Massachusetts in the year 1630. He was born on the 19th of October, 1735, in the town of Braintree, Massachusetts, and in 1751, was admitted a member of Harvard College, graduating therefrom four years afterwards

He soon after commenced the study of law at Worcester,

JOHN ADAMS.

Massachusetts, supporting himself chiefly by teaching in one of the public schools of that town. He was admitted to the bar of Suffolk County in 1758, and in 1766, he removed to Boston, where he soon distinguished himself in his profession.

In 1764, he married Abigail Smith, daughter of Rev. William

Smith, of Weymouth, an educated lady, possessing superior intellectual faculties.

Having filled many important offices, he was in 1777, appointed a commissioner to the Court of France, and in 1779, was appointed a Minister Plenipotentiary for negotiating a treaty of peace with Great Britain. In 1781, he was associated with Franklin, Jay, and others in a commission for concluding treaties of peace with the several European powers. In 1784, he was in Holland and France, negotiating commercial treaties with foreign nations. In 1785, he was appointed by Congress a Minister to represent the United States at the Court of Great Britain.

He resigned in 1788, and in June returned to the United States, after an absence of over eight years.

*Ability*, coupled with *public honesty* and *private worth*, constitute a man equal to any emergency, and fitted for any public position. Adams possessed this character, and these qualifications in an eminent degree. He was the man for the times; no purer patriot ever lived; he was the eloquent and fearless defender of the Declaration of Independence. He was a patriot and a scholar.

He was elected to the Presidency as the successor of Washington after a close and spirited contest, in which his warm personal friend, Thomas Jefferson, was his principle rival. Mr. Jefferson was supported by the Democratic, then called the Republican party, and Mr. Adams by the Federal party. Mr. Jefferson was elected Vice-President.

His inauguration took place in Congress Hall, Philadelphia, on the 4th of March, 1797, he being then in his sixty-second year. He served his term of four years, was again nominated, but defeated. After his term of service had expired, he retired to his estate at Quincy, Massachusetts, and passed the remainder of his days in literary and scientific pursuits. Having lived to the good old age of *ninety-one years*, he died on the 4th of July 1826.

# JEFFERSON'S ADMINISTRATION,

## WITH

## BIOGRAPHICAL SKETCH.
## 1801–1809.

---

### TWO TERMS—EIGHT YEARS.

ELECTED BY THE REPUBLICAN OR ANTI FEDERAL PARTY.

# CABINET.

### PRESIDENT:
THOMAS JEFFERSON, Virginia.

### VICE-PRESIDENTS:
| | |
|---|---|
| AARON BURR, New York. | 1801. |
| GEORGE CLINTON, New York. | 1805. |

### SECRETARY OF STATE:
| | |
|---|---|
| JAMES MADISON, Virginia. | 1801. |

### SECRETARIES OF THE TREASURY:
| | |
|---|---|
| SAMUEL DEXTER, Massachusetts. | 1801. |
| ALBERT GALLATIN, Pennsylvania. | 1802. |

### SECRETARY OF WAR:
| | |
|---|---|
| HENRY DEARBORN, Massachusetts. | 1801. |

### SECRETARIES OF THE NAVY:
| | |
|---|---|
| BENJAMIN STODDERT, Maryland. | 1801. |
| ROBERT SMITH, Maryland. | 1802. |
| JACOB CROWNINSHIELD, Mass. | 1805. |

### POST MASTERS-GENERAL:
| | |
|---|---|
| JOSEPH HABERSHAM, Georgia. | 1801. |
| GIDEON GRANGER, Connecticut. | 1802. |

### ATTORNEYS-GENERAL:
| | |
|---|---|
| THEOPHILUS PARSONS, Massachusetts | 1801. |
| LEVI LINCOLN, Massachusetts. | 1801. |
| ROBERT SMITH, Maryland. | 1805. |
| JOHN BRECKENRIDGE, Kentucky. | 1805. |
| CÆSAR A. RODNEY, Delaware. | 1807. |

## FINANCIAL CONDITION OF THE COUNTRY.

| Year. | Imports. | Exports. | Expenditures. | Debt. |
|---|---|---|---|---|
| 1801 | $111,363,511 | $94,115,925 | $12,273,376 | $83,038,050 |
| 1802 | 76,333,333 | 72,483,160 | 13,276,084 | 80,712,632 |
| 1803 | 64,666,666 | 55,800,038 | 11,258,983 | 77,054,686 |
| 1804 | 185,000,000 | 77,699,074 | 12,624,646 | 86,427,120 |
| 1805 | 120,600,000 | 95,566,021 | 13,727,124 | 82,312,150 |
| 1806 | 129,410,000 | 101,536,963 | 15,070,093 | 75,723,270 |
| 1807 | 138,500,000 | 108,313,151 | 11,292,292 | 69,218,398 |
| 1808 | 56,990,000 | 22,430,960 | 16,764,584 | 65,196,317 |

# THOMAS JEFFERSON.

## BIOGRAPHICAL SKETCH.

Perhaps the most distinguished statesman this country has ever produced, was Thomas Jefferson, the third President of the United States. His ancestors were also early emigrants from Great Britain, who settled in Virginia. His father, Peter Jefferson, was a man of some distinction in the colony.

Thomas Jefferson was born on the 2nd of April, 1743, at Shadwell, in Albemarle County, Virginia. His father dying when he was twelve years of age, left him a large inheritance.

THOMAS JEFFERSON.

He was educated at the College of William and Mary, studied law under the celebrated George Wythe, and commenced its practice in 1767.

He was early identified with the champions of liberty, and in 1775, took his seat in the Continental Congress. Previous to this, he had made an effort in the Legislature of which he was a member, for the emancipation of the slaves in Virginia, but was unsuccessful. In 1772, he married Mrs. Martha Skelton, a widow lady, daughter of Mr. John Wyles, an eminent lawyer of Virginia.

Although one of the youngest members of the Continental Congress, he was selected by a committee duly appointed, and requested to prepare the *Declaration* of *Independence*. This he did, and it was finally adopted with but few alterations and amendments on the 4th of July, 1776. In 1779, he was elected Governor of Virginia, which office he held for two years. He was the author of many tracts, and other writings, and as a man of letters acquired high distinction.

In 1785, he was joined with Adams and Franklin in a commission for negotiating treaties of commerce with foreign nations, and he met them in Paris, in June of that year, and it was through him, as Mr. Webster has confessed, that our diplomatic intercourse was raised to a dignity and strength, which will bear comparison with any that other governments can produce.

Having been elected President his inauguration took place in the new Capitol at Washington, on the 4th of March, 1801 in the 58th year of his age. He was elected by the Anti-Federal or Democratic party, and many important acts were passed and many important events took place during his administration which was continued for eight years (he having been re-elected in 1805). He almost doubled the territory of the Union; caused the vast regions of the West to be explored; gave us character abroad, and tranquility at home.

Having retired from the presidency, he passed the remainder of his days in the cultivation of his beautiful estate at Monticello; in pleasant intercourse with his friends; in literary pursuits, and in advancing his favorite project of a University of Virginia. His pecuniary circumstances becoming embarrassed in his old age, he was compelled to dispose of his library, which was purchased by Congress for $23,950. He died, after a short illness, on the 4th of July, 1826, being the fiftieth aniversary of our independence; the same day that his friend and compatriot John Adams departed this life.

# MADISON'S ADMINISTRATION,

## WITH

## BIOGRAPHICAL SKETCH.
## 1809–1817.

---

### TWO TERMS—EIGHT YEARS.

ELECTED BY THE REPUBLICANS [ANTI-FEDERALISTS.]

# CABINET.

### PRESIDENT:
JAMES MADISON, Virginia.

### VICE-PRESIDENTS:
GEORGE CLINTON, New York.
ELBRIDGE GERRY, Massachusetts.

### SECRETARIES OF STATE:
| | |
|---|---|
| ROBERT SMITH, Maryland. | 1809. |
| JAMES MONROE, Virginia. | 1811. |

### SECRETARIES OF THE TREASURY.
| | |
|---|---|
| ALBERT GALLATIN, Pennsylvania. | 1809. |
| GEORGE W. CAMPBELL, Tennessee. | 1814. |
| ALEXANDER J. DALLAS, Penn. | 1814. |

### SECRETARIES OF WAR:
| | |
|---|---|
| WILLIAM EUSTIS, Massachusetts. | 1809. |
| JOHN ARMSTRONG, New York. | 1813. |
| JAMES MONROE, Virginia. | 1814. |
| WILLIAM H. CRAWFORD, Georgia. | 1815. |

### SECRETARIES OF THE NAVY:
| | |
|---|---|
| PAUL HAMILTON, South Carolina. | 1809. |
| WILLIAM JONES, Pennsylvania. | 1813. |
| BENJAMIN W. CROWINSHIELD, Mass. | 1814. |

### POSTMASTERS-GENERAL.
| | |
|---|---|
| GIDEON GRANGER, Connecticut. | 1809. |
| RETURN J. MEIGS, JR., Ohio. | 1814. |

### ATTORNEYS-GENERAL.
| | |
|---|---|
| CÆSAR A. RODNEY, Delaware. | 1809. |
| WILLIAM PINCKNEY, Maryland. | 1811. |
| RICHARD RUSH, Pennsylvania. | 1814. |

---

## FINANCIAL CONDITION OF THE COUNTRY.

| Year. | Imports. | Exports. | Expenditures. | Debt. |
|---|---|---|---|---|
| 1809 | $59,400,000 | $52,203,233 | $13,867,226 | $57,023,192 |
| 1810 | 85,400,000 | 66,657,970 | 13,319,986 | 53,178,217 |
| 1811 | 53,400,000 | 61,316,883 | 13,601,808 | 48,005,587 |
| 1812 | 77,030,000 | 38,527,236 | 22,279,121 | 45,209,737 |
| 1813 | 22,005,000 | 27,855,927 | 39,190,520 | 55,962,827 |
| 1814 | 12,965,000 | 6,927,441 | 38,028,230 | 81,487,846 |
| 1815 | 113,041,274 | 52,557,753 | 39,582,493 | 99,833,660 |
| 1816 | 147,103,000 | 81,920,452 | 48,244,495 | 127,334,938 |

# JAMES MADISON.

## BIOGRAPHICAL SKETCH.

The fourth President of the United States, was James Madison, who was born in Orange County, Virginia, on the 16th of March, 1751. He was of Welsh descent, and his father James Madison, was among the early emigrants to Virginia.

He received a liberal education, and graduated at Princeton College, in 1771. He commenced the practice of law, but was called in early life, to attend to the public affairs of his State, and Country. In 1779 he was chosen a delegate to the conti-

JAMES MADISON.

nental Congress, and continued as such, until 1784. He was a delegate to the Convention, held at Philadelphia, in May, 1787, to frame the Constitution, and was one of its most distinguished members. He was also elected to the new Congress held at New York, in 1789.

In the year 1794, being then in his forty-third year, he married Mrs. Dolly Paine Todd, of Philadelphia, a widow lady much admired, and who was twenty-three years younger than Mr. Madison.

In his political views, Mr. Madison was a Democrat (then called Republican) and co-operated with Jefferson in his views of national policy. He was Secretary of State during Jefferson's administration, and in 1809, having received the nomination and support of the Democratic, or Anti Federal party, he succeeded Mr. Jefferson as President. The war of 1812, was declared during his administration against Great Britain, and the same year he was re-elected to the presidency. It was also during his administration, that the city of Washington was captured by the British, and the public buildings destroyed. Peace was also concluded at Ghent in 1814, which he sincerely desired.

He retired in 1817, to his residence at Montpelier, in Orange County, Virginia, being then sixty-six years of age. Subsequently, he was chosen a member of the State Convention, to revise the Constitution of his State, and for several years acted as Rector of the University of Virginia. At the age of eighty-five the earthly career of Mr. Madison was closed. He died respected and beloved, on the 28th of June, 1836.

# MONROE'S ADMINISTRATION,

### WITH

## BIOGRAPHICAL SKETCH.
## 1817–1825.

---

### TWO TERMS—EIGHT YEARS.

#### ELECTED BY THE REPUBLICANS [ANTI-FEDERALISTS.]

# CABINET.

### PRESIDENT:
James Monroe, Virginia.

### VICE-PRESIDENT:
Daniel D. Tompkins, New York.

### SECRETARY OF STATE:
John Quincy Adams, Massachusetts.

### SECRETARY OF THE TREASURY.
William H. Crawford, Georgia.

### SECRETARIES OF WAR:
Isaac Shelby, Kentucky.  1817.
John C. Calhoun, South Carolina. 1817.

### SECRETARIES OF THE NAVY:
Benjamin W Crowninshield, Mass. 1818.
Smith Thompson, New York.  1818.
Samuel L. Southard, New Jersey. 1823.

### POSTMASTERS-GENERAL.
Return J. Meigs, Jr., Ohio.  1817.
John McLean, Ohio.  1823.

### ATTORNEY-GENERAL.
William Wirt, Virginia.

## FINANCIAL CONDITION OF THE COUNTRY.

| Year. | Imports. | Exports. | Expenditures. | Debt. |
| --- | --- | --- | --- | --- |
| 1817 | $99,250,000 | $87,671,560 | $40,877,646 | $123,491,965 |
| 1818 | 121,750,000 | 93,281,133 | 35,164,875 | 103,466,633 |
| 1819 | 87,125,000 | 70,141,501 | 24,004,199 | 95,529,648 |
| 1820 | 74,450,000 | 69,661,669 | 21,763,024 | 91,015,566 |
| 1821 | 62,585,724 | 64,974,382 | 19,090,572 | 89,987,427 |
| 1822 | 83,241,541 | 72,160,281 | 17,676,592 | 93,546,676 |
| 1823 | 77,579,267 | 74,699,030 | 15,314,171 | 90,875,877 |
| 1824 | 89,549,007 | 75,986,657 | 31,898,538 | 90,269,777 |

# JAMES MONROE.

## BIOGRAPHICAL SKETCH.

James Monroe, the fifth President of the United States, was born on the 2d of April, 1759, in the county of Westmoreland, Virginia.

His parents, Spencer Monroe and Elizabeth Jones, descended from the first families of that State. He entered the college of William and Mary, but left his collegiate studies before he had graduated, for the purpose of joining the Standard of his Country, which he did in his eighteenth year, and hastened to

JAMES MONROE.

join Washington at his head-quarters, in the city of New York.

He was in many conflicts in the campaign of 1776, and was severely wounded in the battle of Trenton. During the campaigns of 1777, and 1778, he acted as aid to Lord Stirling, and distinguished himself in many battles, displaying great courage and coolness on the bloody fields of Brandywine, Germantown, and Monmouth. He subsequently studied law under Mr. Jefferson, while the latter was Governor of Virginia. In his twenty-fourth year, he was elected to the Legislature of his State, and in the following year, was elected a delegate to the Continental Congress, and thereafter represented his State in Congress, until 1876.

While in New York attending the Continental Congress, he married Miss Kortright, a beautiful and accomplished lady, daughter of Mr. L. Kortright of that city. Mr. Madison was opposed to the adoption of the Federal Constitution as framed by the Convention of 1787, and strongly urged that certain amendments should be made previous to its adoption.

In 1790, he was chosen, and took his place in the Senate of the United States, and continued therein for four years, acting with the Anti-Federal party in opposition to Washington's administration, notwithstanding which, Gen. Washington appointed him Minister to France in 1794, and subsequently, succeeded Mr. King as Minister to England.

In 1799, Mr. Monroe was elected Governor of Virginia, which office he filled for three years. Under the administrations both of Jefferson and Madison, he was appointed to many offices, and superintended many of the important matters and negotiations of the Government, thereby rendering essential, and invaluable services.

In 1816, Mr. Monroe was nominated for the Presidency by the Anti-Federal or Democratic party, and was elected to succeed Mr. Madison. His administration was exceedingly popular, and in 1820, he was almost unanimously re-elected, having received—excepting one—every vote of the Electoral Colleges. His first inauguration took place on the 4th of March, 1817, and his second, on Monday, the fifth of March, 1821. He died at the residence of his son-in-law, Samuel L. Gouveneur in the city of New York, on July 4th, 1831, being the fifty-fifth anniversary of our national independence.

# J. Q. ADAMS'S ADMINISTRATION,

## WITH

## BIOGRAPHICAL SKETCH.
## 1825–1829.

---

### ONE TERM—FOUR YEARS.

ELECTED BY THE REPUBLICAN PARTY.

# CABINET.

**PRESIDENT:**
John Quincy Adams, Massachusetts.

**VICE-PRESIDENT:**
John C. Calhoun, South Carolina.

**SECRETARY OF STATE:**
Henry Clay, Kentucky.

**SECRETARY OF THE TREASURY:**
Richard Rush, Pennsylvania.

**SECRETARIES OF WAR:**
James Barbour, Virginia.   1825.
Peter B. Porter, New York. 1828.

**SECRETARY OF THE NAVY:**
Samuel L. Southard, New Jersey.

**POST MASTER-GENERAL:**
John McLean, Ohio.

**ATTORNEY-GENERAL:**
William Wirt, Virginia,

---

## FINANCIAL CONDITION OF THE COUNTRY.

| Year | Imports | Exports | Expenditures | Debt |
|------|---------|---------|--------------|------|
| 1825 | $96,340,075 | $99,535,388 | $23,585,804 | $83,788,432 |
| 1826 | 84,974,477 | 77,595,322 | 24,103,398 | 81,054,059 |
| 1827 | 79,484,068 | 82,324,727 | 22,656,764 | 73,987,357 |
| 1828 | 88,509,824 | 72,264,686 | 25,459,179 | 67,475,043 |

# JOHN QUINCY ADAMS.

## BIOGRAPHICAL SKETCH.

The sixth President of the United States, was John Quincy Adams. He was the son of John Adams, the second President, and was born in his father's mansion, in the city of Boston, although the family seat was in the present town of Quincy, Massachusetts, on the 11th day of July 1767.

At the age of eleven years, he embarked for France with his father and remained there several months. He subsequently visited Holland, and in 1781, went with Mr. Dana (who had

JOHN QUINCY ADAMS.

been appointed minister) to Russia as his private secretary and remained there eighteen months. From 1783, to 1785, he was with his father in England, Holland, and France. He returned to the United States in 1785, entered Harvard College, and graduated in 1787. He then commenced the study of law at Newburyport under Mr. Theophilus Parsons, and after completing his studies, commenced the practice of his profession in Boston, devoting his leisure time in writing and publishing a series of tracts, and other papers, on the great political questions of the day.

In 1794, General Washington appointed him Minister Resident to the Netherlands, where he remained for two years. He was afterwards appointed Minister Plenipotentiary to Portugal, but on his way there, received an appointment transferring him to Lisbon, where he remained till 1801.

Mr. Adams was a moderate Federalist, and in 1803, was elected a Senator of the United States but not by a party vote. He supported Mr. Jefferson in such measures as his judgment approved. He was appointed one of the commissioners, by whom the treaty of peace was negotiated, between Great Britain and the United States at Ghent, in 1814. In 1815, he was appointed by Mr. Madison, Minister to Great Britain, where he remained about two years, he was then recalled by Mr. Monroe, and appointed by him, Secretary of State, which office he filled for eight years.

The canditates put in nomination to succeed Mr. Monroe, were General Jackson, Henry Clay, William H. Crawford and Mr. Adams. No choice was effected by the Electoral Colleges, by reason of there being so many in nomination, but General Jackson received the greatest number of votes. The election was thereupon referred to the House of Representatives, and on the first ballot, Mr. Adams received the vote of thirteen States and was elected. His inauguration took place on the 4th of March, 1825. John C. Calhoun was made Vice-President.

In May 1797, Mr. Adams was married to Louisa Catherine Johnson, daughter of Joshua Johnson of Maryland, who then resided in London. By this lady, he had four children, of whom, only one, Mr. Charles F. Adams of Boston, is now living.

On the twenty-second of Februry, 1848, this most accomplished scholar and statesman was prostrated by paralysis, while in his seat in the House of Representatives, and breathed his last on the following day. He died in the Speaker's room, in the Capitol, being in his eighty-first year. His dying words were "This is the last of earth."

# JACKSON'S ADMINISTRATION,

## WITH

## BIOGRAPHICAL SKETCH.
## 1829–1837.

TWO TERMS—EIGHT YEARS.

ELECTED BY THE DEMOCRATIC PARTY.

# CABINET.

### PRESIDENT:
ANDREW JACKSON, Tennessee.

### VICE PRESIDENTS:
JOHN C. CALHOUN, South Carolina.
MARTIN VAN BUREN, New York.

### SECRETARIES OF STATE:
| | |
|---|---|
| MARTIN VAN BUREN, New York. | 1829. |
| EDWARD LIVINGSTON, Louisiana. | 1831. |
| LEWIS MCLANE, Delaware. | 1833. |
| JOHN FORSYTH, Georgia. | 1834. |

### SECRETARIES OF THE TREASURY:
| | |
|---|---|
| SAMUEL D. INGHAM, Pennsylvania. | 1829. |
| LOUIS MCLANE, Delaware. | 1831. |
| WILLIAM J. DUANE, Pennsylvania. | 1833. |
| ROGER B. TANEY, Maryland. | 1833. |
| LEVI WOODBURY, New Hampshire. | 1834. |

### SECRETARIES OF WAR:
| | |
|---|---|
| JOHN H. EATON, Tennessee. | 1829. |
| LEWIS CASS, Ohio. | 1831. |

### SECRETARIES OF THE NAVY:
| | |
|---|---|
| JOHN BRANCH, North Carolina. | 1829. |
| LEVI WOODBURY, New Hampshire. | 1831. |
| MAHLON DICKERSON, New Jersey. | 1834. |

### POST MASTERS-GENERAL:
| | |
|---|---|
| WILLIAM T. BARRY, Kentucky. | 1829. |
| AMOS KENDALL, Kentucky. | 1835. |

### ATTORNEYS-GENERAL:
| | |
|---|---|
| JOHN M. BERRIEN, Georgia. | 1829. |
| ROGER B. TANEY, Maryland. | 1831. |
| BENJAMIN F. BUTLER, New York. | 1834. |

## FINANCIAL CONDITION OF THE COUNTRY.

| Year. | Imports. | Exports. | Expenditures. | Debt. |
|---|---|---|---|---|
| 1829 | $71,492,527 | $72,358,671 | $25,044,358 | $58,421,413 |
| 1830 | 70,876,920 | 73,849,508 | 24,585,281 | 48,565,406 |
| 1831 | 103,191,124 | 81,310,583 | 30,038,446 | 39,124,191 |
| 1832 | 101,029,266 | 87,176,943 | 34,356,698 | 24,322,235 |
| 1833 | 108,118,311 | 90,140,443 | 24,257,298 | 7,001,032 |
| 1834 | 126,521,332 | 104,336,973 | 24,601,982 | 4,760,081 |
| 1835 | 149,895,742 | 121,693,577 | 27,575,141 | 3,351,289 |
| 1836 | 189,980,035 | 128,663,040 | 30,934,664 | 3,291,089 |

# ANDREW JACKSON.

## BIOGRAPHICAL SKETCH.

Andrew Jackson, the seventh President of the United States, was of Scottish descent. His grandfather, Hugh Jackson, removed to Ireland, where his sons became respectable farmers. In 1765, his youngest son emigrated to North America, and settled in South Carolina, where he purchased a plantation at Waxhaw Settlement. On this plantation, Andrew Jackson was born on the 15th of March, 1767.

His father died about the time of his birth, leaving his

ANDREW JACKSON.

mother, whose maiden name was Elizabeth Hutchinson, a widow with three sons.

In the spring of 1779, South Carolina was invaded by the English, and his brother, Hugh Jackson, who had enlisted with others to repel them, lost his life in the fatigues of the service. At the age of thirteen, Andrew, with his brother

Robert, joined a company of volunteers and were engaged in a battle at a place called Hanging Rock, where the volunteers particularly distinguished themselves. Both of the young men were soon after taken prisoners, and as such, upon one occasion Andrew was ordered by a British officer to clean his boots, which he indignantly refused to do, whereupon, he was struck by the officer with his sword, causing a deep wound, the scar of which he carried with him to his grave.

His brother Robert, for refusing to perform like menial service, was treated in the same manner, and received a wound from which he never recovered. They were both finally exchanged, and Robert died two days after his arrival home. His mother going on board of a prison ship to nurse some sick, captive friends, took a fever from which she died soon after, leaving Andrew, then a young man, the sole survivor of the family.

When eighteen years of age, he commenced the study of law at Salisbury, North Carolina, and in due time was admitted to the bar, and commenced the practice of law in that State, but being appointed by the Governor, Solicitor for the Western District, which embraced Tennessee, he removed to Jonesborough in 1788, being then only twenty-one years of age. In this new and half-civilized region, he endured hardships and encountered dangers of every kind. His sensitive nature, strong passions, iron will, with his fearless and determined spirit, led him into many difficulties and personal quarrels, all of which he met manfully, ever ready to fight an enemy, or chastise an offender. His motto was, "Ask nothing but what is right; submit to nothing wrong."

On the admission of Tennessee into the Union, Jackson was chosen the first Representative to Congress, and took his seat in the House, on the 5th of December, 1796. His term there however, was short, for being elected by the Legislature, he took his seat in the Senate of the United States, on the 22nd of November, 1797.

In his views he was a democrat, and acted with the Democratic party. After resigning his seat as a Senator, he was appointed Judge of the Supreme Court of Tennessee, which office he held for six years and then resigned. In 1802, he was appointed Major General of the militia of the State. During the war of 1812, he took an active part in the campaigns against the Indians and British, in the capacity of Major General, and on the 23rd of December, 1814, obtained a great victory over them at New Orleans, and was hailed by the people of the South-West as their deliverer.

In 1828, he was nominated for the Presidency, by the Democratic party, the opposing candidate being John Quincy Adams. It was a most exciting campaign, but Jackson was elected, and again re-elected in 1832. His first inauguration took place on the 4th of March, 1829; his second, on the 4th of March, 1833. During his administration, many grave and important questions were agitated, which caused great excitement throughout the country; among these were those relating to the Tariff, U. S. Bank, Public Lands, nullification, Internal Improvement, etc., etc.

On the 3rd of March, 1837, he published his farewell address full of patriotism, good advice, and love of country. He then retired to the Hermitage in Tennessee, where he passed the remainder of his days, breathing his last on the 8th of June, 1845.

# VAN BUREN'S ADMINISTRATION,

WITH

## BIOGRAPHICAL SKETCH.
## 1837–1841.

ONE TERM—FOUR YEARS.

ELECTED BY THE DEMOCRATIC PARTY.

# CABINET.

PRESIDENT:
MARTIN VAN BUREN, New York.

VICE-PRESIDENT:
RICHARD M. JOHNSON, Kentucky.

SECRETARY OF STATE:
JOHN FORSYTH, Georgia.

SECRETARY OF THE TREASURY:
LEVI WOODBURY, New Hampshire.

SECRETARY OF WAR:
JOEL R. POINSETT, South Carolina.

SECRETARIES OF THE NAVY:
MAHLON DICKERSON, New Jersey. 1837.
JAMES K. PAULDING, New York. 1841.

POST MASTERS-GENERAL:
AMOS KENDALL, Kentucky. 1837.
JOHN M. NILES, Connecticut. 1840.

ATTORNEYS-GENERAL.
BENJAMIN F. BUTLER, New York. 1837.
FELIX GRUNDY, Tennessee. 1838.
HENRY D. GILPIN, Pennsylvania. 1840.

## FINANCIAL CONDITION OF THE COUNTRY.

| Year | Imports | Exports | Expenditures | Debt |
|---|---|---|---|---|
| 1837 | $140,989,217 | $117,119,376 | $37,265,037 | $1,878,223 |
| 1838 | 113,717,401 | 108,486,616 | 39,455,438 | 4,857,600 |
| 1839 | 162,092,132 | 121,088,416 | 37,614,936 | 11,983,737 |
| 1840 | 107,641,519 | 132,085,936 | 28,226,558 | 5,125,077 |

# MARTIN VAN BUREN.

## BIOGRAPHICAL SKETCH.

The ancestors of Martin Van Buren, the eighth President of the United States, were among the early emigrants from Holland to the colony of New Netherlands, now the State of New York. His father, Abraham Van Buren, was a farmer in moderate circumstances. Martin, was born at Kinderhook, December 5th, 1782.

MARTIN VAN BUREN.

At the age of fourteen, he commenced the study of law in the office of Francis Sylvester, and completed his studies in the office of William P. Van Ness of New York city. He possessed an active, observing mind, attended all the meetings of the Democratic party, and gave much attention to the political subjects of the day.

In the twenty-first year of his age, he was admitted to the bar, as an Attorney at Law, and commenced its practice in his native village. He soon became one of the most distinguished members of his profession. In 1808, he was appointed Surrogate of Columbia County; in 1815, he was appointed Attorney General of the State; in 1821, he was elected a Senator of the United States, by the Legislature of New York, and in 1828, was elected Governor of that State.

President Jackson having appointed him Secretary of State of the United States, he resigned his office as Governor on the 12th of March, 1829. Having retired from this office in June, 1831, he was appointed by the President, Minister to Great Britain, and arrived in London in September of that year. In May, 1832, he was nominated by the Democratic party as Vice-President, and was elected to that office. He was nominated as the successor of General Jackson by the same party, and received 170 votes of the Electoral College, against 124 for all other candidates. His inauguration took place the 4th of March, 1837.

At this time, the business of the Country was on the verge of prostration and ruin. Previous to this, their having been large facilities for obtaining bank loans, importation of foreign goods had immensely increased, and the spirit of speculation, especially in real estate, had assumed in 1836, the features of a mania. The money thus used in speculation, had been obtained from the Deposit Banks of the United States funds, but in 1836, Congress had authorized the Secretary of the Treasury, to distribute all the public funds, excepting $5,000,000, among the several States. This money after January, 1837, was accordingly taken from the Deposit Banks, thus compelling them to curtail their loans, which resulted in a serious pecuniary embarrassment.

Over trading, and speculation were therefore suddenly checked, and in the spring of 1837, heavy, and innumerable, mercantile failures took place in all our cities, and many banks suspended specie payment. The President recommended to Congress the measure known as the *Sub treasury scheme*, which subsequently passed. Mr. Van Buren was renominated for the Presidency but received only 60 votes of the Electoral College, against 234 for Harrison. He died on the 24th of July, 1862.

# HARRISON'S AND TYLER'S ADMINISTRATIONS,

## WITH

## BIOGRAPHICAL SKETCHES.
## 1841–1845.

ONE TERM—FOUR YEARS.

ELECTED BY THE WHIGS.

*President Harrison died April 4, 1841.*

# CABINET.

### PRESIDENTS:
William Henry Harrison, Ohio. 1841.
John Tyler, Virginia. 1841.

### VICE-PRESIDENT:
John Tyler, Virginia. 1841

### SECRETARIES OF STATE:
Daniel Webster, Massachusetts. 1841.
Hugh S. Legare, South Carolina. 1843.
Abel P. Upshur, Virginia. 1843.
John Nelson, Maryland. 1844.
John C. Calhoun, South Carolina. 1845.

### SECRETARIES OF THE TREASURY.
Thomas Ewing, Ohio. 1841.
Walter Forward, Pennsylvania. 1841.
John C. Spencer, New York. 1843.
George M. Bibb, Kentucky. 1844.

### SECRETARIES OF WAR:
John Bell, Tennessee. 1841.
John C. Spencer, New York, 1841.
James M. Porter, Pennsylvania. 1843.
William Wilkins, Pennsylvania. 1844.

### SECRETARIES OF THE NAVY:
George E. Badger, N. Carolina. 1841.
Abel P. Upshur, Virginia. 1841.
David Henshaw, Massachusetts. 1843.
Thomas W. Gilmer, Virginia. 1844.
John Y. Mason, Virginia. 1844.

### POSTMASTERS-GENERAL.
Francis Granger, New York. 1841.
Charles A. Wickliffe, Kentucky. 1841.

### ATTORNEYS-GENERAL.
John J. Crittenden, Kentucky. 1841.
Hugh S. Legare, South Carolina. 1841.
John Nelson, Maryland. 1844.

## FINANCIAL CONDITION OF THE COUNTRY.

| Year. | Exports. | Imports. | Expenditures. | Debt. |
| --- | --- | --- | --- | --- |
| 1841 | $127,946,117 | $121,851,803 | $31,787,530 | $6,737,398 |
| 1842 | 100,152,087 | 104,691,531 | 32,936,876 | 15,028,486 |
| 1843 | 64,753,799 | 84,346,480 | 12,118,105 | 27,203,450 |
| 1844 | 108,435,035 | 111,200,046 | 33,642,010 | 24,748,188 |

# WILLIAM H. HARRISON.

## BIOGRAPHICAL SKETCH.

William Henry Harrison, the ninth President of the United States, was the youngest son of Benjamin Harrison, one of the Signers of the Declaration of Independence, and one of the Governors of Virginia. William Henry, was born on the ninth of February, 1773, at Berkeley on the James River, Virginia.

He was educated at Hampden, Sydney College, Va., and applied himself to the study of medicine as a profession, but

WILLIAM H. HARRISON.

before its completion, he gave up his studies, and joined the army raised for the defence of the Ohio frontier against the Indians. He received his commission of Ensign in a regiment of artillery, from Gen. Washington, in 1791, and in 1792, was promoted to the rank of Lieutenant.

He soon after joined the new army under the command of

General Anthony Wayne at Pittsburgh, and remained with him some years, engaged in many battles with the Indians, at, and about Fort Washington, where Cincinnati now stands. After the campaign, which resulted in a treaty of peace with the Indians, he was promoted to the rank of Captain, and soon after, at the age of twenty-one, he married the daughter of John Cleves Symmes, the founder of the Miami Settlements.

In 1797, he was appointed by President Adams, Secretary, and *Ex Officio*, Lieutenant-Governor of the North Western Territory. In 1799, he was elected by the legislature of that territory, their first delegate to Congress at the age of twenty-six. Subsequently, the new territory of Indiana was established, which included what are now the States of Indiana, Illinois, Michigan, and Wisconsin, over which he was appointed Governor, and also Superintendent of Indian affairs, and Commander-in-chief of the militia.

He held the office of Governor for a period of thirteen years, having been successively appointed by Adams, Jefferson, and Madison, at the earnest solicitation of the people of the territory. He concluded many treaties with the Indians, and at one time obtained from them the cession of over 50,000,000 of acres, lying between the river Illinois and the Mississippi.

In 1811, he fought the memorable and desperate battle of Tippecanoe, and was very active in the war of 1812. In 1816, he was elected to represent the Congressional District of Ohio, in the House of Representatives of the United States, and subsequently held many other offices. In 1839, he was nominated for the Presidency, by the National Convention of Whig delegates, who had assembled at Harrisburgh, and was elected by an overwhelming majority. He received 234 Electoral votes against 60 for Mr. Van Buren.

The inauguration of General Harrison took place on the 4th of March, 1841, but his administration, however, was very brief. On the 27th of March, he was seized with a severe illness, which terminated his life on Sunday morning the 4th of April, just one month after his inauguration, in the **sixty-eight year of his age.**

# JOHN TYLER.

## BIOGRAPHICAL SKETCH.

John Tyler, the tenth President of the United States, was born in Charles City County, Virginia, on the 29th of March, 1790. His ancestors were among the early English settlers of the Old Dominion. His father was one of the patriots of the Revolution, and devoted himself to its success.

At a very early age, Young Tyler was very much attached to his studies, and was so precocious, that he entered William and Mary College at the age of twelve years, and graduated

JOHN TYLER.

when he was but seventeen. He commenced the study of law, and at nineteen years of age, was admitted to the bar, no objection having been raised as to his age.

In 1811, he was elected a member of the House of Delegates, and took his seat in the Virginia Legislature, where he remained several years, and until 1816, when he was elected to Congress, then being but twenty-six years of age, and was twice re-elected, but by reason of ill health, was finally obliged to resign, and returned to the practice of his profession.

Mr Tyler was elected Governor of Virginia, in December, 1825, and during his administration, he urged forward, and greatly encouraged internal improvements, and many of the finest works in the State, were commenced, and completed, through his instrumentality. He was subsequently re-elected Governor, but before his term of office had expired, he was elected a Senator, having defeated John Randolph.

On the accession of Gen'l Jackson to the Presidency, Mr. Tyler supported his administration in many particulars, but yet, at times, took an independent course. With the nullifiers of South Carolina, he also sympathised; and when the President took his position against the anti-tariff and nullifying proceedings of that State, he withdrew his support from the Administration, acting with Mr. Calhoun, and contending for State Rights.

In 1839, he was elected one of the delegates from Virginia, to the Whig National Convention, at Harrisburg, and exerted his influence in favor of the nomination of Henry Clay, who was defeated by General Harrison, the nominee. It was deemed necessary by the Convention, after the nomination of Harrison, that the candidate for the Vice-President should be a Southern man, and without much reflection, it was offered to Mr. Tyler, who accepted.

On the 6th of April, 1841, after the death of General Harrison, Mr. Tyler took, and subscribed an oath of office, and then issued an inaugural address, to the people of the United States. He took such a course, however, that he lost the confidence of the party who nominated him, without gaining that of his political opponents, and in the late great rebellion, he took part with the enemies of the Republic.

In 1813, at the age of twenty-three, Mr. Tyler married Miss Letitia Christian, a lady much esteemed, and a member of the Episcopal Church. She died at Washington, in 1842. While President of the United States, he was again married to Miss Julia Gardiner, daughter of David Gardiner of New York. He died in Richmond, Virginia, on the 18th of January, 1862.

# POLK'S ADMINISTRATION,

### WITH

## BIOGRAPHICAL SKETCH.
## 1845–1849.

### ONE TERM—FOUR YEARS.

**ELECTED BY THE DEMOCRATIC PARTY.**

# CABINET.

### PRESIDENT:
James K. Polk, Tennessee.

### VICE PRESIDENT:
George M. Dallas, Pennsylvania.

### SECRETARY OF STATE:
James Buchanan, Pennsylvania.

### SECRETARY OF THE TREASURY:
Robert J. Walker, Mississippi.

### SECRETARY OF WAR:
William L. Marcy, New York.

### SECRETARIES OF THE NAVY:
George Bancroft, Massachusetts. 1845.
John Y. Mason, Virginia. 1846.

### POST MASTER-GENERAL:
Cave Johnson, Tennessee.

### ATTORNEYS-GENERAL:
John Y. Mason, Virginia. 1845.
Nathan Clifford, Maine. 1846.
Isaac Toucey, Connecticut. 1848.

## FINANCIAL CONDITION OF THE COUNTRY.

| Year. | Imports. | Exports. | Expenditures. | Debt. |
|---|---|---|---|---|
| 1845 | $117,254,564 | $114,646,606 | $30,490,408 | $17,093,794 |
| 1846 | 121,691,797 | 113,488,516 | 27,632,282 | 16,750,926 |
| 1847 | 146,545,638 | 158,648,622 | 60,520,851 | 38,926,623 |
| 1848 | 154,998,928 | 154,032,131 | 60,655,143 | 48,526,879 |

# JAMES K. POLK.

## BIOGRAPHICAL SKETCH.

James Knox Polk, the eleventh President of the United States, was born on the 2nd of November, 1795, in Mecklenburg County, North Carolina. His ancestors were emigrants from Ireland, who settled in Somerset County, on the eastern shore of Maryland.

His father was a plain farmer, but an energetic, enterprising man, a strong Democrat, and an ardent admirer and supporter of Jefferson. In 1806, he removed with his family to

JAMES K. POLK.

Tennessee. Having prepared himself, under Mr. Black, a classical teacher, his son James K. Polk, in 1815, entered the University of North Carolina, being then in his twentieth year, and in 1818, graduated with the highest honors of his class.

Having returned to Tennessee, he commenced the study of law in the office of Felix Grundy, was admitted to the bar at the close of 1820, and soon became a leading practitioner. In 1823, he was elected to the legislature of his State, and after two years, was elected to represent his District in Congress. He was a staunch Democrat, the personal and political friend of General Jackson, and a firm opponent of Mr. Adams.

He was elected Speaker of the House in 1835, and re-elected to that position in 1837. For fourteen years, he served his District in Congress; then declined a re-election, but subsequently, in 1839, was nominated for Governor, and was elected by a large majority. After serving two years, he was re-nominated, but was defeated by James C. Jones, the Whig candidate.

On the 29th of May, 1844, Mr. Polk received the nomination of the Democratic National Convention assembled at Baltimore, for President of the United States, and was subsequently elected, receiving 170 Electoral votes, against 105 for Henry Clay. George M. Dallas was elected Vice-President, by the same majority over Mr. Frelinghuysen.

He was inaugurated on the 4th of March, 1845. During his administration, war was commenced with Mexico, which resulted in a treaty, whereby California and New Mexico were ceded to the United States. The controversy with Great Britain, respecting the North West boundary, was also settled by treaty, and an independent treasury system was established.

After the inauguration of General Taylor, he returned to Tennessee where he expected to spend the remainder of his days in retirement; but his days were few. He was seized with the chronic diarrhoea about three months after his term of office had expired, and he died on the 15th of June, 1849, in the fifty-fourth year of his age.

# TAYLOR'S AND FILLMORE'S ADMINISTRATIONS,

## WITH

## BIOGRAPHICAL SKETCHES.

## 1849—1853.

---

ONE TERM—FOUR YEARS.

ELECTED BY THE WHIGS.

*President Taylor died July* 9, 1850.

# CABINET.

### PRESIDENTS:
| | |
|---|---|
| Zachary Taylor, Louisiana. | 1849. |
| Millard Fillmore, New York. | 1850. |

### VICE-PRESIDENT:
| | |
|---|---|
| Millard Fillmore, New York. | 1849. |

### SECRETARIES OF STATE:
| | |
|---|---|
| John M. Clayton, Delaware. | 1849 |
| Daniel Webster, Massachusetts. | 1850 |
| Edward Everett, Massachusetts. | 1852. |

### SECRETARIES OF THE TREASURY.
| | |
|---|---|
| William M. Meredith, Penn. | 1849. |
| Thomas Corwin, Ohio. | 1850. |

### SECRETARIES OF WAR:
| | |
|---|---|
| George W. Crawford, Georgia. | 1849. |
| Charles M. Conrad, Louisiana. | 1850. |

### SECRETARIES OF THE NAVY:
| | |
|---|---|
| William B. Preston, Virginia. | 1849. |
| Wm. A. Graham, North Carolina. | 1850. |
| John P. Kennedy, Maryland. | 1852. |

### SECRETARIES OF THE INTERIOR.
| | |
|---|---|
| Thomas Ewing, Ohio. | 1849. |
| Alex. H. H. Stuart, Virginia. | 1850. |

### POSTMASTERS-GENERAL.
| | |
|---|---|
| Jacob Collamer, Vermont. | 1849. |
| Nathan K. Hall, New York. | 1850. |
| Samuel D. Hubbard, Connecticut. | 1852. |

### ATTORNEYS-GENERAL.
| | |
|---|---|
| Reverdy Johnson, Maryland. | 1849. |
| John J. Crittenden, Kentucky. | 1850. |

## FINANCIAL CONDITION OF THE COUNTRY.

| Year. | Imports. | Exports. | Expenditures. | Debt. |
|---|---|---|---|---|
| 1849 | $147,857,439 | $145,755,820 | $56,386,422 | $64,704,693 |
| 1850 | 178,138,318 | 151,898,790 | 41,604,718 | 64,228,238 |
| 1851 | 216,224,932 | 218,388,011 | 48,476,104 | 62,560,395 |
| 1852 | 212,945,442 | 209,658,366 | 46,712,608 | 65,130,692 |

# ZACHARY TAYLOR.

## BIOGRAPHICAL SKETCH.

Zachary Taylor, the twelth President of the United States, was born in Orange County, Virginia, on the twenty-fourth of November, 1784. His father, Richard Taylor, served with valor and zeal throughout the Revolutionary war. He held the commission of Colonel, was engaged in many battles, and rendered valuable aid to General Washington at Trenton.

The year following the birth of Zachary, Colonel Richard Taylor emigrated with his family to Kentucky, and settled

ZACHARY TAYLOR.

near Louisville. He was one of the framers of the Constitution of Kentucky, and was for many years a member of the Legislature of that State.

The early education of Zachary was necessarily limited. He assisted his father on the farm, until he was past twenty-one years of age. He received a commission as Lieutenant in the Seventh Regiment of United States Infantry, from President Jefferson, on the third of May, 1808.

In 1810, he was married to Miss Margaret Smith, a lady of Maryland. In 1812, he was placed in command of Fort Harrison, where he was attacked by a large number of Indians, and for his heroic defence of the fort, the President conferred upon him the rank of Major by brevet.

On the 20th of April, 1819, Major Taylor received the commission of a Lieutenant Colonel, and in 1832, was promoted by President Jackson to the rank of Colonel. He was engaged in the war against Black Hawk, and subsequently against the Seminole Indians in Florida, and had command of the United States troops in the desperate and bloody battle of Okeechobee, where he was again victorious.

For the distinguished services rendered in this battle, he received the thanks of the President in 1838, and was promoted to the rank of Brigadier-General by brevet soon after. In the war with Mexico, General Taylor displayed great military skill, sound judgment, and heroic bravery, as evinced in the memorable battles of Palo Alto, Resaca de la Palma, and Buena Vista.

His determined bravery, and brilliant achievements during the campaigns in Mexico, secured him the love and admiration of the people of the United States. He had taken no active part in politics, but was considered a Whig.

At the Whig National Convention, which met at Philadelphia on the 1st of June, 1848, he received the nomination for the presidency on the fourth ballot, having received 171 votes, against 35 for Clay, 60 for Scott, and 14 for Webster. At the election in November, he received 163 of the Electoral votes, against 127 for General Cass, the Democratic candidate.

His inauguration took place on Monday, the 5th of March, 1849, before a very large assemblage of people.

Early in July, 1850, he was seized with an alarming illness, which, assuming the form of a billious fever, soon terminated his life. He died in the city of Washington, on the 9th of July, 1850, in the 66th year of his age, having discharged the duties of President, one year, four months and four days.

# MILLARD FILLMORE.

## BIOGRAPHICAL SKETCH.

Millard Fillmore, the thirteenth President of the United States, was born at Summer Hill, in Cayuga County, New York, January, 7th, 1800.

His father, Nathaniel Fillmore, was a farmer, but lost his property by reason of some defect in the title. In 1819, he removed to Erie County, New York, and purchased a small farm which he cultivated with his own hands. His mother's

MILLARD FILLMORE.

name was Phebe Millard; she was a daughter of Dr. Abiathar Millard, and died in 1831.

The early education of Mr. Fillmore was extremely limited, and at a suitable age he was apprenticed to a wool-carder, but he improved every leisure moment in reading and cultivating his mind, having an insatiable thirst for knowledge. He remained four years as an apprentice, when he was advised by the late Judge Wood, of Cayuga County, whose acquaintance he had formed, to quit his trade and study law, and he very generously offered to give him a place in his office, and to advance money to defray his expenses.

Having accepted this offer, he entered Judge Wood's office and remained there for two years, partially supporting himself, however, by teaching three months in each year. In the fall of 1821, he removed to Erie County and entered a law office in Buffalo. In 1826, he was married to Abigail Powers, daughter of Rev. Lemuel Powers, a lady very highly esteemed for her many virtues.

In 1827, Mr. Fillmore was admitted as an attorney, and in 1829, as a Counselor of the Supreme Court of that State. He formed a copartnership with an elder member of the bar in Buffalo, and continued a successful practice in that city till 1847, when he removed to Albany, having been elected Comptroller. Previous to this, however, he had served for several years in the Legislature of that State, and had won the confidence of all other members.

He was elected to Congress in the fall of 1832, and continued for several years to represent his District. In 1844, he reluctantly accepted the Whig nomination for Governor of New York, but was defeated. In 1848, he was nominated by the Whigs, in the National Convention, for Vice-President, being put upon the ticket with General Taylor, and received the same number of Electoral votes. After he had entered upon his duties of Vice-President, he exhibited great wisdom and firmness, and as the presiding officer of the Senate, he exercised great courtesy, and ability.

On the 10th of July, 1850, after the decease of General Taylor, Mr. Fillmore took his oath of office as President. The old Cabinet having resigned, he selected a new Cabinet of eminent men, including Daniel Webster, as Secretary of State. It was a critical period in the history of the Country, as many difficult and exciting questions were under discussion, but his messages were calm, conciliatory, yet firm, and many vexed questions were settled during his administration.

Mr. Fillmore died at Buffalo, N. Y., March 8, 1874.

# PIERCE'S ADMINISTRATION,

## WITH

## BIOGRAPHICAL SKETCH.
## 1853–1857.

### ONE TERM—FOUR YEARS.

#### ELECTED BY THE DEMOCRATIC PARTY.

# CABINET.

**PRESIDENT:**
Franklin Pierce, New Hampshire.

**VICE-PRESIDENT:**
William R. King, Alabama.

**SECRETARY OF STATE:**
William L. Marcy, New York.

**SECRETARY OF THE TREASURY:**
James Guthrie, Kentucky.

**SECRETARY OF WAR:**
Jefferson Davis, Mississippi.

**SECRETARY OF THE NAVY:**
James C. Dobbin, North Carolina.

**SECRETARY OF THE INTERIOR:**
Robert McClennand, Michigan.

**POSTMASTER-GENERAL:**
James Campbell, Pennsylvania.

**ATTORNEY-GENERAL:**
Caleb Cushing, Massachusetts.

## FINANCIAL CONDITION OF THE COUNTRY.

| Year | Imports | Exports | Expenditures | Debt |
|---|---|---|---|---|
| 1853 | $267,978,647 | $230,976,157 | $51,577,061 | $67,340,628 |
| 1854 | 30',562,381 | 278,241,064 | 75,473,119 | 47,242,206 |
| 1855 | 261,468,520 | 275,156,846 | 66,164,775 | 39,969,731 |
| 1856 | 314,639,943 | 326,964,908 | 72,726,341 | 30,963,900 |

# FRANKLIN PIERCE.

## BIOGRAPHICAL SKETCH.

Franklin Pierce is the son of General Benjamin Pierce, an officer in the old War of Independence, and was born at Hillsborough, New Hampshire, November 23rd, 1804, and was the fourteenth President of the United States.

In early life he received a liberal education, and at sixteen years of age, entered Bowdoin College, at Brunswick, Maine. He graduated in 1824, studied law, and was admitted to prac-

FRANKLIN PIERCE.

tice at the bar in 1827, and by degrees attained the highest rank in his profession.

He became an active politician, and a warm supporter of General Jackson in 1828. The following year he was elected to represent his District in the State Legislature, where he remained four years. In 1833, he was elected to Congress, and represented his constituents for four years in the House of

Representatives, and was then elected by the Legislature of his State, to a seat in the Senate of the United States.

In 1834, he married the daughter of Rev. Dr. Appleton, formerly President of Bowdoin College, and subsequently removed to Concord, which has since been his place of residence. When the war with Mexico broke out, he was active in raising the New England regiment of Volunteers, and having been commissioned a Brigadier-General, he joined the army in Mexico under General Scott, where he distinguished himself in many hard-fought battles.

At the Democratic Convention held in Baltimore, in 1852, he was unexpectedly nominated as the candidate for the next Presidency. He was elected by an overwhelming majority, having received 254 of the Electoral votes, while General Scott, the opposing candidate, received only 42. William R. King, of Alabama, was elected Vice-President, but was unable to take his seat by reason of increasing ill-health, which terminated his life in April, 1853.

Mr. Pierce was inaugurated as President on the 4th of March, 1853, and at the expiration of his term of office, he retired to private life. He died at Concord, N. H., October 8, 1869.

# BUCHANAN'S ADMINISTRATION,

WITH

## BIOGRAPHICAL SKETCH.
## 1857–1861.

ONE TERM—FOUR YEARS.

ELECTED BY THE DEMOCRATIC PARTY.

# CABINET.

### PRESIDENT:
James Buchanan, Pennsylvania.
### VICE-PRESIDENT:
John C. Breckinridge, Kentucky.
### SECRETARIES OF STATE:

| | |
|---|---|
| Lewis Cass, Michigan. | 1857. |
| Jeremiah S. Black, Pennsylvania. | 1860. |

### SECRETARIES OF THE TREASURY:

| | |
|---|---|
| Howell Cobb, Georgia. | 1857. |
| Philip F. Thomas, Maryland. | 1860. |
| John A. Dix, New York. | 1861. |

### SECRETARIES OF WAR:

| | |
|---|---|
| John B. Floyd, Virginia. | 1857. |
| Joseph Holt, Kentucky. | 1861. |

### SECRETARY OF THE NAVY:

| | |
|---|---|
| Isaac Toucey, Connecticut. | 1857. |

### SECRETARY OF THE INTERIOR.

| | |
|---|---|
| Jacob Thompson, Mississippi. | 1857. |

### POST MASTERS-GENERAL:

| | |
|---|---|
| Aaron V. Brown, Tennessee. | 1857. |
| Joseph Holt, Kentucky. | 1859. |
| Horatio King, Maine. | 1861. |

### ATTORNEYS-GENERAL:

| | |
|---|---|
| Jeremiah S. Black, Pennsylvania. | 1857. |
| Edwin M. Stanton, Pennsylvania. | 1860. |

## FINANCIAL CONDITION OF THE COUNTRY.

| Year | Imports | Exports | Expenditures | Debt |
|---|---|---|---|---|
| 1857 | $362,890,141 | $362,960,608 | $71,274,587 | $29,060,386 |
| 1858 | 282,613,150 | 324,644,421 | 82,002,186 | 44,910,777 |
| 1859 | 338,768,130 | 356,789,461 | 83,678,643 | 58,754,699 |
| 1860 | 362,162,541 | 400,122,296 | 77,055,125 | 64,769,703 |

# JAMES BUCHANAN.

## BIOGRAPHICAL SKETCH.

James Buchanan, the fifteenth President of the Republic, was of Irish parentage, and was born in Franklin County, Pennsylvania, on the 23rd of April, 1791. He received a liberal education, and graduated at Dickinson College with the highest honors, at the early age of eighteen years.

He studied law in the office of James Hopkins, of Lancaster, and in due time was admitted to the bar, and soon became

JAMES BUCHANAN.

a successful practitioner, attaining a high rank in his profession.

In 1814, when but twenty-three years of age, he was elected to the Legislature of his State, and in 1820, was sent to represent his District in Congress, where he remained for ten years, taking an active part in all of its proceedings and becoming distinguished as a debater.

He was a warm and consistent supporter of President Jackson, who appointed him a Minister to Russia in 1831. In 1834, he was elected to a seat in the United States Senate, and represented his constituents in that body for ten years.

In 1845, he was appointed Secretary of State, by President Polk, and acted as such during his term of service, and at the expiration thereof, retired to private life. In 1853, he was appointed Minister to England by President Pierce, in which official position he exhibited all the great qualities of an eminent Statesman.

Mr. Buchanan was nominated as a candidate for the Presidency, by the Democratic National Convention which assembled at Cincinnati, in June, 1856, and after a most exciting canvass he was elected by a large majority. The opposing candidates were Ex-President Fillmore, nominated by a National Convention of the American Party, and John C. Fremont, nominated by a National Convention of Republicans.

The last year of his term of office was an eventful one: the Slavery question had been revived, and the most intense excitement existed in the public mind. For months previously, a band of conspirators, including three or four members of his Cabinet, had been plotting treason against the government, and when in November, 1860, Abraham Lincoln was elected to the Presidency, this treason broke out into open rebellion, and in December, 1860, the first of the Southern States seceded, and others soon followed.

Mr. Buchanan, insisting that he had no right to coerce a State, even in rebellion, and possessed no Constitutional power to use the army and navy to put down the rebellion, passively sat, with closed eyes and folded arms; which inaction greatly encouraged the conspirators, to go on and complete their work of destroying the Nation.

After the close of his administration, he retired to Wheatland, near Lancaster, Pennsylvania, where he died, June 1st, 1868.

# LINCOLN'S ADMINISTRATION,

## WITH

## BIOGRAPHICAL SKETCH.
## 1861–1865.

ELECTED BY THE REPUBLICAN PARTY FOR TWO TERMS.

Administered Four Years, One Month and Eleven Days.

Was assassinated the 14th of April 1865.   Died April 15th, 1865.

# CABINET.

### PRESIDENT:
Abraham Lincoln, Illinois.

### VICE-PRESIDENTS:
Hannibal Hamlin, Maine.
Andrew Johnson, Tennessee.

### SECRETARY OF STATE:
William H. Seward, New York.

### SECRETARIES OF THE TREASURY:
| | |
|---|---|
| Salmon P. Chase, Ohio. | 1861. |
| William Pitt Fessenden, Maine. | 1864. |
| Hugh McCulloch, Indiana. | 1865. |

### SECRETARIES OF WAR:
| | |
|---|---|
| Simon Cameron, Pennsylvania. | 1861. |
| Edwin M. Stanton, Pennsylvania. | 1862. |

### SECRETARY OF THE NAVY:
| | |
|---|---|
| Gideon Wells, Connecticut. | 1861. |

### SECRETARIES OF THE INTERIOR.
| | |
|---|---|
| Caleb B. Smith, Indiana. | 1861. |
| John P. Usher, Indiana. | 1863. |

### POSTMASTERS-GENERAL:
| | |
|---|---|
| Montgomery Blair, Maryland. | 1861. |
| William Dennison, Ohio. | 1864. |

### ATTORNEYS-GENERAL:
| | |
|---|---|
| Edward Bates, Missouri. | 1861. |
| James J. Speed, Kentucky. | 1864. |

---

## FINANCIAL CONDITION OF THE COUNTRY.

| Year | Imports | Exports | Expenditures | Debt |
|---|---|---|---|---|
| 1861 | $286,598,135 | $213,971,277 | $85,387,313 | $90,867,828 |
| 1862 | 275,357,051 | 229,938,985 | 550,811,700 | 514,211,371 |
| 1863 | 252,919,920 | 322,355,254 | 8 5,796,630 | 1,098,795,181 |
| 1864 | 329,562,895 | 301,981,561 | 1,298,144,656 | 1,710,690,489 |

LINCOLN'S INAUGURATION.

# ABRAHAM LINCOLN.

## BIOGRAPHICAL SKETCH.

Abraham Lincoln, the sixteenth President of the United States, was born in Hardin County, Kentucky, February 12th, 1809. His education in early life was quite limited. In 1816, his parents removed with him to Spencer County, Indiana, and subsequently he removed to Illinois.

In 1830, he was a clerk in a store; in 1832, was a Captain of Volunteers in the Black Hawk war, and in 1834, was elected to the Legislature of the State of Illinois, where he served four years.

In 1836, he was licensed to practice law in the courts of that State, and he commenced his profession at Springfield, in 1837.

Mr. Lincoln soon rose to distinction, and became a prominent leader of the Whig party in Illinois. He canvassed the entire State for Henry Clay in 1844, and in 1846, was elected to Congress, where he served his constituents with fidelity.

On the 16th of May, 1860, the Representatives of the Republican party assembled in Convention, in an immense building called "The Wigwam," erected for that purpose in Chicago, and on the 19th, they nominated Mr. Lincoln as their candidate for the Presidency, and Hannibal Hamlin of Maine, for the Vice-Presidency. There were three other candidates for the Presidency in the field, viz; John Bell, nominated by the *Constitutional Union Party*; Stephen A. Douglass, by the regular *Democratic Convention*, and John C. Breckenridge, by the *Seceders* from that Convention, calling themselves the *National Democratic Convention*. Mr. Lincoln was elected, having received 180 of the Electoral votes, or 57 more than all his opponents.

He was inaugurated on the 4th of March, 1861, amid intense excitement. Violence was apprehended, but General Scott having made ample provision to preserve the peace, all passed off quietly. The rebellion having broken out into open hostilities, commencing with the seizure of Government property, and the attack on Fort Sumter, the President, on the 15th of April, 1861, issued his first call for seventy-five thousand men. On the 1st of January, 1863, he issued his Emancipation Proclamation, declaring all slaves in the rebellious States free.

In November, 1864, Mr. Lincoln, having again received the

MEDAL FROM THE FRENCH DEMOCRATS.

nomination was re-elected to the Presidency, with Andrew Johnson as Vice-President; they were inaugurated on the 4th of March, 1865, and the following month General Lee surrendered his army, thus virtually terminating the rebellion.

On the 2nd of April, the President, by proclamation, declared the war to be at an end.

There was great rejoicing throughout the Republic, in the great success of our arms, and the bright prospect of peace, soon, however, to be changed to grief and mourning. On the 14th of April, our lamented President was shot through the head by one John Wilkes Booth, while seated with his wife in a private box, in Ford's theatre in Washington, causing his death the following morning, he then being fifty-six years of age. It was the result of a conspiracy to assassinate, not only the President, but also members of his Cabinet and others. His remains were interred in the Oak Ridge Cemetery, at Springfield, Illinois.

*MEDAL FROM THE FRENCH DEMOCRATS.

*The above Engraving, represents a magnificent Gold Medal, which was presented by forty thousand French Democrats, to the President's widow, to express their sympathy for Our Republic, in the loss of so illustrious a Chief Magistrate. It is in outline, about one third less in size than the original—For a full description of it, see "Civil War in America," by Lossing.—

# JOHNSON'S ADMINISTRATION,

## WITH

## BIOGRAPHICAL SKETCHES.
## 1865–1869.

AS VICE-PRESIDENT, HE SUCCEEDS MR. LINCOLN FOR REMAINDER OF TERM.

# CABINET.

### PRESIDENT:
ANDREW JOHNSON, Tennessee.

### SECRETARY OF STATE:
WILLIAM H. SEWARD, New York.

### SECRETARY OF THE TREASURY:
HUGH McCULLOCH, Indiana.

### SECRETARIES OF WAR:
| | |
|---|---|
| EDWIN M. STANTON, Pennsylvania. | 1865. |
| ULYSSES S. GRANT, Illinois. | 1867. |
| EDWIN M. STANTON, Pennsylvania. | 1868. |
| JOHN M. SCHOFIELD, Missouri. | 1868. |

### SECRETARY OF THE NAVY:
| | |
|---|---|
| GIDEON WELLS, Connecticut. | 1865. |

### SECRETARIES OF THE INTERIOR.
| | |
|---|---|
| JOHN P. USHER, Indiana. | 1865. |
| JAMES HARLAN, Iowa. | 1865. |
| ORVILLE, H. BROWNING, Illinois. | 1866. |

### POST MASTERS-GENERAL:
| | |
|---|---|
| WILLIAM DENNISON, Ohio. | 1865. |
| ALEX. W. RANDALL, Wisconsin. | 1866. |

### ATTORNEYS-GENERAL:
| | |
|---|---|
| JAMES SPEED, | 1865. |
| HENRY STANBERRY, Ohio. | 1866. |
| WILLIAM M. EVARTS, New York. | 1868. |

## FINANCIAL CONDITION OF THE COUNTRY.

| Year | Imports | Exports | Expenditures | Debt |
|---|---|---|---|---|
| 1865 | $234,339,810 | $336,697,123 | $1,897,674,224 | $2,682,593,026 |
| 1866 | 445,512,158 | 550,684,299 | 541,072,666 | 2,783,425,879 |
| 1867 | 411,733,309 | 438,577,312 | 393,079,655 | 2,692,199,215 |
| 1868 | 373,400,448 | 454,301,713 | 369,889,970 | 2,636,320,964 |

# ANDREW JOHNSON.

## BIOGRAPHICAL SKETCH.

Andrew Johnson, the seventeenth President of the United States, was born in Raleigh, North Carolina, on the 29th of December, 1808. At an early age he was apprenticed to learn the business of a tailor, and continued at the trade for several years.

Unlike most of the young men of this country, he grew up in

ANDREW JOHNSON.

utter ignorance of the most common branches of an English education, and was not able either to read or write until he was twenty years of age, after removing to Greenville in East Tennessee. He subsequently became an Alderman of that place, and in 1836, was elected Mayor, which office he filled for three years.

In 1835, he was chosen to the State Legislature, and in 1843, he was elected to Congress, and represented his State therein for several years. In 1853, he was chosen Governor of Tennessee, and was re-elected to that office.

In 1857, he was elected United States Senator, and was subsequently, in 1862, appointed by President Lincoln, Military Governor of Tennessee. He had previously been a Democrat in politics, and in the election of 1860, had used his influence to elect Mr. Breckenridge to the Presidency. He professed, however, to have changed his views materially, condemned the course of the South in the rebellion, and supported the measures of President Lincoln.

The Union National Convention, held at Baltimore, in June, 1864, nominated Mr. Lincoln for the Presidency, and Mr. Johnson for the Vice-Presidency, and in November, they were elected by a large majority.

On the 15th of April, 1865, a few hours after the death of Mr. Lincoln, he took the oath of office as President of the United States. Disagreements soon arose between Congress and the President, respecting the reconstruction of the States lately in rebellion, and it soon became evident that he was more friendly to the late enemies of the country, than he was to her true, and tried friends. He issued an order to Mr. Stanton, removing him from his office of Secretary of War, and performed many acts, considered by the majority of the people, as highly improper in a Chief Magistrate.

On the 22nd of February, 1868, by a vote of 126 to 47, it was resolved by the House of Representatives, that Andrew Johnson, President, be impeached of high crimes and misdemeanors. Articles of impeachment were prepared and presented, and on the 5th of March, 1868, the Senate of the United States, for the first time, was organized as a court for the trial of the President. Chief-Justice Salmon P. Chase presided. The trial continued from the 30th of March, to the 6th of May, 1868, when the case was submitted to the Senate. Its decision was given on the 26th of May. Thirty-five found him guilty, and nineteen voted "Not guilty."

In order to convict, it was necessary that two thirds should vote in the affirmative; one vote of the required number being wanted, he was acquitted.

Mr. Johnson died, July 31, 1875.

# GRANT'S ADMINISTRATION,

## WITH

## BIOGRAPHICAL SKETCH.
## 1869–1877.

---

### TWO TERMS—EIGHT YEARS.

#### ELECTED BY THE REPUBLICAN PARTY.

### PRESIDENT:
Ulysses S. Grant, Illinois.

### VICE-PRESIDENTS:
Schuyler Colfax, Indiana.
Henry Wilson, Massachusetts.

### SECRETARY OF STATE:
Hamilton Fish, New York.

### SECRETARIES OF THE TREASURY:
George S. Boutwell, Massachusetts.
William A. Richardson, Massachusetts.
Benjamin H. Bristow, Kentucky.

### SECRETARIES OF WAR:
| | |
|---|---|
| John A. Rawlins, Illinois. | 1869. |
| William W. Belknap, Iowa. | 1869. |
| Alphonso Taft, Ohio. | 1876. |

### SECRETARIES OF THE NAVY:
| | |
|---|---|
| Adolphe E. Borie, Pennsylvania. | 1869. |
| George M. Robeson, New Jersey. | 1869. |

### SECRETARIES OF THE INTERIOR:
| | |
|---|---|
| Jacob D. Cox, Ohio. | 1869. |
| Columbus Delano, Ohio. | 1870. |
| Zachariah Chandler, Michigan. | 1875. |

### POSTMASTERS-GENERAL:
| | |
|---|---|
| John A. J. Creswell, Maryland. | 1869. |
| Marshall Jewell, Connecticut. | 1874. |

### ATTORNEYS-GENERAL:
| | |
|---|---|
| E. Rockwood Hoar, Massachusetts. | 1869. |
| George H. Williams, Oregon. | 1869. |
| Edwards Pierrepont, New York. | 1875. |

---

### STATEMENT OF THE PUBLIC DEBT, Nov. 30 1875.

Total amount of Principal ................................. $2,207,986,255
" " " Interest ...................................... 34,960,516

Total Debt ................................. $2,242,946,771

Cash in the Treasury, Coin.................. $70,404,676
" " " Currency ............. 12,014,962
Deposits for Redemption Certificates. ....... 42,610,000
$125,029,638

Debt Less Cash in Treasury........................ $2,117,917,133

Decrease of Debt from March 1, 1869 to Dec. 1, 1875, $509,862,271

# ULYSSES S. GRANT.

## BIOGRAPHICAL SKETCH.

Our present chief magistrate, Ulysses S. Grant, being the eighteenth President of the United States, is of English descent. His grandfather, Noah Grant, was born in Coventry, Connecticut, on the 23d of June, 1748. He took an active part in the battle of Lexington, in the capacity of a Lieutenant, and

ULYSSES S. GRANT.

served through the Revolutionary war, having been promoted to the rank of Captain.

He subsequently removed to Westmoreland County, Penn., where, on the 23d of January, 1794, his father, Jesse Root Grant was born. In 1799, the family removed to Ohio, and on the 27th of April, 1822, at Point Pleasant, Clarmont County,

Ohio, in a small frame, one-story dwelling, was born Ulysses S. Grant, the subject of this sketch.

His mother's maiden name was Hannah Simpson; she was the only daughter of a thrifty farmer, a lady much beloved and respected.

A few months after his birth, his father removed to Georgetown, in Brown County, where he prosecuted successfully his business as a tanner. The early education of Ulysses was very much neglected, and being passionately fond of horses, most of his time was spent in driving the "team," and making himself useful to his father. He subsequently attended school at Maysville, Kentucky, and at the Academy at Ripley.

Through the influence of Thomas L. Hamer, a Member of Congress from the Georgetown district, he received an appointment to the Military Academy at West Point and at once applied himself to study, under a professional teacher, and on the 15th of May, 1839, he started for West Point, being then in his eighteenth year.

He soon became initiated, and grew quite popular among the cadets, for his modesty and amiability, and was nicknamed "Uncle Sam." He was a fair scholar, but excelled in mathematics.

On the 30th of June, 1843, Grant graduated, being the twenty-first, on a list of thirty-nine. These were all that were left of more than one hundred who had entered the class with him. He was at once appointed brevet second Lieutenant in the Fourth Infantry, and took an active part in the Mexican War which followed, exhibiting at all times, great coolness and bravery, and at the close of which, he bore the brevet rank of Captain. In 1853, he was promoted to the rank of full Captain.

At St. Louis, on the 22nd of August, 1848, Grant married Miss Julia B. Dent, daughter of Colonel Frederick Dent, a young lady, very attractive in her manners, and amiable in disposition, whom he had known, and to whom he had been engaged for some years.

In 1854, he resigned his commission, and having lost some sixteen hundred dollars by the sutler of his regiment, he found himself reduced to poverty and want, against which he struggled for several years, without means, and without any legitimate business.

His father, Colonel Dent, had given his daughter Julia, sixty acres of land from his farm at Whitehaven, and also three or four slaves. On this land he built himself a small house, hauling the logs for its walls, and splitting the shingles for the roof with his own hands. This place he named "Hardscrabble," suggested by the hard struggle he experienced in obtaining from it sufficient for the bare sustenance of his family.

After four years of hard labor upon his small farm, and after expending some two thousand dollars his father had advanced him, he gave up farming as a failure, and went into partnership with one Mr. Boggs, at St. Louis, Mo., as real estate agents.

This copartnership commenced January 1st, 1859, and continued for about nine months, when, finding the business would not support two families, the copartnership was dissolved. From this time, to March, 1860, Captain Grant had no permanent business, although he had a wife and four children to support.

In March, 1860, he removed with his family to Galena, Illinois, his father and brothers having offered him a situation in their store, at an annual salary of six hundred dollars per annum, with the promise of an interest in the business, at some future time. His father had been successful in business, and was worth from seventy-five to one hundred thousand dollars at this time.

About the 1st of May, 1861, after the breaking out of the rebellion, through the influence of Elihu B. Washburne, and others, Governor Yates, of Illinois, took him into his office, as his military adviser, and Adjutant-General. He had previously to this, tendered his services to the Government at Washington, but his letter had been unanswered.

On the 4th of May, he was put in command of Camp Yates, during the absence of Captain Pope, and subsequently mustered several regiments into the service. On the 16th of June, he was appointed Colonel of the Twenty-First Illinois Volunteers, and requested to take command at once. Of his commission, Governor Yates subsequently said, "It was the most glorious day of my life when I signed it."

Being without horse, or uniform, he obtained the indorsement of an old friend to his note for three hundred dollars, which he got discounted, and with the proceeds, purchased them. His regiment was first ordered to Mexico, in Missouri, and there being no means of transportation, he marched them across the country on foot. In two months afterwards, Colonel Grant was appointed a Brigadier-General, his commission dating back to the 17th of May.

From this time, his promotion from rank to rank was rapid. In the battles in which he was engaged, he exhibited the same military qualities, as had been displayed by General Taylor in Mexico. Cool, calculating, persevering, and brave, he went into a fight expecting to be victorious, and when he was whipped, he did not "see it," and consequently did not "stay whipped."

In his first battle at Belmont, where he handled three thousand men so successfully, when a member of his staff, who had never been under fire before, rode up to him exclaiming, "Why, General, we are entirely lost! They have surrounded us!" he replied, apparently unmoved, "Well then, we will cut our way out  We have whipped them once to-day, and I think we can again."

His subsequent brilliant campaigns, did not secure him from the vilest of slanders. He was denounced as a drunkard, as being blood-thirsty, reckless of human life, incompetent, an utterly unfit to command a large body of troops. President Lincoln was strongly urged to remove him. After his capture of Vicksburg, however, where in the capitulation, he received fifteen Generals, about thirty-thousand soldiers, and one hundred and seventy-two cannon, President Lincoln sent him that remarkable autograph letter, dated July 16th, 1863, wherein, after acknowledging the great services, he had rendered the Country, he concludes with these words, "I now wish to make the personal acknowledgement, *that you were right, and I was wrong.*"

In 1864, a bill passed Congress, reviving the grade of Lieutenant-General, and authorizing the Executive to confer it upon some officer. This high rank in 1798, was created for Washington, in anticipation of a war with France. It was discontinued when he died. After the Mexican war, it was conferred by brevet on Winfield Scott. At the time of the passage of the bill, no other Americans had ever held it.

This bill, being passed, and Grant having been appointed to this office, by the President, he was telegraphed to report to the War Department in person, which he did, and received personally from the President, the commission. Soon after this he started West, and upon his arrival at Nashville, found an order from the War Department, formally assigning him to the command of *all the forces of the United States*, with headquarters in the field.

He made short work with the rebellion, and upon the surrender of Lee and his army, it was virtually at an end. General Grant's military career, from beginning to end, was a glorious one. He has fought more battles, and gained more victories, has captured more prisoners, and taken more guns than any General of modern times.

On the 12th of August, 1867, President Johnson suspended Stanton, and made Grant Secretary of War *ad interim*. The Senate subsequently refused to sanction this suspension, whereupon Grant surrendered the office to Stanton, against the wishes of President Johnson.

On the 20th of May, at a National Convention of the Republican party held in Chicago, General Grant was *unanimously* nominated for the Presidency, and Schuyler Colfax for the Vice-Presidency, both of whom were elected by large majorities over Seymour and Blair, the opposing candidates, and he was inaugurated on the 4th of March, 1869.

The administration of President Grant has been financially, a successful one. At the commencement of his term, March 4th, 1869, the aggregate debt of the Country was nearly two billions, six hundred and thirty millions of dollars. Since then it has rapidly decreased. On the 1st of December 1871, it had decreased *two hundred and seventy-seven millions.* The decrease from March 1, 1869, to December 1, 1876, was over *five hundred millions.*

On the 5th day of June, 1872, at a National Convention of the Republican party held in the Academy of Music, in Philadelphia, General Grant, amid the wildest enthusiasm, was unanimously renominated for the Presidency, and Henry Wilson was nominated for the Vice-Presidency, both of whom were elected by large majorities.

# ELECTORAL VOTES

### FOR

# President and Vice-President of the United States,

#### UNDER THE CONSTITUTION.

### FIRST TERM—1789 TO 1793

At the time of this election, only eleven states had ratified the Constitution. North Carolina and Rhode Island had rejected it, and the Legislature of New York, by reason of some disagreement between the two branches, had failed in passing a law respecting the choosing of the Electors, and consequently no Electors were appointed to represent that State. Only *ten States*, therefore, participated in the election.

By the Constitution, as it then stood, the presidential electors voted for *two persons*, and the one receiving the highest number of votes, was to be the President, and the one having the next highest number, was to be the Vice-President. It was necessary that the President should receive a *majority* of the whole number of electoral votes, but this was not necessary to elect the Vice-President.

Whole number of Electors, 69.

ELECTORAL VOTE—George Washington, 69; John Adams, 34; John Jay, 9; R. H. Harrison, 6; John Rutledge, 6; John Hancock, 4; George Clinton, 3; Samuel Huntington, 2; John Milton, 2; James Armstrong, 1; Edward Telfair, 1; Benjamin Lincoln, 1.

George Washington was thereupon declared the President, and John Adams, the Vice-President.

---

### SECOND TERM—1793 TO 1797.

Fifteen states participated in this election; Rhode Island and North Carolina having ratified the Constitution, and two new States, Vermont and Kentucky, having been admitted into the Union.

ELECTORAL VOTES. 185

Whole number of Electors, 132.
ELECTORAL VOTE—George Washington, 132; John Adams, 77; George Clinton, 50; Thomas Jefferson, 4; Aaron Burr, 1.

George Washington was therefore again declared the President, and John Adams the Vice-President.

---

### THIRD TERM—1797 TO 1801.

Tennessee having been admitted, the whole number of States, 16.

Whole number of Electors, 138.

ELECTORAL VOTE—John Adams, 71; Thomas Jefferson, 68; Aaron Burr, 30; Samuel Adams, 15; Oliver Ellsworth, 11; George Clinton, 7; John Jay, 5; James Iredell, 3; George Washington, 2; John Henry, 2; S. Johnson, 2; Charles C. Pinckney, 1.

John Adams was therefore declared the President, and Thomas Jefferson the Vice-President.

---

### FOURTH TERM—1801 TO 1805.

Whole number of States, 16.

Whole number of Electors, 188.

ELECTORAL VOTE—Thomas Jefferson, 73; Aaron Burr, 73; John Adams, 65; Charles C. Pinckney, 64; John Jay, 1.

The votes for Jefferson and Burr being the highest, and *equal*, there was no election. It was necessary, therefore, under the Constitution, that the House of Representatives should decide which one was to be President, and which one Vice-President. On the 36*th ballot*, Mr. Jefferson was chosen President, and Mr. Burr Vice-President.

---

### FIFTH TERM—1805 TO 1809.

Previous to this election, an amendment to the Constitution relative to the election of President and Vice-President had been proposed, *so as to designate which person had been voted for* as *President, and which one as Vice-President*. This Amendment had passed both branches of Congress, and in 1804, it had been ratified by the Legislatures of three-fourths of the States as required by the Constitution, and on the 25th of September, 1804, it was announced by the Secretary of State, as having been duly adopted and ratified. Hence at this election, they were voted for separately. Ohio had also been admitted into the Union.

Whole number of States, 17.
Whole number of Electors, 176.
ELECTORAL VOTE.—For President, Thomas Jefferson, 162; Charles C. Pinckney, 14.

For Vice-President, George Clinton, 162; Rufus King, 14.

Mr. Jefferson was therefore declared the President elect, and Mr. Clinton the Vice-President.

## SIXTH TERM—1809 TO 1813.

Whole number of States, 17.
Whole number of Electors, 175.
ELECTORAL VOTE.—For President, James Madison, 122; George Clinton, 6; C. C. Pinckney, 47;

For Vice-President, George Clinton, 113; James Madison, 3; James Monroe, 3; John Langdon, 9, ; Rufus King, 47;

Mr. Madison was therefore declared the President elect, and Mr. Clinton the Vice-President.

## SEVENTH TERM—1813 TO 1817.

Whole number of States, 18.
Whole number of Electors, 217.
ELECTORAL VOTE.—For President, James Madison, 128; De Witt Clinton, of New York, 89.

For Vice-President, Elbridge Gerry, 131; Jared Ingersoll, 86.

Mr. Madison was therefore declared the President elect, and Mr. Gerry the Vice-President.

## EIGHTH TERM—1817 TO 1821.

**Whole** number of States, 19.

Whole number of Electors, 217.

ELECTORAL VOTE.— For President, James Monroe, 183; Rufus King, 34.

For Vice-President, Daniel D. Tompkins, 183; John E. Howard, 22; James Ross, 5; John Marshall, 4; Robert G. Harper, 3.

Mr. Monroe was therefore declared the President elect, and Daniel D. Tompkins, Vice-President.

---

## NINTH TERM—1821 TO 1825.

Whole number of States, 24.

Whole number of Electors, 282.

ELECTORAL VOTE.—For President, James Monroe, 231; John Quincy Adams, 1.

For Vice-President, Daniel D. Tompkins, 218; Richard Stockton, 8; Robert G. Harper, 1; Richard Rush, 1; Daniel Rodney, 1.

Mr. Madison, was therefore declared the President elect, and Mr. Tompkins the Vice-President.

---

## TENTH TERM—1825 TO 1829.

Whole number of States, 24.

Whole number of Electors, 261.

ELECTORAL VOTE.—For President, Andrew Jackson, 99; John Quincy Adams, 84; William H. Crawford, 41; Henry Clay, 37.

For Vice-President, John C. Calhoun, 182: Nathan Sanford, 30; Nathaniel Macon, 24; Andrew Jackson, 13; Martin Van Buren, 9; Henry Clay, 2.

Neither of the candidates for the Presidency receiving a *majority*, there was no election, and the vote was carried to the House of Representatives, where Adams received the vote of 13 States, Jackson of 7 States, and Crawford of 4 States.

Adams was therefore elected President, and John C. Calhoun, the Vice-President.

## ELEVENTH TERM—1829 TO 1833.

Whole number of States, 24.

Whole number of Electors, 261.

ELECTORAL VOTE.—For President, Andrew Jackson, 178; John Quincy Adams, 83;

For Vice-President, John C. Calhoun, 171; Richard Rush, 83; William Smith, 7.

POPULAR VOTE.—For President, Jackson, 650,028; Adams, 512,158.

Mr. Jackson, was therefore declared the President elect, and Mr. Calhoun, the Vice-President.

---

## TWELFTH TERM—1833 TO 1837.

Whole number of States, 24.

Whole number of Electors, 288.

ELECTORAL VOTE.—For President, Andrew Jackson, 219; Henry Clay, 49; John Floyd, 11: William Wirt, 7.

For Vice-President, Martin Van Buren, 189; John Sargent, 49; William Wilkins, 30; Henry Lee, 11: Amos Ellmaker, 7.

POPULAR VOTE.—For President, Jackson, 687,502; Clay, 550,189; Wirt and Floyd combined, 33,108.

Mr. Jackson was therefore declared the President elect, and Martin Van Buren, the Vice-President.

---

## THIRTEENTH TERM—1837 TO 1841.

Whole number of States, 26.

Whole number of Electors, 294.

ELECTORAL VOTE.—For President, Martin Van Buren, 170; William H. Harrison, 73; Hugh L. White, 26; Daniel Webster, 14: W. P. Mangum, 11.

For Vice-President, Richard M. Johnson, 147; Francis Granger, 77; John Tyler, 47; William Smith, 23.

POPULAR VOTE.—For President, Van Buren, 762,149; all others combined, 736,736.

Mr. Van Buren was therefore declared the President elect, and Mr. Johnson the Vice-President.

ELECTORAL VOTE. 189

### FOURTEENTH TERM—1841 TO 1845.

Whole number of States, 26.
Whole number of Electors, 294.
ELECTORAL VOTE.—For President, Wm. H. Harrison, 234; Martin Van Buren, 60.
For Vice-President, John Tyler, 234; R. M. Johnson, 48; L. W. Tazwell, 11; James K Polk, 1.
POPULAR VOTE.—Harrison, 1,274,783; Van Buren, 1,128,702 James G. Birney, 7,609.
Mr. Harrison was therefore declared the President elect, and Mr. Tyler, the Vice-President.

### FIFTEENTH TERM—1845 TO 1849.

Whole number of States, 26.
Whole number of Electors, 275.
ELECTORAL VOTE.—For President, James K. Polk, 170; Henry Clay, 105.
For Vice-President, George M. Dallas, 170; Theodore Frelinghuysen; 105.
POPULAR VOTE. — For President, Polk, 1,335,834; Clay, 1,297,033; Frelinghuyson, 105.
Mr. Polk was therefore declared the President elect, and Mr. Dallas the Vice President.

### SIXTEENTH TERM.—1849 to 1853.

Whole number of States, 30.
Whole number of Electors, 290.
ELECTORAL VOTE. — For President, Zachary Taylor, 163; Lewis Cass, 127.
For Vice President, Millard Fillmore, 163; William O. Butler, 127.
POPULAR VOTE.—Taylor, 1,362,031; Cass, 1,222,445; Van Buren, 291,455.
Mr. Taylor was therefore declared the President elect, and Mr. Fillmore the Vice-President.

## SEVENTEENTH TERM.—1853 to 1857.

Whole number of States, 31.

Whole number of Electors, 296.

ELECTORAL VOTE.—For President, Franklin Pierce, 254; Winfield Scott, 42.

For Vice-President, William R. King, 254; William A. Graham, 42.

POPULAR VOTE.—For President, Pierce, 1,590,490; Scott, 1,378,589; John P. Hale, 157,296.

Mr. Pierce was therefore declared the President elect, and Mr. King the Vice-President.

## EIGHTEENTH TERM.—1857 to 1861.

Whole number of States, 31.

Whole number of Electors, 296.

ELECTORAL VOTE.—For President, James Buchanan, 174; John C. Fremont, 109; Millard Fillmore, 8.

For Vice-President, John C. Breckenridge, 174; William L. Dayton, 109. Andrew J. Donalson, 8.

POPULAR VOTE.—Buchanan, 1,832,232; Fremont, 1,341,514; Millard Fillmore, 874,907.

Mr. Buchanan was therefore elected President, and Mr. Breckenridge the Vice-President.

## NINETEENTH TERM.—1861 to 1865.

Whole number of States, 33.

Whole number of Electors, 303.

ELECTORAL VOTE.—For President, Abraham Lincoln, 180, John C. Breckenridge, 72; John Bell, 39; Stephen A. Douglass, 12.

For Vice-President, Hannibal Hamlin, 180; Joseph Lane, 72. Edward Everett, 39; H. V. Johnson, 12.

POPULAR VOTE.—Lincoln, 1,857,610; Douglass, 1,365,976; Breckenridge, 847,953; Bell, 590,631.

Mr. Lincoln was therefore elected President, and Mr. Hamlin the Vice-President.

## TWENTIETH TERM.—1865 to 1869.

The States in rebellion did not vote in this election.
Number of States participating in the election, 25.
Whole number of Electors who voted, 233.
ELECTORAL VOTE.—For President, Abraham Lincoln, 212; George B. McClellan, 21.
For Vice-President, Andrew Johnson, 212; George H Pendleton, 21.
POPULAR VOTE.—For President, Lincoln 2,223,035; McClellan, 1,811,754.—Total Vote, 4,034,789.
Mr. Lincoln was therefore re-elected President, and Mr. Johnson elected the Vice-President.

## TWENTY FIRST TERM.—1869 to 1873.

Whole number of States which voted, 34.
Whole number of Electors who voted, 294.
ELECTORAL VOTE.—For President, Ulysses S. Grant, 214; Horatio Seymour, 80.
For Vice-President, Schuyler Colfax, 214; Blair, 80.
POPULAR VOTE.—For President, Grant, 3,021,020; Seymour, 2,716,475.—Total, 5,737,495.
Virginia, Mississippi, and Texas, did not take part in the election. The Legislature of Florida chose the Electors.
Grant and Colfax were therefore elected.

## TWENTY SECOND TERM.—1873 to 1877.

Whole number of States, 37.
Whole number of Electors, 366.
ELECTORAL VOTE.—For President, Ulysses S. Grant, 292; Horace Greeley, 74.
POPULAR VOTE.—For President, Grant, 3,579,793. Greeley, 2,842,425; O'Connor, 29,489; Black, 5,608 Total Vote, 6,457,315. Grant's majority over Greeley 737,368 over all, 702,271.
Grant was therefore elected President, and Wilson, Vice-President.

# PRESIDENTIAL ELECTION OF 1876.

## Popular and Electoral Vote by States.

| States. | Popular Vote. | | | | Electoral Vote. | |
|---|---|---|---|---|---|---|
| | Hayes Rep. | Tilden Dem. | Cooper Green. | Smith Pro. | Hayes. | Tilden. |
| Alabama | 68,230 | 102,002 | | | | 10 |
| Arkansas | 38,669 | 58,071 | 289 | | | 6 |
| California | 78,614 | 75,845 | 44 | | 6 | |
| Colorado | By | Legislature. | | | 3 | |
| Connecticut | 59,034 | 61,931 | 774 | 378 | | 6 |
| Delaware | 10,752 | 13,351 | | | | 3 |
| Florida | 23,849 | 22,923 | | | 4 | |
| Georgia | 50,446 | 130,088 | | | | 11 |
| Illinois | 278,232 | 258,601 | 17,233 | 141 | 21 | |
| Indiana | 208,011 | 213,526 | 9,533 | | | 15 |
| Iowa | 171,327 | 112,099 | 9,001 | 36 | 11 | |
| Kansas | 78,322 | 37,9 2 | 7,776 | 110 | 5 | |
| Kentucky | 97,156 | 159,690 | 1,944 | 818 | | 12 |
| Louisiana | 75,135 | 70,636 | | | 8 | |
| Maine | 66,300 | 49,823 | 663 | | 7 | |
| Maryland | 71,981 | 91,780 | 33 | 10 | | 8 |
| Massachusetts | 150,063 | 108,777 | 779 | 84 | 13 | |
| Michigan | 166,534 | 141,095 | 9,060 | 766 | 11 | |
| Minnesota | 72,962 | 48,799 | 2,311 | 7 | 5 | |
| Mississippi | 52,605 | 112,173 | | | | 8 |
| Missouri | 145,029 | 203,077 | 3,498 | 64 | | 15 |
| Nebraska | 31,916 | 17,554 | 2,320 | 1,599 | 3 | |
| Nevada | 10,383 | 9,308 | | | 3 | |
| New Hampshire | 41,539 | 38,509 | | | 5 | |
| New Jersey | 103,517 | 115,962 | 712 | 43 | | 9 |
| New York | 489,207 | 521,949 | 1,987 | 2,359 | | 35 |
| North Carolina | 108 417 | 125,427 | | | | 10 |
| Ohio | 330,698 | 323,182 | 3,057 | 1,636 | 22 | |
| Oregon | 15,206 | 14,149 | 510 | | 3 | |
| Pennsylvania | 384,122 | 366,158 | 7,187 | 1,319 | 29 | |
| Rhode Island | 15,787 | 10,712 | 68 | 60 | 4 | |
| South Carolina | 91,870 | 90,006 | | | 7 | |
| Tennessee | 89,566 | 133,166 | | | | 12 |
| Texas | 44,800 | 104,755 | | | | 8 |
| Vermont | 44,092 | 20,254 | | | 5 | |
| Virginia | 95,558 | 139,670 | | | | 11 |
| West Virginia | 40,698 | 56,455 | 1,373 | | | 5 |
| Wisconsin | 130,668 | 123,927 | 1,509 | 27 | 10 | |
| Total | 4,033,295 | 4,284,265 | 81,737 | 9,522 | 185 | 184 |

Total Vote for Presidential Electors........................8,411,139.
Tilden's Majority over all others........................157,391.

THE WHITE HOUSE.

# RUTHERFORD B. HAYES.

## BIOGRAPHICAL SKETCH.

Rutherford Birchard Hayes, was born in Deleware, Ohio, October 4th, 1822. His parents, Rutherford Hayes and Sophia Birchard, were natives of Windham County, Vermont, and emigrated to Ohio in 1817.

Mr. Hayes graduated at Kenyon College, with the first honors of his class, in 1842. Soon afterward he entered the Law School of Harvard University, from which he graduated in 1845. He was admitted to the Bar at Marietta, and began the practice of his profession at Fremont, Ohio.

In 1849 he removed to Cincinnati, where he soon acquired a fine practice. In 1852 he was married to Miss Lucy Webb, daughter of Dr. James Webb, of Chillicothe. In 1858 he was elected City Solicitor, and held the office till the Spring of 1861. At this period of his life, he was considered one of the most brilliant young lawyers at the Cincinnati Bar, and had acquired an enviable reputation.

When the rebellion broke out, Mr. Hayes, an original Republican, took sides with the Union cause, and his feelings and sympathy were strongly enlisted. With the aid of Judge Matthews, he undertook to raise a regiment of volunteers, and soon the 23d Ohio Infantry was organized, with W. S. Rosecrans as Colonel, and Mr. Hayes as Major.

This regiment was early in the field. It reached Clarksburg, West Va., July 27th 1861, and passed the remainder of the year in arduous campaigning under Gen. Rosecrans. In November, Hayes was promoted to Lieut. Col., and was assigned to the command of his regiment.

In April, 1862, Lieut. Col. Hayes moved his regiment from winter quarters, and on the 1st of May made a brilliant dash on Princeton, driving the rebels from the town, and capturing prisoners and arms. On the 10th of May, at Giles' Court-House, he was attacked by a greatly superior force, and fought all day, gradually falling back a distance of five miles. He managed to choose his own position, kept the enemy at bay, and inflicted much greater injury than he received. His skill and coolness in handling his forces on this occasion were deserving of great praise.

In August, he received orders to march with all possible dispatch to the Great Kanawha. The regiment made about 104 miles in three days, embarked on transports for Parkersburg, and took the cars for Washington, where it joined McClellan's army. It was here attached to the Division of Gen. J. D. Cox; and, marching into Maryland, arrived at Middletown, September 13th. On the 14th began the battle of South Mountain, resulting in the greater battle of Antietam on the 17th.

The first shots at South Mountain were fired by Hayes's regiment, which, at an early hour, was ordered to ascend the mountain by an unfrequented road. It surprised and captured the enemy's picket, and vigorously assailed the main line sheltered behind stone parapets; but received from their greatly superior force so heavy a fire of musketry and canister shot, that in a few minutes 100 officers and men, out of 350 men who went into action, were killed or wounded. Among the latter was Hayes, who had an arm badly broken. He was not, however, ready for ambulance or hospital; and soon reappeared on the field with his wound half dressed, and fought until he was so weak that his men had to carry him away.

After the battle of Antietam, Hayes was promoted to a Colonel, and ordered with his regiment to the Kanawha Valley, where, in December, 1862, he was placed in command of the First Brigade of the Kanawha Division—a famous organization.

In the battle of Opequan, Col. Hayes's brigade, after advancing across several open fields, gained the crest of a hill, and caught a glimpse of the enemy's line. Moving

RUTHERFORD B. HAYES.

forward, under a heavy fire, it dashed through a fringe of underbrush, and halted on the edge of a slough forty yards wide, and nearly waist deep. Seeing his whole line wavering, Col. Hayes plunged into the morass under a shower of bullets and grape, and was the first man over. The infantry floundered across after him, and the enemy were driven back. At Winchester a succession of brilliant charges were made by his brigade, and in leading one of them his horse was shot under him.

Gen. Early, with his shattered army, now fell back to Fisher's Hill, eight miles south of Winchester, and took up a strong position between two mountains. Sheridan followed sharply, and impetuously assailed this new stronghold. Crook's division was sent around to the right to envelop Early's right and rear; Col. Hayes' command led this movement, and, by making a detour through a series of ravines, arrived at a point on Early's flank, deemed unassailable. Clambering up the steep side of North Mountain, covered with trees and underbrush, the division, unperceived, gained a position close to and in the rear of the enemy, and then charged them with such fury that they fled, routed and terrified, leaving many guns and hundreds of prisoners to the victorious soldiers.

Col. Hayes was at the head of his column throughout this brilliant charge, directing the movements of his troops, and by his example of personal daring greatly adding to their enthusiasm and impetuosity. During this terrible campaign he was wounded four times, and three horses were shot from under him. He was now promoted to brigadier-general "for gallant and meritorious service in the battles of Winchester, Fisher's Hill, and Cedar Creek;" and was breveted major-general "for gallant and distinguished services during the campaigns of 1864 in West Virginia." In the spring of 1865 he was given the command of an expedition against Lynchburg, and was preparing to cross the mountains of West Virginia, when the war was brought to a close.

While still connected with the army, in the fall of 1864, Gen. Hayes was nominated for Congress by the Republicans of the Second District of Ohio. Soon afterwards he received a letter importuning him to return home and make the canvass. To this letter he replied as follows:

"IN CAMP, Oct. 2.

Yours of 29th ult. is received; thanks. I have other business just now. Any man who would leave the army at this time to electioneer for Congress ought to be scalped.
Truly yours, R. B. HAYES."

He was elected to Congress by a large majority, and took his seat in 1865. He was re-elected to Congress in 1866, but resigned in August, 1867, on receiving the Republican nomination for Governor of Ohio, and entered actively upon the canvass. The opposing candidate was Judge Thurman, and the contest was a very close one; but Mr. Hayes was elected by a majority of nearly 3,000 votes.

In 1869 he was re-elected Governor by an increased majority, his opponent being Geo. H. Pendleton. After his term of office had expired he resumed the practice of his profession. In 1872 he was a candidate for Congress, but was defeated by Henry B. Banning, a Liberal Republican.

In 1875 he was again nominated for Governor, notwithstanding his letter of withdrawal in favor Judge Taft. During the canvass which followed, Gov. Hayes was for two months constantly on the stump, making speeches in almost every county, and sometimes two or three a day in as many different places; and the great victory for hard-money which was won by the Republicans of Ohio was due in a great measure to his efforts. He was elected by 5500 majority over the defeated candidate, Gov. Allen, who had been considered invulnerable by his party.

As a Governor, Mr. Hayes has shown good executive abilities, and gained great popularity, not only among Republicans, but with men of all parties. He stands upon record as a gentleman and patriot, unblemished in name, character, and conduct.

# WILLIAM A. WHEELER.

## BIOGRAPHICAL SKETCH.

William A. Wheeler was born at Malone, Franklin County, New York, June 30th, 1819. At the age of seventeen years he entered the University of Vermont, where he remained two years. He then left college and began the study of law. On completing his studies he opened an office in his native town, became popular, and was nominated by the democrats for District Attorney of Franklin County. He was elected to the position and held it for several years, discharging his duties in an able and impartial manner.

Subsequently, Mr. Wheeler was elected a member of the

WILLIAM A. WHEELER.

State Legislature on the Whig ticket. At the close of his term he became cashier of a bank in Malone, and remained connected with it for fourteen years, displaying judicious judgment in all his business transactions. He also became interested in railroads, and was president of one company for eleven years.

When the Republican party was made up from the Whig organization he followed its fortunes, and in 1858 was elected to the State Senate, where he was an active member, and served for two terms as President *pro tem*. His ability and integrity were so well understood that his party removed him to a higher sphere of action by electing him as Representative to the thirty-seventh Congress from the Sixteenth District. He proved to be a faithful representative, consistently supporting the Republican Party, and upholding all measures for the suppression of the rebellion. After his term had expired he passed three or four years in private life.

In 1867 Mr. Wheeler was elected a member of the State Constitutional Convention, and was chosen as its presiding officer. In 1868 Mr. Wheeler was again a successful candidate for Congress. He represented his District in the forty-first Congress; and being re-elected at each successive election by large majorities, he has been continuously a member of Congress up to the present time.

In 1869, Mr. Blaine, then speaker of the House, appointed him Chairman of the Committee on the Pacific Railroad; he afterward held the same position, and served on various committees.

In 1874, he was appointed Chairman of the Congressional Committee who visited New Orleans to settle the disturbing questions which then prevailed in Louisiana, and it was mainly owing to his exertions that a peaceable settlement was obtained. The compromise agreed upon by the Committee (known as the Wheeler Compromise) was adopted in good faith by Republicans and Democrats, peace was restored, and good feeling soon prevailed among all classes of citizens.

Mr. Wheeler is a sterling man, able, discreet, experienced in public affairs, and universally respected for his excellent qualities and unquestioned integrity.

www.ingramcontent.com/pod-product-compliance
Lightning Source LLC
Chambersburg PA
CBHW020525300426
44111CB00008B/551